IBAN OR SEA DAYAK FABRICS
AND THEIR PATTERNS

LONDON
Cambridge University Press
FETTER LANE

NEW YORK · TORONTO
BOMBAY · CALCUTTA · MADRAS
Macmillan

TOKYO
Maruzen Company Ltd

Group of Iban women, pp. 3, 4.

IBAN OR SEA DAYAK FABRICS
AND THEIR PATTERNS

A DESCRIPTIVE CATALOGUE OF
THE IBAN FABRICS IN THE MUSEUM OF
ARCHAEOLOGY AND ETHNOLOGY
CAMBRIDGE

by

ALFRED C. HADDON

and

LAURA E. START

CAMBRIDGE
AT THE UNIVERSITY PRESS
1936

CAMBRIDGE UNIVERSITY PRESS
Cambridge, New York, Melbourne, Madrid, Cape Town, Singapore,
São Paulo, Delhi, Dubai, Tokyo, Mexico City

Cambridge University Press
The Edinburgh Building, Cambridge CB2 8RU, UK

Published in the United States of America by Cambridge University Press, New York

www.cambridge.org
Information on this title: www.cambridge.org/9780521183451

© Cambridge University Press 1936

First published 1936
First paperback edition 2010

A catalogue record for this publication is available from the British Library

ISBN 978-0-521-18345-1 Paperback

CONTENTS

CONTENTS

PREFATORY NOTE

During the last half of December, 1898, I had the good fortune to be the guest of Mr R. Shelford, the Curator of the Sarawak Museum at Kuching. Most of my time in Kuching was spent in the Museum, where more especially I studied the fine collection of Iban cloths, as many patterns on the cloths were named. I took ninety-three photographs of sixty-nine cloths in the Museum and of some twenty cloths belonging to various people; more than two hundred sketches of patterns and designs were made of which the names were obtained.

I collected a few cloths and names, and subsequently purchased a large number of cloths from Dr Charles Hose, on which names had been affixed to their respective patterns and designs. These cloths I have given to the Museum of Archaeology and Ethnology, University of Cambridge. There are, however, two or three cloths in the collection obtained from other sources.

This material, together with numerous data from other tribes, was accumulated in the hope that I should be in a position to study the decorative art of the natives of Sarawak, which ambitious scheme can now be only partially realized.

The Cambridge Museum thus possesses a fine representative collection of Iban cloths, consisting of 14 *kalambi*, jackets, 49 *bidang*, petticoats, 7 *sirat*, loin-cloths, 1 *bedong*, woman's girdle, 2 *dangdong*, shawls, and 11 *pua*, blankets; some 84 in all. These bear names of more than 1500 patterns and designs.

The British Museum possesses about the same number of Iban cloths. On the fifty-nine specimens purchased from Dr C. Hose there are comparatively few named patterns, and there are none on the cloths obtained from other sources.

The names on the foregoing cloths and those which I gathered in Sarawak afford a basis for a study of these interesting and beautiful fabrics.

I was fortunate to enlist the enthusiastic co-operation in this study of Miss Laura E. Start, M.Ed., Lecturer in the Education Faculty, Victoria

PREFATORY NOTE

University of Manchester. To it she has applied her practical experience and thus, so far as I am aware, there is for the first time a full technical description of the manufacture of Iban cloths and garments, and in addition an adequate account of their decorative motives. Miss Start also made all the drawings.

A. C. HADDON

LIST OF LINE BLOCKS IN THE TEXT

LIST OF LINE BLOCKS

LIST OF PLATES

PLATES OF MOTIVES (IN LINE)

LIST OF PLATES

PHOTOGRAPHIC PLATES

INTRODUCTION

This study is based on the large collection of Sarawak cloths in the Museum of Archaeology and Ethnology at Cambridge. The equally large collection of cloths in the British Museum has also been examined by us, and we have compared the available specimens with the numerous photographs and sketches made by one of us in Sarawak. We therefore venture to claim that there is sufficient material for a preliminary study of this nature. There is a considerable number of designs and patterns which are not here mentioned and for most of them we do not know by what names they are called.

Although some of the designs are sufficiently realistic to make identification possible, most of them are highly conventionalized. Indeed, in many cases it is almost impossible to see any resemblance between the design and the object it is intended to represent. No doubt some students will question whether there is any such connection, but we must remember that these are traditional representations which have been transmitted through very many generations and it could not be expected that a realistic treatment could often persist.

The Iban certainly admit that most of the designs or patterns are intended to represent some concrete object. Cloths that have been collected in different places and at various times show designs that resemble each other to a remarkable extent, and, furthermore, in most cases the Iban apply similar names to them. Every Iban cannot be expected to know the names of all the designs and patterns, so it is not surprising that identifications should occasionally vary. There are numerous tribes or groups of Iban and this fact may cause some discrepancy in the names given, not only in identification but through dialectic differences; added to this are divergencies in the spelling of words by the transcribers.

If a native is not sure what a pattern really means he will be apt to describe it as looking like some particular thing or as representing that thing. It is obvious that the nearest approach to certainty can only be attained by inquiry from the actual woman who made the pattern.

It sometimes happens that apparently very similar designs may have different names applied to them. These usually are simple designs or patterns, and in such cases there may be no recognized general name for them. To take one example, a zigzag has its own name, *lelingkok*, but it is often termed *semerai sungai*, which implies the conception of going in a canoe from one bank of a river to the other so as to avoid or make use of stronger currents. It has also been described as the movement or progression of a snake.

The vast majority of the names in our collection, as well as all those on the specimens in the British Museum, were collected by Dr Charles Hose and naturally we have accepted these as accurate, but either he or the persons whom he employed made variations in the spelling of a given word; usually we could ascertain the most common or likely variant and in some cases we adopted instead the spelling of the word given by the authors of the *Sea Dyak Dictionary*, as that must be regarded as authoritative.

In many cases, but by no means in all, a translation was given by Dr Hose of the native name—sometimes literally, sometimes freely—these we have copied and printed in quotes. Occasionally the translation of a word differed from that given in the *Sea Dyak Dictionary*; these cases have usually been noted by us. Unfortunately there are many native names for which we cannot find a translation; they are given as written by the transcribers. Translations by us are printed without quotes.

Originally the labels were pinned on to the cloths in what was intended to be their appropriate position, but even so, on account of the relatively large size of the labels it is not always apparent to which design or what part of it the label applied. Subsequently numbers written on tape to correspond with the labels were sewn on to the cloth by Mrs Haddon, who took great care to retain the original position of the labels. In some cases there evidently was a mistake in the original position of a label. These sources of error are not quite so serious as might be feared, since we have such a large number of names on different cloths that checking is almost always possible. We venture to hope that few mistakes due to these causes have been perpetuated by us.

A card catalogue of drawings of every design bearing the same name was made, and the most typical examples in each group were selected and have been included in pls. i to xxv.

Our procedure in the following pages is to give the weave, colour and methods of producing the patterns of a considerable number of individual cloths, and in the case of the jackets how they were constructed. The patterns and designs are described and illustrated as copiously as space permits, and we have added what information we have been able to find with regard to their significance; very rarely have we hazarded suggestions of our own.

We gratefully thank those Museum authorities who have afforded us opportunities for examining the cloths under their charge and the various unknown Iban who have given information. We feel that especial thanks are due to the late Dr Charles Hose for having supervised the identification of the designs on the cloths that have formed the basis of our study; the help afforded by these names has been invaluable.

The cloths themselves, together with the photographs and sketches made in Sarawak, are placed in the Cambridge Museum of Archaeology and Ethnology and are available to those who would like to consult them.

We candidly admit that we are merely pioneers in this investigation and it remains for others who can interrogate the Iban themselves to confirm, modify, or correct our provisional statements and to enter more deeply and securely into the motives that lie behind these expressions of Iban aestheticism.

The admirable compilation *The natives of Sarawak and British North Borneo* (1896), by H. Ling Roth, has been of very great assistance to us, especially his chapter xvii. His *Studies in primitive looms* (1918) is invaluable, as it is based on his own investigations. We have quoted with due acknowledgment from various authors whose observations have elucidated our subject and to those whose names are most frequently mentioned we offer our thanks. Particular mention should be made of the excellent *Sea Dyak Dictionary* by the Rev. W. Howell and D. J. S. Bailey, to which we have so often referred under *S.D.D.*, and we have found their English-Sea Dyak Vocabulary useful.

THE IBAN OR SEA DAYAKS

THE general appearance and psychical characteristics of the Iban have been well described by Hose and McDougall (I, p. 32, and measurements taken by Haddon are given in II, pp. 339, 340). They are industrious and energetic, and are great wanderers; this latter peculiarity struck the Kayans, who termed them "Ivan" (immigrant or wanderer), and this name has been adopted by large numbers of them in recent years and modified into Iban (II, p. 250). "When the Ibans became associated in piratical matters with the Malays of the coast, these latter assigned to their allies the heads of their enemies, as a sort of perquisite. This state of affairs lasted until well into the nineteenth century; and it is from their association with the Malays of the coast in their piratical expeditions that the Iban became known to Europeans as a Sea Dayak" (Hose, 1926, p. 145). The term Dayak, Dyak, etc., merely designates a non-Malayan inhabitant of Borneo and has no ethnic or tribal significance. It is probably derived from the Malay word *daya*, "inland".

The Iban can be distinguished from the other peoples of Borneo by their physical and mental traits and by many differences in culture. There appear to be two main ethnic stocks in Borneo: (1) a narrow-headed type, often termed Indonesian, but, to avoid ambiguity, the term Nēsiōt is preferable (Haddon, 1929, pp. 22, 119); (2) a broad-headed type, Proto-Malay (or Oceanic Mongol), which is a branch of the Pareoean or Southern Mongoloid (*l.c.* 1929, p. 32), to which stock the Iban may be assigned (cf. Haddon, 1901). Hose and McDougall (II, p. 248) regard the Iban as belonging to the same "stock from which the true Malays of Sumatra and the Peninsula were differentiated by the influence of Arab culture. A large number of the ancestors of the present Ibans were probably brought to Borneo from Sumatra less than two hundred years ago [Hose, 1926, p. 7, says, "less than three hundred years ago"].... Some two centuries ago, a number of Malay nobles were authorised by the Sultan of Brunei to govern the five rivers of

Sarawak proper, namely, the Samarahan, the Sadong, the Batang Lupar, the Saribas, and the Klaka rivers. These Malays were pirate leaders, and they were glad to enrol large numbers of pagan fighting men among their followers...[they] found, no doubt, that their pagan relatives of Sumatra lent themselves more readily to this service than the less warlike Klemantans of Borneo, and therefore, as we suppose, they brought over considerable numbers of them and settled them about the mouths of these rivers". "It seems to us probable that the greater part of the ancestors of the Ibans entered Borneo in this way. But there is reason to think that some of them had settled at an earlier date in this part of Borneo and rather farther southward on the Kapuas River....In most respects they closely resemble the other Iban tribes, but they are distinguished by some peculiarities of language and accent; their manners are gentler, their bearing less swaggering; they are less given to wandering" (II, p. 249).

We are not in a position to criticize the supposition that some 200 or 300 years ago Malay chiefs introduced Iban warriors from Sumatra to Sarawak, but Hose and McDougall recognize an earlier population of Iban in Borneo. It seems doubtful whether the characteristic Iban culture is so recent as Hose and McDougall seem to imply, and it would be interesting to know from what part of Sumatra "their pagan relatives" came, and if there are any traces there now of such people. We suggest that the Iban migration into Borneo may be regarded as an early wave of the movements that culminated in the Malay Empire.

Hose and McDougall (I, p. 31) state that the Iban "have spread northwards over Sarawak during the latter half of the last century, chiefly from the region of the Batang Lupar, where they are still numerous. They are still spreading northward, encroaching upon the more peaceful Klemantan tribes. They are most densely distributed in the lower reaches of the main rivers of Sarawak, especially the Batang Lupar and Saribas rivers, which are now exclusively occupied by them; but they are found also in scattered communities throughout almost all parts of Sarawak, and even in British North Borneo, and they extend from their centre in Sarawak into the adjacent regions of Dutch Borneo, which are drained by the northern tributaries of the Great Kapuas River". The different tribes or groups of Iban are distinguished by the names of the rivers along which they dwell, thus they

are known as Batang Lupar, Saribas, Rejang, Kanowit, etc. The physical
characters of the various ethnic groups in Sarawak are described by Haddon
in an Appendix to Hose and McDougall's monograph.

IBAN COSTUME

The Iban are extremely fond of dress and both men and women wear many
ornaments as well.

The usual male attire consists of:

Sirat (*chawat* of the Malays), or waist cloth, usually of red or blue cotton
cloth, sometimes having an embroidered end made of native material.

Labong, a headkerchief, which is usually richly decorated; or a cap of
woven cane, both of which are often ornamented with feathers.

Takai buriet or seat mat, usually made of skin or cane matting, the edge
being finished off with cloth and beads or buttons.

Kalambi or jacket, with or without sleeves, used chiefly on ceremonial
occasions.

Dangdong or shawl is also sometimes worn over the shoulder.

The women wear:

Bidang or petticoat, reaching to the knees and usually made of home-
made cloth elaborately decorated with warp-dyed patterns.

Bedong or woman's waist band or girdle.

Rawai or corset, made of a series of split ratan rings upon which brass
rings are threaded. The ratan rings fit so tightly that it is difficult
to bend the body.

Kalambi or jacket, sometimes rather longer than the men's but of the
same shape.

Girdles of coins, silver and brass chain or strips of coloured cane are also
worn round the waist, and *tanggok* or necklaces of beads, cane and silver
coins round the throat. Heavy earrings in the distended lobe of the ears are
worn by most tribes.

Some idea of the women's costume can be gathered from the frontispiece,
which shows a group of four women and two children. The women are
wearing skirts, *bidang*, with patterns; spider designs can be seen on the

3

second from the left and shrews and spiders on the second from the right, which also shows clearly the way the garment is folded when worn. Three figures show the corset, *rawai*, and the girdles of coins round the waist outside it. Two women have bead necklaces and the two on the right wide bead collars. The jackets of the two women to the left are of imported material, but the central figure wears a *kalambi* of striped native cloth somewhat similar to Z. 2342, which is described briefly on p. 37. The tall girl, second from the right, is a Kayan who lives with an Iban family.

THE PRODUCTION OF CLOTH

The garments worn by the Iban, whether petticoats, coats, loin-cloths or shawls, as well as their blankets, are made either from bark-cloth or hand-woven cotton stuff; the latter material is usually of native manufacture.

BARK-CLOTH

The bark-cloth is the cheaper material, and garments made from it are therefore worn when working in the jungle and by those who cannot afford woven cloth. "The old blankets, curtains, waist-cloths, and coats of the Dyaks were made of bark-cloth" (*S.D.D.* p. 133).

There are several sources from which suitable material for making bark-cloth can be obtained: the *pedalai*, bread-fruit tree (*Artocarpus* sp.), and a tree of a similar type called *tekalong* provide bark which can be wrought into loin-cloths, strips of about 10 ft. in length being obtainable when the trees are mature (*Sarawak Gazette*, 1894, p. 146).

The Kayans use the inner bark of a tree which they call *tajam*, but is called *ipoh* by the Iban. According to the Catalogue of the Brooke Low Collection this appears to be identical with the *upas* tree of Java, *Antiaris toxicaria*. In the *S.D.D.* (p. 60) it is stated that "there is another species of tree called *ipoh*, a sort of bread-fruit, the bark of which is made into white blankets, *pua*". Hose and McDougall (1, p. 220) state that cloth "is made from the bark of trees of several species (principally the *Kumut*, the *ipoh*, and the wild fig)".

The process of making the bark-cloth is to peel off the bark in broad strips, soak it well in water and then hammer it out with a heavy wooden mallet, which is grooved in deep cross cuts on its broad surface. This hammering breaks up the tissue of the bark and makes it more pliant but also accentuates any holes or rents, which are strengthened transversely by darning lines and patterns with thread made from the fibre of pineapple leaves or imported material (fig. 1).

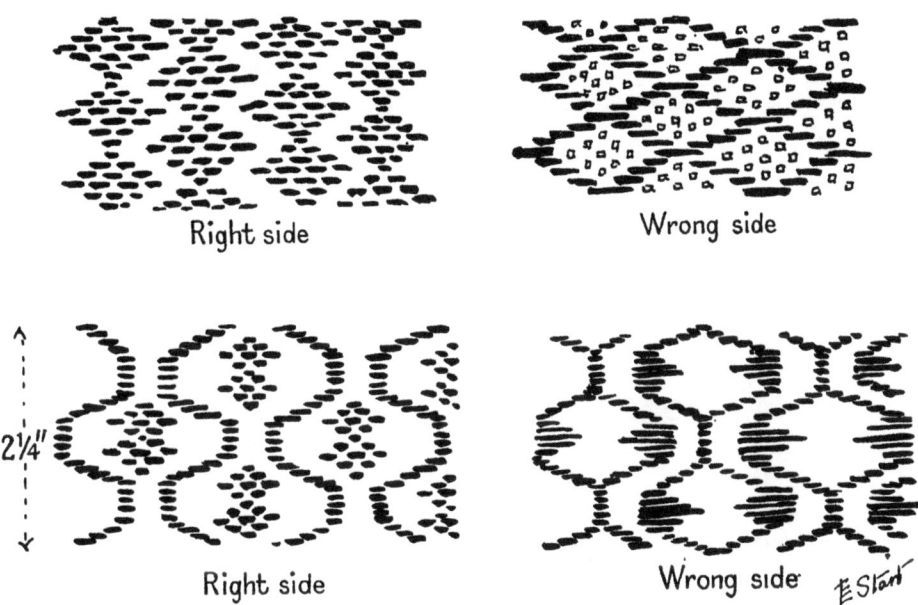

Right side — Wrong side

Right side — Wrong side

2¼″

Fig. 1. Two patterns in transverse darning on a bark-cloth sleeveless jacket, open down the sides. British Museum (3425).

COTTON CLOTH

The cloths which are used for garments are usually of purely native manufacture and are entirely the work of the women, from the setting of the cotton seed to the making up of the garment when the cloth has been woven. The men make the wooden beams, battens, heddles and spools used in weaving, but otherwise take no part in the work.

In order to make our account more complete we incorporate information given by the Rev. W. Howell (1912, p. 61) which has not been recorded by other writers. He says that "separate farms or gardens (*empalai*) are set apart for growing cotton (*taya*)....After the cotton has been picked, taken

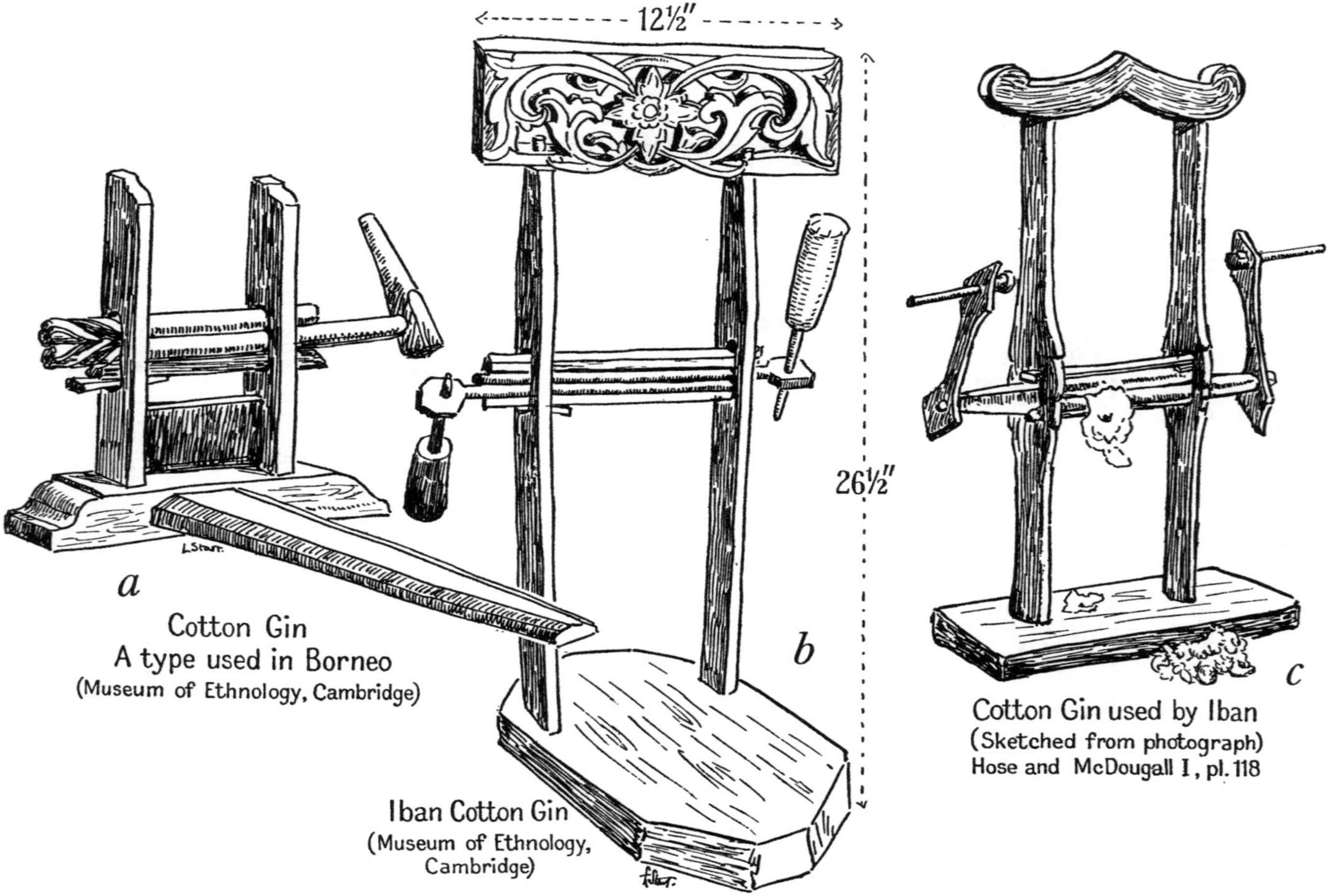

Cotton Gin used by Iban
(Sketched from photograph)
Hose and McDougall I, pl. 118

c

$26\frac{1}{2}''$

$12\frac{1}{2}''$

Iban Cotton Gin
(Museum of Ethnology,
Cambridge)

b

Cotton Gin
A type used in Borneo
(Museum of Ethnology, Cambridge)

a

Fig. 2. Types of cotton gin, *pemigi*, used by the Iban: *a*, *Kilangan kabu-kabu* (Malay), Skeat collection, 336; *b*, Haddon collection, Z. 2352.

out of its skin and dried, it is passed through a cotton gin (*pemigi*) in order to get rid of its seeds" and fragments of husk.

The gin consists of two small wooden rollers which revolve in opposite directions, each with a crank-like handle, fixed into the two upright supports of a frame (fig. 2). Extra strips of wood are generally fixed above and below

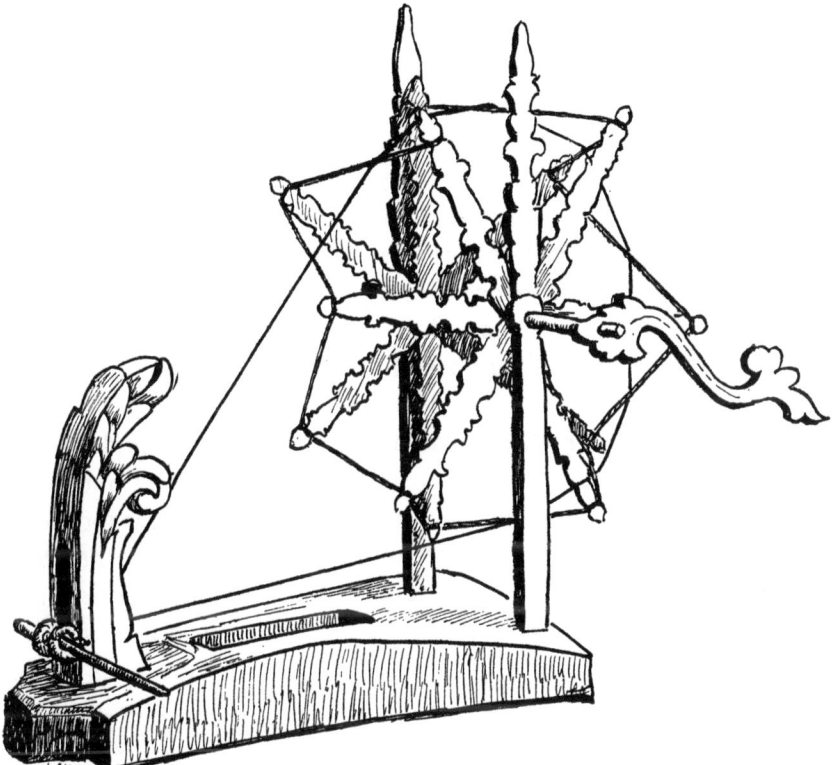

Fig. 3. An Iban spinning wheel, *gasing*. Museum of Ethnology, Cambridge, Haddon collection, Z. 2355.

the rollers to ensure sufficient pressure, and these are tightened by wedges. A similar form of gin is used throughout Indonesia and the Malay peninsula. The yarn is then spun from the mass of fibre.

The simple spinning wheel, *gasing*, is turned by the right hand, the fibre being twisted with the left hand (so Hose and McDougall say, 1, p. 221, but their pl. 119, owing to the method of reproduction, shows the reverse action. Gomes (1911), pl. p. 128, gives the same photograph in the correct position). The wheel, which has a shaft passing through two uprights at one end of the stand, consists of two elements, each composed of three flat wooden spokes which cross at their centres and are so arranged that one set alternates with the other (fig. 3). A strong thread is carried across alternately from the ends of the spokes of one element to those on the other, forming a zigzag which is the periphery of the driving wheel. At the other end of the stand there is a support on which the spindle is mounted horizontally; in the one here illustrated it passes through two rings attached to the support and so can rotate freely. The two rings are placed on either side of a long vertical hole near the base of the support through which the endless belt of cord, which goes round the driving wheel, passes to the spindle. The rotation of the spindle supplies the necessary twist to the drawn-out fibre. The process is intermittent, since each length or stretch of yarn has to be wound on to the spindle before another length is spun. When the spindle is full the thread is wound off into a ball or on to a separate piece of wood (pl. xxiv, *a*, *b*).

A more elaborate method, similar to that used in Java, is described by Howell, who says that after ginning, the cotton is threshed out on a mat with a cotton-beater (*pemalu taya*), the women using both hands for the work; this is done only very early in the morning. The cotton is threshed to form a flat mass, *lapis*, averaging 2 to 3 ft. square and some 2 in. in thickness. In the evening the *lapis* is folded and placed on the thigh to be cut into very thin pieces, which are put into a basket. The following morning the pieces are put on a mat and are again threshed till the *lapis* are reduced to the thickness of a sheet of thick paper. Later the *lapis* is to be *diluli*, that is, to be rolled up into the thickness of a finger so as to be ready for spinning. A *luli* is a pointed stick from 6 in. to 1 ft. long and no thicker than a little finger. After the *lapis* is rolled round the *luli* twice or thrice, it is cut off and placed in a basket. The cotton thus rolled is also called *luli*. The *luli* are then attached to a spinning wheel (*gasing*) and spun into a thread one by one.

We hesitate to criticize any statement by the Rev. W. Howell, but he seems to be describing the Javanese method of preparing and spinning the cotton (cf. Loebèr, 1903, pl. II, 3, 4, which show the thrashing and the *luli*, but not the rolling, in Java). No other accounts or illustrations give any indication of the Iban employing this method. We have consulted a cotton spinner of great experience, who says that the continual thrashing of the cotton and the cutting up into *luli* would break and weaken the fibres, which would be detrimental to making a good thread in spinning and would not produce yarn of the quality used in the Iban cloths.

"When the shuttle-pin [this is an impossible term. The Iban use a spool and not a shuttle in weaving. Howell is referring to the spindle] (*mata gasing* or 'eye of the spinning-wheel') is full up the thread is stretched in the *koali* or cotton-stretcher. It is then taken out and dipped in rice gruel (*kanji*) for some little time—this is called the process of *nyikat*; after being well saturated it is taken out and stretched lengthways in the *ruai* [the verandah or long reception room of the house] by means of two bamboos. After this it is combed with a cocoanut husk in order to smooth it and to take off any rice grains that are sticking to it; it remains thus until quite dry, when it is rolled up into a ball or balls; this last process being called *nabu*. The thread is now ready for the further processes of dyeing and weaving" (Howell, p. 62).

According to Howell (but no one else records it), the thread is unrolled from the ball and "stretched in the loom to ascertain the length and breadth of the cloth to be woven; this process is called *mungga*. This being ascertained the thread is carefully taken out of the loom as it is, and fixed to the *tangga ubong* or 'the ladder of the thread'".

The tying frame, according to Hose and McDougall (I, p. 221), is usually about 6 ft. [183 cm.] long and 20 in. [5·08 cm.] wide. That in the British Museum (96.3.17) is 5 ft. 7 in. long and 9½ in. wide; it is figured by Loebèr, 1903, pl. III, fig. 4. Our specimen (pl. XXVI, A) has a total length of 8 ft. and is 1 ft. 4 in. wide; the cross bars for the longer warp threads are 4 ft. 7 in. apart, the others are 7 in. shorter. Cross bars are fixed to the frame the distance apart required for the length of the cloth to be woven and the yarn goes round them from end to end.

If the cloth is to be plain, the web is set up in the loom, but if a self-coloured cloth is required, such as the dark blue worn by widows, the yarn is dyed before it is set up in the loom; there are, however, cases where a patterned cloth has been re-dipped in a blue dye.

9

The following technique is employed for the production of the pattern-dyed cloths which have a rep or poplin weave, that is, the warps form the surface of the cloth.

The patterns are produced by a resist method, the parts of the web to be reserved from any dye being tied with a dried strip of a fibrous leaf known as *lemba*. This fibre is stripped from the underside of a broad-leaved plant with yellow flowers (*Curculigo latifolia*) which grows in great abundance on old cultivated fields near houses.

As the continuous warp is wrapped right round the cross bars there is an upper and a lower web; the threads from both are tied together and so a repeat of the pattern is obtained. A skein of the *lemba* fibre can be seen attached to one of the lower cross bars in pl. xxvi, A.

As will be evident from the elaborate designs shown in the *bidang* and *kalambi* cloths illustrated later, quite a small number of warps may be tied together, six or eight, and the distance tied up may be very short. The work is often highly skilled and the women usually work from memory without the aid of any pattern, although the Rev. A. Horsburgh (1858, p. 43) says "the Balaus women sketch out the design on the extended web", see Gomes (1911, p. 52). A portion of the tied-up warp is shown in pl. xxvi, B.

When all the parts intended to be left undyed are tied up, the looped ends of the warp are also tied tightly, although already held securely by the numerous wrappings. The web is then immersed in the dye bath, which is most probably of a brown colour from *pinang* (*Areca catechu*) or of a richer red brown from the mangrove. After soaking in the dye for the required length of time, which may be a few hours or several days, according to the depth of colour needed, the web is stretched out to dry in a shady place. When dry the fibre is cut and stripped off and the design then appears in the natural colour of the cotton, on a dark-brown background.

Several dyeings sometimes take place so as to produce a number of shades and colours.

The yarns for the self-coloured stripes in the borders are dyed separately, and when all are dry the web is set up in the loom with these specially dyed yarns arranged to form warp stripes.

The following description of the technique of warp tie-dyeing is taken from Howell (1912): The first process of *kebat* [or *ikat*, "tying"] is to retain the white colour of the future pattern. After this is done the *kebat* thread is taken out of the *tangga ubong* and dipped into *engkerbai* water for a night and then dried; this is a mixture made by boiling the leaves of the *engkerbai* shrub and mixing some *chunam* [lime] with it; this gives a reddish colour to the thread. After it is quite dry the thread is fixed again to the *tangga ubong* and *kebat* for the second time. This second *kebat* is to retain the reddish colour for the pattern, and is called *mampul*. The thread is again removed and dipped into *tarum*, indigo water, which is made from the indigo plant in the same way as the *engkerbai* water; this gives the exposed portions of the thread a black colour. After it is quite dry it is fixed for the last time to the *tangga ubong* to undergo *ngetas tampok lemba*, "the cutting off of the knots", that is, the cutting of the knots of *lemba*. This accomplished, the thread is carefully put into the loom for weaving.

The use of tie-dyeing by other peoples is mentioned on pp. 138–142.

WEAVING

The *tumpoh* or loom used for weaving is extremely simple, being the most primitive form in Indonesia (Ling Roth, 1918, p. 65). Its component parts are a warp beam, breast beam, heddle, shed stick, beater-in, a back strap, and two or four laze rods (fig. 4). As there is no rigid framework the warp beam can be set up wherever there are two convenient upright posts, usually on the *ruai*, the verandah or long reception room. The breast beam, being attached to a back strap that goes round the weaver's waist, lies almost in her lap and so by a slight movement of her body she can manipulate the tension on the web (fig. 4).

The warp is wrapped continuously round the warp and breast beams and the threads are prevented from becoming entangled by one or two pairs of laze rods, the odd threads or odd groups of threads being first lifted and one rod passed through, and then the evenly numbered threads are lifted and another rod is passed through the new shed. The ends of each pair of laze rods are usually tied together by a cord. Cane heading rods are also frequently used at the commencement of the weaving to keep the warps evenly stretched. There are generally a few rows of weaving between the two rods, if more than one is used. The raising of alternative warps, or groups of warps, is effected by a shed stick and the single heddle, to which one set of warp threads is fastened by loops or leashes. The latter may be arranged spirally or alternately on the heddle (fig. 5); and more than one end is sometimes threaded through a leash. A sword-shaped beater-in (fig. 6, e) is generally used to press home each pick of weft, the latter being carried on a spool, which is often as long as the web is wide, so that it easily passes from hand to hand (fig. 6, f).

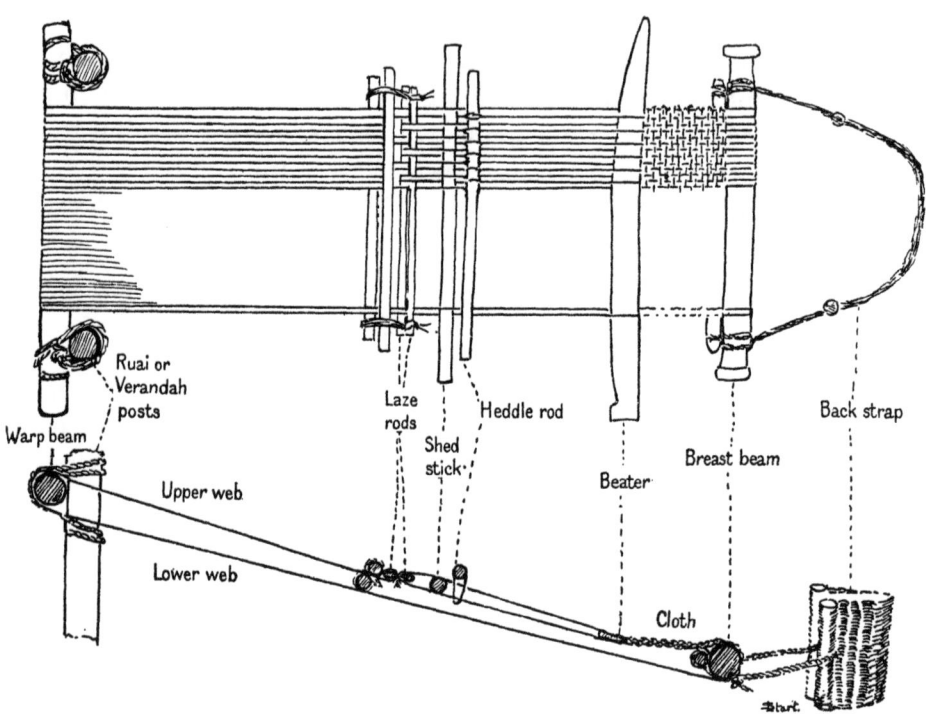

Fig. 4. Plan and elevation of a typical Iban loom, *tumpoh*.

Mr Ling Roth (1918, p. 68) indicates that loom pattern laze rods are sometimes used by the Iban, but the examples he describes seem to be for exceptional pieces of cloth which average less than 9 in. wide and vary from 30 in. to 24 in. in length. These are much narrower and shorter webs than any used for the clothing usually worn or than any of the cloths we have examined. In none of these, where the pattern has been produced by the method of warp dyeing just described, has there been any variation from a plain one up and one down like a "tabby weave", but, owing to the slackness of the warp groups and the few picks of weft to the inch combined with the width of the weft threads, which are usually arranged in pairs side by side, the resulting cloth is a rep or poplin, that is, a warp-surfaced material, which has been produced by the use of one heddle and a shed stick.

Fig. 5. Continuous heddle leashes: *a*, spiral; *b*, alternate. After Ling Roth, 1918, fig. 1 A.

Although Ling Roth has made a drawing (1918, p. 69) to explain how a pattern could be worked by means of laze rods, we do not know if the Iban ever use pattern laze rods. We are definitely of opinion that the pattern is produced by the *sunkit* method, see p. 88.

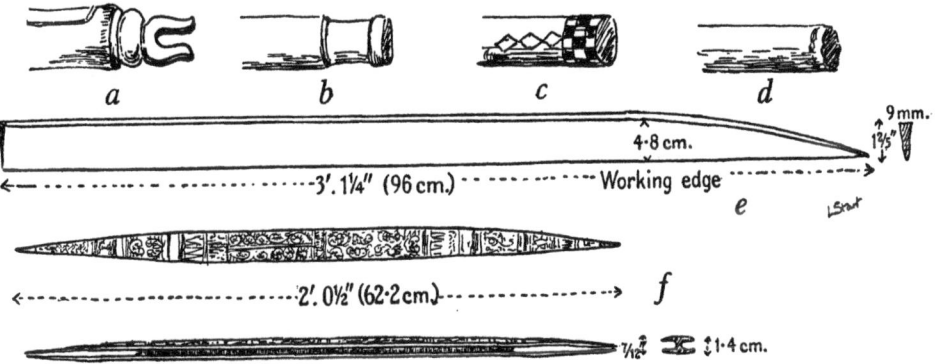

Fig. 6. Iban weaving implements: *a, b*, breast beam ends; *c, d*, warp beam ends; *e*, sword beater-in; *f*, spool. *a, f*, Museum of Ethnology, Cambridge (f. 25.551); *b, c*, Royal Scottish Museum, Edinburgh; *d, e*, Horniman Museum, London.

Sir James Brooke gave a *pua* to the British Museum (3430) woven with palm fibre; the patterns are those characteristic of ordinary *pua*, but are much less clear.

THE MAKING OF PATTERNS OTHER THAN
WARP-DYED

In addition to the warp-dyed method patterns are produced on the finer cloths woven on the *tumpoh* or primitive loom of the Iban by

(1) Pure embroidery.

(2) The use of free spools to give an embroidered effect.

(3) A form of tapestry weaving or weft-mosaic carried out with the needle.

(4) Brocade weaving with free spools or needles.

(5) Slight variations produced by manipulation of the weft.

When the Malay or *tanjak* loom is used with its series of heddles and treadles, more sophisticated and generally geometric patterns are produced, and Ling Roth mentions the use of pattern laze rods for the same purpose. These methods are refinements which are not typically Iban, and it is noticeable that the cloths woven by the Iban on the Malay loom are always inferior in quality to those woven on their own simpler type of loom.

Referring to the different possibilities of producing pattern it may be noted that (1) and (2) are chiefly used on *kalambi* and *sirat*, (3) and (4) are almost entirely confined to the working of badges and (5) occurs occasionally on *kalambi* and *sirat*, but more often as the heading to the *pua*.

Embroidery and the use of free spools

The raised patterns produced by embroidery can also be made by the use of free spools, used to pick up threads when needed and then allowed to hang from the web until required again; the weft passes across the back of the cloth from one motive to another.

This is a method used by the Malays and is much more difficult than embroidery, and as the Iban do not often use the *tenjak* for their weaving but prefer their more simple *tumpoh*, it seems reasonable to suppose that they would choose the easier method in working the raised type of pattern.

J. A. Loebèr, Jn. reproduces some examples with patterns of this type and describes them as having "flottante inslag"—floating weft—which might apply to either method, and in order to find out whether an example

14

has been actually embroidered or worked with free spools it is necessary to follow out a number of individual threads.

This has been done in all cases when the work has been described as embroidered, and it has been found that although working threads generally end at the lowest point other threads have been worked downwards in a vertical and oblique direction first and then upwards again in an oblique line, a method only possible if a needle has been used. One motive from cloth 35.906 (fig. 19) has been enlarged to show the actual stitches (fig. 7).

The ends of all threads are cut off very closely to the cloth and may be either on the right or wrong side, and as the work is extraordinarily well stitched it is sometimes extremely difficult to find where any pattern begins and ends. Both back and front of the work appear alike, although the slanting stitches which carry the thread below the next row of weft usually appear on the wrong side. This form of good workmanship, namely the reversible quality of the pattern, is characteristic of the finer work amongst more civilized Eastern peoples, such as the Chinese and Japanese.

▭ White threads   ▬ Black threads

Fig. 7. Bird motive, *burong kaki panjai*, "bird with long legs", on an embroidered coat, showing the direction of the stitches, 35.906. See also bottom row of fig. 23, B.

The tapestry method or weft-mosaic.

This method of forming patterns on a bare warp with a needle is of widespread occurrence; it is found in old Peruvian work and was used in Egypt at least 1500 years B.C. (L. E. Start, 1914, pp. 14, 15). The needle carrying any particular colour darns that thread backwards and forwards over any special series of warps until the little design is completed.

15

Thus the black thread at the top right-hand corner of fig. 8 wraps the third bundle of warps four times, then passes under the second and back over the top of it, under the third and over the fourth bundle. It turns back under 4, goes over 3 and under 2, turning back over the top of it to repeat the previous row. In this manner, which is like darning, the black triangle is completed. As each little bit of the pattern is worked separately it forms a kind of weft-mosaic, and as long as the bulk of the work follows an oblique

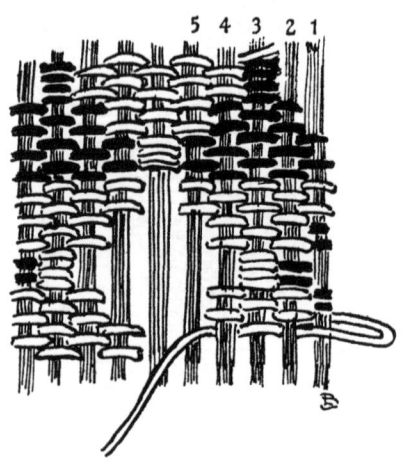

Fig. 8. Tapestry method of needle-weaving or weft-mosaic. Part of the central flower in the badge of 35.903.

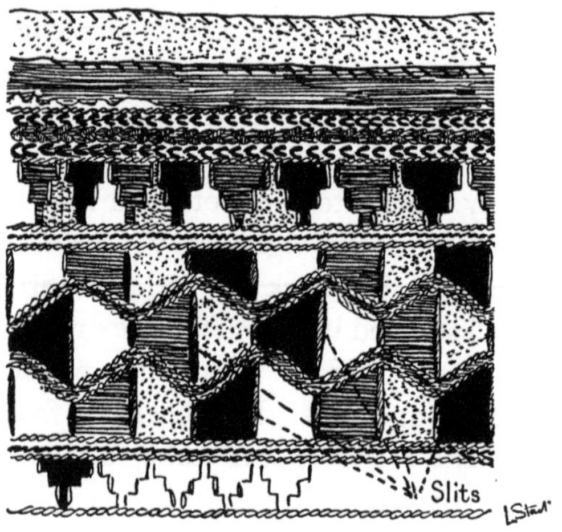

Fig. 9. Needle-woven pattern showing slits. The badge of *kalambi* 35.910.

outline it is firm, but if long vertical lines occur a gap appears in the work, just as it does in actual tapestry weaving, and this has to be sewn up at the back (fig. 9). This method is described variously as the tapestry method, needle-weaving, and weft-mosaic; the diagram (fig. 8) is a part of the central flower in the badge at the back of cloth 35.903. The unfilled lozenge in the centre would be filled in with red in the same way after the black and white triangles around were completed, or the process could be carried out in the reverse order and the central lozenge be worked first.

The brocade method

This name has been used because the effect produced is like that of brocade or patterned damask weaving, the pattern being the result of an unbroken surface of weft threads filling the desired shape and passing behind the web between the patterns or else carrying on between them as tabby weaving.

Gold and silver threads are usually used as weft by the Iban when they adopt this method of working a badge at the back of a coat, and the weaving is done whilst the warp is stretched in the loom.

A small spool is used to pick up those warps where the gold is not required to show and passes over the top of any number where pattern is wanted on the surface. Gold thread will not stand much handling because of the possibility of stripping the thin metal from its core of silk or cotton, and as each row is picked up individually there is no great strain on the weft, but the resulting cloth is of a very loose texture.

The simple pattern of lines and lozenges illustrated (fig. 24) in the section on *kalambi* has been carried out in this way. There does not seem any evidence that special weaving contrivances, such as pattern laze rods, have been used for these brocade patterns, and the process, in any case, is much quicker than that of the tapestry method.

Weft manipulation to form pattern

One of the most effective and commonest variations produced by means of the spool is that of "twining", which frequently occurs at or near the beginning of a blanket cloth and is also used as decorative lines in the badges (figs. 10, *a*, *b*, 15).

Two spools are used at the same time and the warps are usually bunched. In fig. 10, *a*, where a white and a black thread are shown, it is quite easy to follow the working. Beginning with the white spool, it goes over, whilst the black goes under the same bunch of warps, and before proceeding to the next bunch the spool threads are crossed, then the black goes over and the white under the next bunch of warps before the spool threads are crossed again. In this way a line of alternate black and white stitches having a rope-like or twisted effect is produced, and if two such lines are worked in opposite directions the effect is that of a black and white plait (fig. 10, *b*).

Another way in which a different colour effect is produced is by means of weft stripes, and one example is enlarged in fig. 10, *c*, where the warp ends are first grouped into fives by means of a row of twining and then a shed is made of three and two warp ends alternately, through which there are first two picks of black and then two of red. A single pick of the ordinary weft then takes up the two groups and goes over, under, over the ends in the three groups right across the cloth, and this is followed by two picks of black through a shed similar to the first.

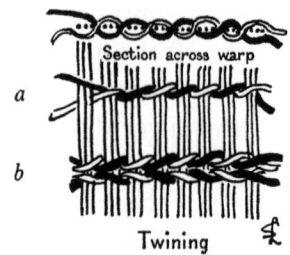

In the *kalambi*, *sirat* and girdles occasional weft stripes occur which may be either worked with a needle or woven by a spool; the needle would be the easier, as no new shed would have to be made.

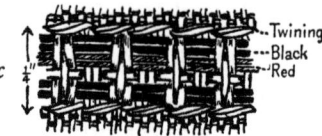

Fig. 10. Weft patterns.

Weft-patterned cloths

The Iban occasionally make use of a Malay loom or *tenjak*, and by means of a series of heddles and treadles set up in a suitable framework produce weft-patterned cloths, but these are rare and are not represented in our collection. When this type of loom is used the pattern itself loses its naïve quality and becomes a regular all-over design based on geometrical forms.

The patterns generally produced by this method are much more akin to Malay and Chinese designs than any produced by the warp-dyed method.

Iban methods of spinning and weaving fabrics, the apparatus employed and some finished cloths are given by the following: Ling Roth, 1896, 1, pp. 29–54, with numerous illustrations; 1918, pp. 65–70, with illustrations. Other Indonesian looms are described.

J. A. Loebèr, Jn., 1903, pl. III, 4, *tangga ubong*, Sarawak (British Museum, no. 1896.3.17), pl. IV, weaving, Saribas Dayak (copied from Beccari, 1904, fig. 13), pl. XIII, 1, "Geïkatte schering", pl. XIV, an Iban *pua*, pl. XIV, 1, an Iban *pua* (British Museum, 96.7); other Indonesian methods and fabrics are illustrated. Gomes, 1911, pls. pp. 52, 128. Hose and McDougall, 1912, I, pp. 221, 223, drawing of a *bidang*, fig. 61, photographs of *pua*, pls. 131, 132; owing to the process employed in reproduction the positions of the women are reversed in plates 118–121, thus the right hand appears to be the left hand. In Hose, 1926, they are shown correctly in the pl. facing p. 182; photograph of part of a *pua* and of a *bidang*, pl. p. 183.

DYES

The range of colour used by the Iban in dyeing their cotton yarn and tied-up webs is limited; shades of brown, from a pale buff to a vandyke, most frequently form the backgrounds to the patterns; the most effective is a reddish brown; brown is also the usual colour of the yarn used as weft.

For the brightly coloured stripes, generally found near the selvedges of the cloths, yarns dyed red, yellow, black, pale blue, or green are used, and sometimes an unusual effect has been produced by dipping a cloth which already has such stripes in an indigo bath.

All the dyes used in the cloths described are vegetable in origin and either act by oxidization or in conjunction with some simple alkali, such as wood ash or alum. Hose and McDougall (I, p. 222) say: "lime and gypsum are sometimes mixed with the watery extracts as mordants but these are probably modern refinements"; but Perkins and Everest (1918, p. 463) state that "at an early date in India and the Far East such other mordants as naturally occurring sulphates of aluminium and iron were used".

The rich reddish brown so successfully exploited by the Iban is obtained from the bark of the mangrove or of the *samak* tree and is a favourite colour with the Saribas women, who make the best fabric. A dark purple is obtained from the leaves of the *tarum* (indigo) plant. Many shades of duller brown are obtained from the *pinang*, *Areca catechu*, which may also be used as a mordant for other dyes. The catechu is dissolved in boiling water, the yarn is immersed in the hot bath of liquid from a half to a full hour for light shades of brown and steeped overnight for dark shades. The colour is developed with the liquor obtained from wood ash.

Yellow is obtained from turmeric and wood of the Jack-tree (*Artocarpus integrifolia*), known to the Iban as *pedalai*. This wood is rasped and used in conjunction with an alkali. The Javanese use this wood together with alum in dyeing their *batik* patterns. An aqueous solution of the wood if heated with an alkali gives a beautiful blue.

Blue is usually obtained from the leaves of various species of *Indigofera*, which are soaked in water for 12 hours. During this time bacterial fermentation takes place and begins to form a yellow liquid which is run off. This is areated by agitation; it first turns green and then blue.

If the leaves of the *Indigofera tinctoria* are used the presence of an alkali is necessary in the water, as the glucoside which is contained in them splits up into indigo and sugar, and without the alkali the indigo is insoluble in the water. Under the right conditions it becomes indigo white, which oxidises on exposure to air into indigo blue.

Ling Roth (11, footnote p. 37) quotes von Donop's reference to a small shrub called *home*, the leaves of which resemble *Cinchona succirubra* and are sometimes used in place of indigo; the leaves are boiled and the cloth immersed in the liquor.

The scarlet yarn used in the self-colour stripes is generally procured from the Malays, but a brilliant red is also obtainable from the ratan *jernang*. The dye is made from the scales which cover unripe fruit of this species of ratan ("*Calamus didymophyllus*, or, perhaps, *Damonorops draco*, called Dragon's blood", *S.D.D.*).

Green is obtained by over-dyeing a yellow with light blue, either indigo or that obtained from an alkaline aqueous solution of jack-wood (*Artocarpus integrifolia*). In the latter case both colours, the yellow and the blue, might have the same source.

A black dye can be made from the large juicy leaves of a Melastomacea (*Medinillopsis Beccariana*). Beccari (1904, p. 277) says that the Tubao Kayans use the juice of these leaves to blacken their teeth.

The effect of black can also be secured by over-dyeing indigo on a red-brown. The latter method appears to be the one most frequently adopted by the makers of the cloths in the collection.

The *S.D.D.* gives *ladu*, mud found in down-river streams and used as a black dye for petticoats.

When any yarn has been dyed it is spread out in some shady place to dry.

The Iban usually dye the background colour first, whether it be a light or reddish brown, reserving the pattern so that it appears light or white; darker spots and other colours are the result of a second dyeing.

W. Howell (1912) says that *kain chelum*, black cloth, is obtained by dipping the cloth into *engkerbai* water for a night; after washing and drying it is soaked in *tarum* water (indigo). *Kain mata* or *ubong mata*, the unripe cloth or unripe thread, is the undyed material.

The thread of *kain engkudu*, "the red cloth", is called *ubong embun* because it has to be exposed to the dew, *embun* (*ambun*), for so many nights, the exact length of time depending on the woman who conducts the operation. The dyeing of the *kain* or *pua mansau*, *engkudu* or *embun* is done in the following way: "After being first dipped in saffron water, *kunyit* [turmeric], it is subjected to the following concoction: (i) *kapayang* oil, made from *kapayang* (*Pangium edule*) seeds burnt and pounded in salt, and for proper preservation there should be plenty of salt; (ii) *klemintin* fruit; (iii) *klampai* fruit; (iv) *engkringan* fruit; and (v) ginger, all burnt and pounded in the same way. These are carefully measured out with a cocoanut shell in the correct proportions, and are then put into a wooden trough containing cold water. After this concoction has been well stirred and mixed the thread is dipped into it for twenty-four hours, during which time great care is taken to see that it is well saturated. It is then taken out and stretched on a mat for twelve hours and afterwards put out on the outside platform (*tanjeu*) for sixteen days, so that the sun and dew may complete the process. It should be noted that although dew is apparently regarded as a necessity, great care is taken to prevent the newly-dyed thread from getting wet from rain, and on the slightest suggestion of a shower, either by day or night, the thread is taken into the house. After eight days on the *tanjeu*, the thread is turned, so that the other side may receive similar treatment for the remaining eight days. The dyed thread is now washed, dried, dipped in rice gruel, combed and rolled into balls ready for weaving."

"The mixing of this particular dye is supposed to be very difficult and perhaps only one in fifty knows much about it. The woman who becomes the recognized authority on this subject takes the name of 'Orang tau nakar tau ngar', which means 'She who knows the secret of measuring out the drugs in order to obtain the rich colour', and for this work she is well paid, the usual fee being a small jar (*tepayan*), a sacred stone (*plaga*), a small bell (*grunong*), and a brass ring (*chinchin tembaga*). Some of the 'professors' affirm that they learnt the art from the fairy goddesses such as Kumang, Indai, Abang, etc. With some Sea-Dayak tribes they even go so far as to make offerings to these goddesses, asking their help in the difficult work of dyeing the cotton red (*ngar*, or *nakar ubong*). The woman who undertakes this particular kind of dyeing, first of all gets a piece of steel which she bites in order to strengthen her soul. This steel is called *kris samengat*. They make a great deal of fuss over the work of laying out the thread on the platform (*tanjeu*) and the business of it is called the *kayau indu*, or 'warpath of the women'."

"The Sea-Dayak bachelor in order to win the affections of a maiden must needs get a head first, similarly the Sea-Dayak maiden to win the affection of a bachelor must needs be accomplished in the arts of weaving and dyeing."

In the following pages we describe the specimens in the Cambridge Museum in the order of *kalambi, bidang, sirat, bedong, dangdong* and *pua*.

KALAMBI, JACKETS

The *kalambi* or jacket is a garment worn by both men and women; the former, however, only use it on full-dress occasions, when a *dangdong* or shawl is also thrown over the shoulder. The women do not usually wear a jacket when in the house, the *bidang*, or petticoat, and *rawai*, or corset of brass rings threaded on ratan circles, alone being worn; they don the jacket for out-door pursuits or for special occasions.

The men's and women's jackets are alike in material and shape except that the women's is usually a little longer. The jackets are made of bark-cloth or woven fabric; the latter type only is here described.

The method of weaving is exactly the same as for the *bidang*, and similar coloured stripes are introduced at the edges of the cloths, which average just under 20 in. (50·8 cm.) in width. It takes a whole length of cloth for a jacket with sleeves. If the garment is to be decorated with a badge at the back, this is worked on the warp threads before the cloth is removed from the loom (pl. xxvii).

Two methods are used in the production of these badges, either a form of needle-weaving or weft-mosaic, or the brocade method. Both have been described under the heading "The making of patterns other than warp-dyed" (pp. 15, 17).

Pure embroidery is used as a means of producing pattern on some of the woven cloth jackets in addition to the badges. The elaborate designs frequently worked on bark-cloth jackets serve, however, not only for decoration but also as a strengthening device, as the stitching is mostly done in a horizontal direction in order to make the longitudinal fibres firmer (fig. 1).

According to Mr Leggatt (Notes) "the dresses of the Sarebas are the best embroidered as they are the cleverest in all needlework".

Further ornamentation is also provided by the use of fabrics of foreign manufacture; English red and yellow flannel, Chinese printed cotton and silks, are used as narrow edgings to the badges and for making neat the cut edges at the front of the coat and the neck. Gold thread obtained from the Chinese and Malays is sometimes introduced in the working of the badge and also to a very slight extent in the pure embroidery; Brooke Low (Catalogue) says that "the *kalambi subang* manufactured by the Sarebas is of a finer and closer texture than any other and therefore more expensive. The thread of which it is wrought is procured from the Malays and is of a red colour".

Fringes of beads or hawk-bells occur on some of the finer examples and a short twisted fringe of warp ends is left on others, whilst small tassels of coloured threads are occasionally used to make a neat finish to a side seam (fig. 18, *a*).

Most of the *kalambi* are, however, made of cloth with a warp-dyed pattern, and those decorated with good omen birds are greatly prized and are worn on such important occasions as the beginning of house-building, and the first planting of paddy, whilst others with sacred birds have value as a cure for sickness. It is probable that these special uses of *kalambi* for ceremonial purposes have led to their more elaborate treatment.

The Sakarang wear jackets without sleeves and some tribes have a striped cloth, that is, there are narrow warp-dyed stripes alternating with plain colour stripes across the whole width; see cloths Z. 2341, Z. 2342.

Analysis of weaving in *kalambi*

No. of cloth	Width	No. of warp ends to inch	Description of warp	No. of weft picks to inch	Description of weft	Notes
35.903	1 ft. 7¾ in. (50·1 cm.)	88–132 ends (44 groups) 132–176 ends (44 groups)	Paired and threes in pattern stripes. Fours and threes in self-coloured stripes	20–22	Brown. Three parallel threads	Pattern stripes have had three dyeings: light brown, deep red brown, indigo on red brown (vandyke)
35.904	1 ft. 7¼ in. (48·8 cm.)	204 ends (68 groups)	Triple warps throughout. Very fine yarn	26–30	Two spools used alternately and threads cross at edge of cloth. Three, occasionally four, parallel threads of finely spun yarn; red in colour	One of the most finely woven cloths in the collection. The warp and weft are both red except in the border stripes, when yellow and dark blue warps are used. The patterns are embroidered with a double thread of white or three threads of black
35.905	1 ft. 7¼ in. (48·8 cm.)	112 ends (56 groups)	Paired, odd groups of threes in coloured stripes	22	Three parallel threads. Greyish white	Colour dull, a greyish white pattern on dull vandyke ground. The cloth is striped right across its width, pattern stripes being divided by groups of red, white and brown stripes
35.906	1 ft. 5½ in. (44·4 cm.)	272 ends (68 groups)	Four parallel ends in each group	22	Red. Four, six or eight threads with a slight twist which appears as parallel in the shed	A finely woven red cloth with solid white, black and yellow stripes at the sides. The patterns are embroidered in dark blue and white with a twisted or doubled thread for the white and a fourfold untwisted thread for the blue stitches
35.907	1 ft. 7½ in. (49·5 cm.)	112 ends (56 groups) 192 ends (64 groups)	Paired in the pattern stripes. Threes in self-colour stripes	20	Brown. Three parallel threads	Pattern stripes of white with brown ground alternate with composite stripes of black, white, red and yellow, and extend right across the width of the cloth. Faded

The cloth woven for jackets is nearly always firmer to feel and finer in texture than that made for the *bidang*. This is mostly due to the fact that the finer warps are used and the number may vary from about 100 ends an inch in a cloth of moderate quality to 272 in a finely woven one, and the ends

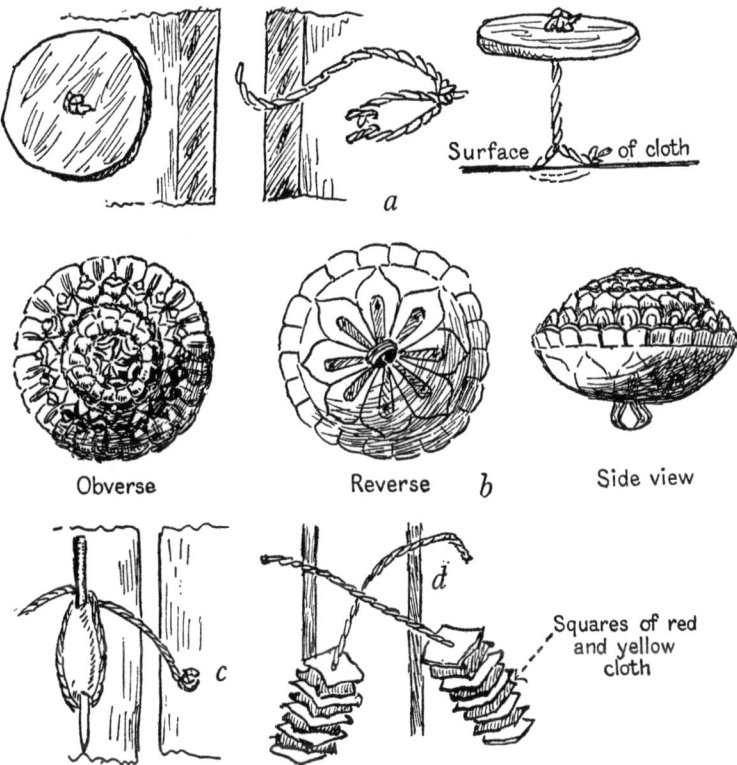

Fig. 11. Methods of fastening *kalambi*: *a*, wooden button and string, 35.911; *b*, silver-gilt button of local workmanship, 35.910; *c*, thorn and string, Sakaran Iban (Ling Roth, II, p. 32); *d*, two strings with ornamented ends, British Museum (No. +7010).

are usually paired or sister warps. Just as in the *bidang* cloths, where solid colour stripes appear it is usual to find more ends to the inch than in the main body of the cloth.

The weft is often threefold, occasionally four, and the strands are wound tape-wise on the spool. (The Javanese use a similar method of making a wide weft, as can be seen in the spool thread in a Javanese loom belonging to the Manchester College of Technology.) An average number of picks to the inch is 22. The colour of the weft is often red and sometimes a dull white, instead of the almost universal brown used in the other cloths.

In addition to the native yarns, some doubled white yarns, either imported or mechanically spun, are used, especially for embroidery and badges. The gold and silver thread used in the latter, and less frequently as an embroidery thread, is obtained from the Malays or Chinese.

The method of cutting out and making up a *kalambi* with sleeves is given in detail for cloth 35.903. All jackets are made up in the same way, except that there may be a variation in the amount of slope cut away for the sleeve.

In making up, a lacing stitch or some type of open stitch is usually used for the sides (fig. 12, *d*), but a counter hem is the method adopted for joining the sleeve seams, which are always left open for an inch or two under the armpit.

The fastening of the coat may be a piece of fine twine attached to one side and wrapped round a thorn stuck through the cloth on the other edge (fig. 11, *c*), or it may be a button, varying from a beautifully worked silver-gilt one of native manufacture (fig. 11, *b*) to an European shirt button or a crudely shaped piece of wood (fig. 11, *a*).

Occasionally ties are made on either side of a coat consisting of twine. The ends of the ties may have a number of small squares of red and yellow flannel threaded on them (fig. 11, *d*).

The *kalambi* are described in the following order:

35.903	35.909	Z.2342	35.901
35.907	35.902	Z.2341	35.911
35.905	35.919	35.904	
35.910	35.908	35.906	

THE IBAN JACKET

35.903. A Saribas jacket. This cloth is a fine specimen of a *kalambi burong*, "bird coat", with a badge worked in at the bottom of the back in the tapestry method, i.e. needle-woven upon the stretched warp.

Length of cloth before folding or sleeves cut from it about 6 ft. (182·9 cm.); width varies from 19½ in. (49·5 cm.) to 20 in. (50·8 cm.).

The manner in which the coat has been cut from the length of cloth is best seen in fig. 12, *a*, which shows how the front width is divided for the

26

opening and a **V**-shaped piece cut for the neck, the piece of cloth thus cut being turned down to form a double thickness at the back of the neck, which

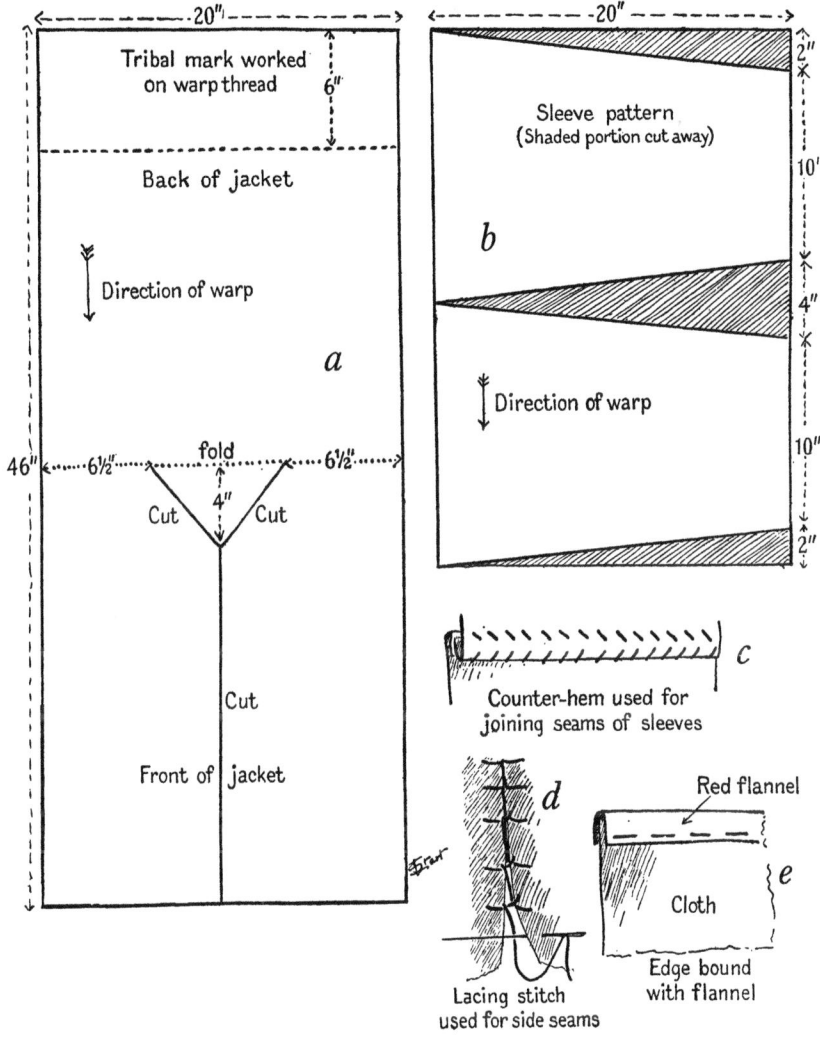

Fig. 12. Cutting out and making up a *kalambi*.

is then hemmed in place. The sleeves are shaped by having a portion cut away from each side so as to make the wrist 4 in. narrower than the part joining the body of the jacket at the shoulder (fig. 12, *b*), and the two raw edges thus produced are joined by a coarsely sewn counter hem, i.e. each edge is turned under once and the raw edges, being placed upon one another, the folds on either side of the garment are felled or hemmed down (fig. 12, *c*). Openings are left under the armpit both in the sleeve seams and the side seams of the jacket, which are joined by a lacing stitch worked from side to side with a cord-like thread made from pineapple fibre (fig. 12, *d*). The sleeves are seamed on with the same material and all the remaining raw edges of the garment are bound with narrow strips of imported scarlet flannel, secured by a coarse tacking stitch (fig. 12, *e*) or in some parts by a hemming stitch.

The material used in making the garment is an excellent example of warp-pattern dyeing. Groups of coloured warp stripes (fig. 13, *a*) in red, yellow, black, white, red, white, black, yellow, red, amounting in all to a compound stripe $9\frac{1}{16}$ in. (23 cm.) wide, separate the patterned stripes (fig. 13, *b*). The latter vary in width, being alternately $\frac{5}{16}$ in. (8 mm.) and $1\frac{1}{16}$ in. (2·6 cm.); there are 88 to 132 warp ends to the inch, grouped in twos and threes, and 20 to 22 picks of weft, each of which consists of three parallel threads.

In the coloured warp stripes which

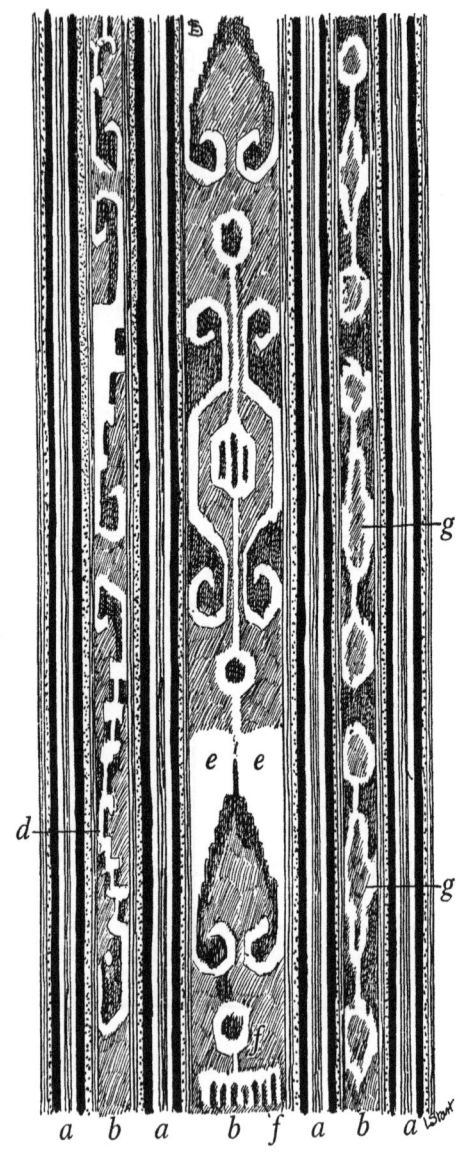

Fig. 13. Pattern repeat on back and sleeves of *kalambi* 35.903: *a*, solid colour stripes; *b*, pattern stripes; *d*, *daun wi*, "leaf of ratan" (see pl. xxii, *m*); *e*, *sayap burong lelayang*, "wing of swift, *Collocalia fuciphaga*"; *f*, *sugu*, "a comb"; *g*, *lachau*, "the green grass lizard".

28

give a solid colour effect the cloth is of a still closer texture, because the warps are grouped mainly in fours instead of threes and there are as many as 176 ends to the inch; this greater closeness of texture enhances the colour effect.

The patterned stripes have white motives (undyed yarn) on a reddish brown background, the dye being obtained by the Saribas women from mangrove bark; parts of the designs are emphasized by deep sepia brown obtained by a second dyeing of indigo over the red-brown.

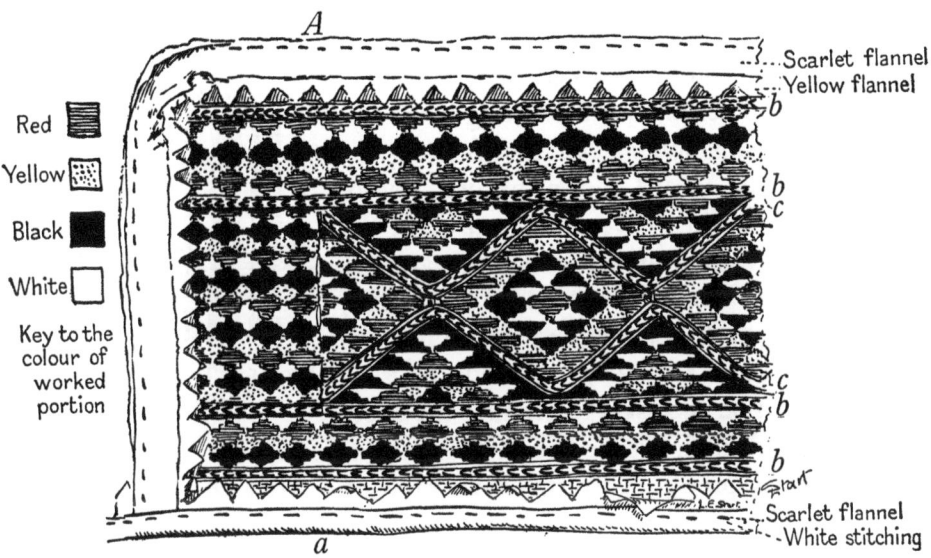

Fig. 14. Badge at the bottom of the back of *kalambi* 35.903, worked in the tapestry manner on the bare warp.

A portion of the repeat on the back and sleeves is shown in fig. 13, which represents: *d, daun wi,* "a ratan leaf" (pl. XXII, *m*); *e, sayap burong lelayang,* "the wing of a swallow or swift"; *f, sugu,* "a comb" (pl. XXIV, *g*); and *g, lachau,* "a green grass lizard" (pl. XII, *f*). At the bottom of the front of the coat is *burong buah bangkit,* "bird with the *bangkit* fruit" (pl. VIII, *a*).

Stripes of various colours are termed *ara* and these particular ones are labelled *ara ular kendawang; kendawang* is "a snake, *Cylindrophis rufus,* with a red head and a red tip to its tail, body striped black, white and red. It is said by the natives to be poisonous" (*S.D.D.*). Two broader stripes are

29

labelled *ara belambang*. *Ara* also signifies "spread out", which is probably its meaning in this case; *belambang* means "irregularly", which adequately describes these two stripes, as some of the colours are broader than others.

The interesting badge (fig. 14) at the back of the jacket has been produced by needle-weaving and has been worked in upon the bare warp while that was still on the loom. The colours used, red, white, yellow and black, are indicated in the figure, which shows one-half of the badge.

The warp threads are grouped into bundles of about fifteen by the first two rows worked. The long parallel horizontal and curved lines of the design at *b* and *c* (fig. 14) are worked first, the effect of slanting stitches and an alternating black and white plait being obtained as shown in fig. 15 where the black thread shows the first row of stitches and the white the returning row. It will be noted that the threads cross one another alternately with the warp secured between them, as in twining, so that the wrong side is just the reverse in colour to the right. Four rows of stitches would be necessary to produce the effect

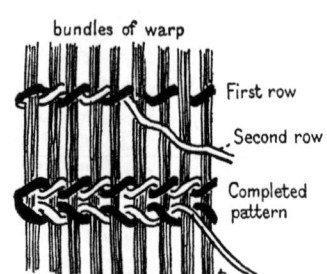

Fig. 15. Plaited or twined lines in badge, 35.903.

of the plait in the figure, or two needles might be kept working alternately and the result produced by two rows of work. After the completion of these long lines the intervening spaces are filled in with lozenges and triangles in red, yellow, white and black, each motive being completed before the next is begun. The stitch used is like darning; an enlarged detail is shown in fig. 8.

As will be seen from fig. 14, the pattern is one which, consisting chiefly of slanting lines, does not exhibit the usual weakness of the tapestry or needle-weaving method, i.e. gaps such as are produced when vertical lines are worked, except at the ends where variation of the central design has caused a long open slit *A–a*. This has been joined afterwards by string, the lacing stitch used for the side seams being the method adopted. The whole badge is surrounded by a vandyked border of yellow woollen material, *keselat lilit* ("*lilit*, gold embroidery on the edge of a handkerchief", *S.D.D.*), edged with scarlet flannel, secured by coarse white running stitches. The yellow and scarlet flannels are foreign and probably of British origin.

The central pattern of the badge (fig. 14) is labelled *pantak lelambak*, "wasp and flower pattern" (pl. XVII, *f*); it is enclosed within two zigzags called *lelingkok kelalin lantai*, zigzag interlaced bamboo. The black and white border within the triangles caused by the zigzag are labelled *dabong betangkal*, serrated notch (pl. XXIV, *l*). The upper border is labelled *lalat tisik tengiling* (which appears to signify a fly scraped off the scales of a *Manis javanicus*) and the lower border, *dabong telik leka labu*, serrated seed of gourd, *Cucurbita lagenaria*; perhaps the hour-glass-like red and black lozenges represent a constricted gourd, but *leka* signifies seed, grain.

A *kalambi burong* is considered one of the best kinds of jackets to possess, as many of the patterns symbolize ritual birds, possessing some special protective virtue.

The Iban are great observers of omens, always consulting them before beginning any important undertaking. The bird omens are the most numerous and important; the omen birds are supposed to be the sons-in-law of Singalang Burong and come from the spirit world as his messengers.

35.907   A *kalambi burong*. A striped cloth jacket similar in construction to the bird coat previously described has an analogous badge at the back, but the dyed designs and details of decoration are different; they consist mainly of birds.

The warp is grouped in threes in the solid colour stripes and in pairs in the patterned ones and averages 148 ends to the inch. The weft is brown and three threads are carried across each pick, tape-wise or parallel, having been previously wound on the spool in that manner.

The coat is bound round the edge with red flannel as in the previous cloth, but it and the badge at the back have also a bordering of a narrow white braid of European make which is usually used in Europe as a foundation for crochet work. Probably the chief value of the braid lies in its zigzag pattern, which was produced in the previous coat by snipping pieces out of the edge of the woollen material; further ornamentation has been added to the braid in the shape of a little looped stitch or picot (fig. 16, *b*), worked either in green or indigo.

A charming addition to the red border at the back is a hand-made braid

31

with a gold weft and a small scalloped edge. The braid is composed of purple, yellow and white warps brightened by the faint glisten here and there of the weft. In weaving the braid, three spools, each carrying two gold threads, appear to have been used in rotation, the thread being interlaced at the edge (much in the same way as baskets are often finished) and forming tiny

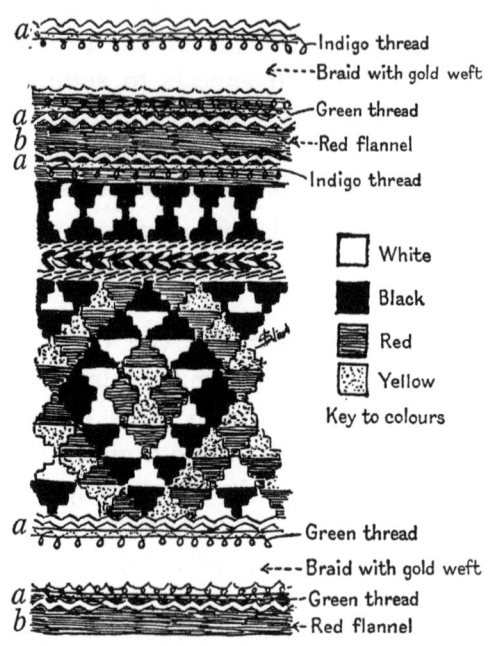

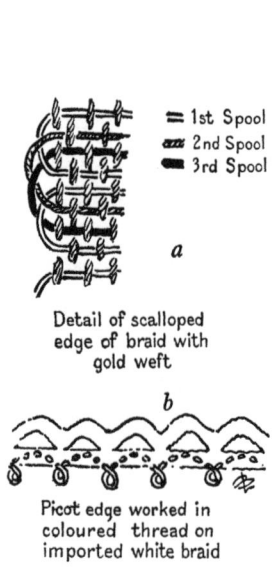

≡ 1st Spool
≋ 2nd Spool
▬ 3rd Spool

a

Detail of scalloped
edge of braid with
gold weft

b

Picot edge worked in
coloured thread on
imported white braid

Fig. 16. Details of badge
braids of *kalambi*, 35.907.

a ———Indigo thread
←----Braid with gold weft
———Green thread
←---Red flannel
———Indigo thread

☐ White

■ Black

▤ Red

▦ Yellow

Key to colours

a ———Green thread
←---Braid with gold weft
a ———Green thread
b ←-Red flannel

Fig. 17. One repeat of the pattern worked on
a badge of a *kalambi*, 35.907, by the tapestry
method, with added borders.

scallops. The method of interlacing is drawn in fig. 16, *a*. The native name for the braid, *lilit*, signifies "gold embroidery" or "to warp or bind with gold thread".

A single motive of the pattern in the badge is drawn in fig. 17; there are 11 complete and one partial repeat of this in the width of 17⅛ in. (43·5 cm.). The design is executed in red, white, yellow and black in the needle-weaving or tapestry method; the similarity of the pattern to that in cloth 35.903 is noticeable and possibly indicates that the original owner was a Saribas Iban. At the top of the badge is a band of white stepped lozenges on

32

a black ground; it is labelled *dabong igi labu*, serrated seed of gourd. The black and white band between this and the broad band is labelled *kelalin lantai*, interlaced bamboo. The double zigzag of the broad band is called *dabong lelingkok*, the triangles are labelled *lalat dabong lancham*, fly, serration or dog-tooth, pointed; the central designs are termed *lalat ketupang lensat*, (*lalat*, fly, *ketup*, to bite; *lensat* is a "fruit-bearing tree, *Lansium domesticum*", *S.D.D.*); this appears to mean a fly biting *lensat* (fruit).

The patterned stripes measure ¾ in. (1·9 cm.) and ¼ in. (6 mm.) alternately and are divided by compound solid colour stripes in the order: red, orange, indigo, white, indigo, orange, red, each ⅝ in. (1·6 cm.) wide and intended as a whole to represent the black, white and red bands of the *kendawang* snake (*Cylindrophis rufus*). The composite stripe is labelled *ara surik kendawang*, see p. 29. Amongst the birds figured in the broader patterned stripes are: *burong betampong*, "a ceremonial bird which cures sickness" (pl. IX, *d*); *burong bekarong*, "a hidden bird", similar to examples on pl. VII, *i–k* and *burong sawang prut*, "a bird with a hole in its breast" (pl. VII, *g*). All the narrower patterned stripes contain *daun wi*, "ratan leaves", very similar to those drawn on pl. XXII, *l, m*.

About two-thirds down the front of the jacket there occurs in all the patterned stripes a very interesting blurred design, which consists of a brown blank space with an indistinct lighter smear in its middle; above and below is an irregular wavy line (fig. 18, *b*). This is labelled *kengkang lang*, the striped kite: "the kite, according to Dyak belief the bodily shape and form of *Singalang Burong*, the Bird King, who, upon one occasion only, appeared on earth in human form but has since adopted the shape and form of the kite" (*S.D.D.*). The formless mass may be a naïve way of acknowledging the impossibility of depicting the Supreme Being.

35.905. A bird coat. This old "*Baju burong*" probably belonged to a Skarang Dayak, as some of the names of designs used are given in that dialect; and it is not so well finished as other examples of similar coats, having no badge or flannel binding. The side seams are joined by a form of blanket-stitch worked from side to side (fig. 18, *a*), which when closely done looks like the backbone of a fish and so is called *jayit tulang ikan*. Three little tassels, *kelapong leka*, made of the coloured warp thread finish off the end of the seam (fig. 18, *a*).

The warp is paired, with odd groups of three in the coloured stripes, and there are 112 ends to the inch; the weft is threefold and there are 22 picks to the inch.

The patterned stripes have a brown background with white motives and these are separated from one another by grouped warp stripes of red, yellow, brown and white, which vary in width from ⅜ in. (9 mm.) to 11/16 in. (1·7 cm.).

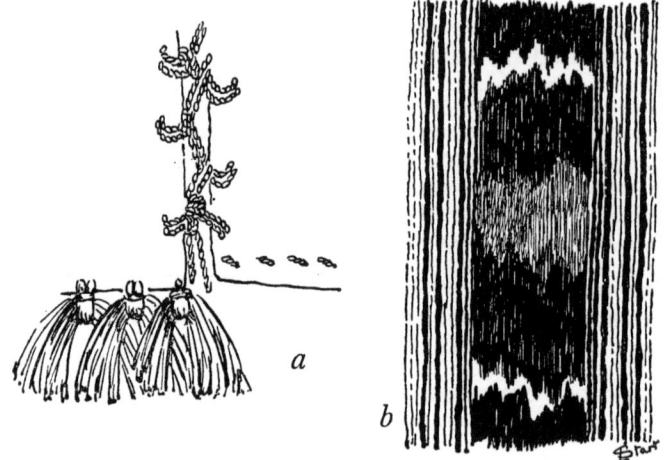

Fig. 18. Details of bird *kalambi*: *a*, tassels at end of seam, 35.905; *b, kengkang lang*, 35.907.

The narrower of the vertical patterned stripes have repeats of *anak lachau*, young grass lizard, similar to pl. XII, *a*; they are separated by variously coloured groups of, or compound, stripes, *surik rinik*, from the stripes decorated with birds, such as *burong bekarong*, "covered or concealed birds" (pl. VII, *j*); *burong enchoyok* (*tinggang ujan*)—the words in brackets indicate that this *burong* is associated with falling rain (pl. IX, *h*, and *g* seems to be a variant); *burong buah bangkit*, "bird on *bangkit* fruit". The designs on the front of the jacket also include *kengkang lang*, "striped kite". At the bottom of the back of the jacket are designs labelled *lancham pemuchok tubu*, "pointed bamboo shoots", pl. XVIII, *g*.

In giving names to the patterns on this cloth the owner described it as *satu macham bekarong samoa*, "a good kind to cover anyone", and also said *enggo lachau samoa*, "to wear a lizard all or everyone". The grass lizard is one of the lower rank of omen animals.

35.910. This is a well-made typical *kalambi* bound at the top with a narrow and at the sides with a broad band of red flannel. The lower edge has a strip of red and of yellow flannel and about 2½ in. above this are similar strips. At the collar is the silver-gilt button shown in fig. 11, *b*.

Among other devices in the broader vertical stripes are *burong burak*, "bird with a white breast"; *burong bekinkiang*, crooked *burong*; *burong pemiyaiarbong*; *burong trugu* and *langkiang*, a lizard with a long reflexed tail. The narrower stripes contain lizards, ratan, and other devices usually found in such stripes. A prominent feature in this and the next jacket is the occurrence of *kengkang lang* in the centre of all the vertical stripes on the front of the jacket. The badge is illustrated in fig. 9.

35.909. This is a new *kalambi* which apparently has never been worn, and there are no labels attached to the patterns. Stripes composed of two black lines edged with white in a rather broad red band separate the broad stripes containing birds from slightly narrower stripes in which are thick white zigzags with black spots. On the lower border of the back is a band or badge of chequer-work: yellow bands slope in one direction and red bands in the other; where they cross each other is a black square, the interspaces being white. Above this is a horizontal row of coarse double twining in brown and white.

35.902. On the body of this man's jacket there are self stripes in the colours of the *kendawang* snake, dividing patterned ones filled with birds. At the bottom of the back two rows of coarse double twining in black and white, about an inch apart, are outlined by and enclose a sparsely worked lozenge pattern done in gold thread.

35.919. This is a piece of cloth 8 ft. long made for a *kalambi* with sleeves, just as it is when taken off the loom. The photograph (pl. xxvii) shows only one-quarter of the length, but it will be seen that the length is continuous as the warp ends joining the part where the badge has been worked in and those of the other end of the cloth are uncut. Fragments of a thin strip of bamboo, used as a laze rod (fig. 4), still remain near the beginning of the pattern and can be seen near the bottom of the photograph. Below the needle-woven badge are two coarse threads which have been used to group the warps for the stitchery. The cloth has self-coloured stripes of white, scarlet and yellow alternating with patterned ones.

The part of the cloth photographed (pl. xxvii) shows the variously coloured stripes, *surik ular kendawang*, which separate the alternate rows of *burong burak prut*, "bird with white breast" (cf. pl. vii, *e*), and *lachau*, "green grass lizard" (cf. pl. xii, *a*); the *lachau* are found only at the ends of the cloth, throughout the greater part of its length being replaced by *daun wi*, "leaf of ratan" (cf. pl. xxii, *k*). At the extreme ends of the cloth below the *burong* are designs which on other cloths are labelled *pemuchok tubu*, "bamboo shoots", perhaps with the head of a locust on the top of the shoot. At the top and bottom of the badge is a very narrow border of two yellow stripes separated by black and white spots; this is called *kelalin lantai*, interlaced cane; two similar horizontal borders separate the main patterns of the badge. The upper and lower patterns consist of a series of white and black triangles separated by a row of red and yellow triangles; they are labelled *lalat dabong igi labu*, fly, serrated or dog-tooth, seed, gourd. On other parts of the cloth are *burong lelayang*, swallow, *burong mansau prut*, "bird with red breast", *daun entibap*, "(isolated) leaf of the *arenga* palm" (see pl. xxii, *a–e*). The *kengkang lang* (p. 33) is especially prominent. The broad central pattern has two zigzags, *lelingkok kelalin lantai*, zigzag interlaced cane, which divide the band into triangles and lozenges, which are filled up with white, yellow, red and black triangles, all the last having a gold thread centre; within the lozenges are black designs enclosing red and yellow triangles; these are labelled *buah belimbing*.

35.908. This is a jacket of somewhat unusual colour; its edges are bound with red flannel, and there is no badge on the back. Width, 21 in. (53·4 cm.); length from shoulder to hem, 22 in. (55·9 cm.).

The warps are paired throughout the cloth except in the pale brown and yellow self stripes, where a coarser yarn has been used in the former, the latter being crowded together. There are 60 groups to the inch, i.e. 120 ends and 24 picks of weft to the inch.

The background is dark red in tone with patterns in light brown with darker markings of red and dark brown. There are two narrow patterned borders at the sides of the cloth, each divided from the other and from the central pattern by coloured warp stripes representing the snake, in red, yellow, black and pale brown, repeated twice.

On the front of the jacket are *aji*, shrews, and the back is covered with

36

remaung, "tiger-cats"; all are typical conventions of these animals. Between the spaces of the tiger-cats are various *burong*; *anak lachau*, "young grass lizards" (pl. xii, *e*); *engkatak*, "frog" (pl. xiii, *d*); and *igi bras*, "grains of uncooked rice".

The narrow vertical bands, which are transverse on the sleeves, contain various birds, including *kengkang lang*, "the striped kite"; *burong belingkian*, "argus pheasant", with its long tail feathers (pl. ix, *e*); *burong besugu*, "bird with comb" (pl. vii, *p*); *burong entepa*, "bird with outstretched wings" (pl. vii, *q*, *r*); *burong buah bangkit*, "bird on *bangkit* fruit" (pl. viii, *c*), but this is very like a form of *burong entepa* and there is no indication of the conventional lozenge-shaped *bangkit* fruit.

It looks as if the cloth from which the back and sleeves of this coat has been made was originally woven for a *bidang*, but the front portions have characteristic *kengkang lang* in the two *burong* stripes and a very broad one between shrew designs which are covered on the outside with a band of red flannel. The only definite example of this type of *kengkang lang* on any *bidang* in our collection is 35.884.

Z.2342. This jacket is called "*kalambi ara*, striped coat", which is a very good description. There are broad white and dull indigo stripes at the sides and centre of the back and the space between has three narrow horizontally striped black and white bands with crimson stripes on each side of them, alternating with composite ones of all three colours about 1 in. in width. A very coarse needle-woven or weft-mosaic pattern of vertical lozenges in black, white, red and yellow decorates the hem at the back and this is finished off by a row of small tassels, consisting of bunches of cotton ends tied in with the bunched ends of the warps.

Z.2341. A woman's reddish brown coat with narrow simple and composite stripes of purple and white, having broader white purple and black stripes at the sides. There is a rather coarse pattern of triangles darned in white at the bottom of the back, edged with a row of double twining in black and white. The end of the back of the jacket is finished off with small cotton tassels in red, yellow, black and white, tied on by bunches of warp ends.

35.904. The red cloth of which this *kalambi* is made is finely woven and is $19\frac{1}{4}$–$19\frac{1}{2}$ in. (48·8–49·5 cm.) wide, having groups of coloured warp stripes at each side.

Most of the back and the front portions of the jacket are elaborately decorated with anthropomorphic designs, and the sides are decorated with groups of coloured stripes between which are zoomorphs (figs. 19, 21).

These patterns, which are in blue, white and orange, may have been produced by either of two methods, embroidery or the use of free or floating spools. If spools have been used, a principle which is simple becomes elaborate in the actual working, for taking the white portion of each design, it seems to need two spools for its production, used in different ways, e.g. to work the outline of a lozenge one spool would be used for each side, but for a solid vertical line the two would be used alternately, the threads of one appearing above a throw of weft, the second below; the indigo parts of the pattern could be produced by single spools carrying a group of three or four untwisted threads.

If this is the method which has been employed, each pattern being picked out on the warp with the free spools, a wonderfully accurate effect has been produced.

The same difficulty would not be experienced if embroidery were the method adopted, and it therefore seems most probable that the needle was the only tool used. The fineness and regularity of the work are not at all out of keeping with other embroidered work, e.g. the *sirat* ends, and with the general accuracy of workmanship in other Iban crafts.

Whichever method was used, a fresh thread has been introduced for each little patch of colour and the reverse is exactly similar in effect to the obverse.

The garment is, in shape and construction, similar to those previously described, except that the whole of the coat appears to have been enlarged; the width has been increased by the insertion of a piece of imported red cotton cloth in the side seams, the sleeves have been lengthened by a similar insertion at the shoulder seam and both front and back have been lengthened by a piece 5 in. in depth—an argument in favour of the descent of the jacket from one person to another. On the front the joining has been concealed by a band of stitching, the centre being worked in gold thread with border lines of yellow chain-stitch. At the back the joining is hidden by the border of red and yellow flannel which surrounds the badge.

The badge (fig. 21) consists of three parallel, horizontal bands, the outer ones of gold thread and the central one of white and red thread. The designs, which reproduce patterns plaited (*anyam*) in mats, are worked in the brocade method, i.e. the weft threads being loosely carried across the back of the cloth until needed to form a portion of the pattern.

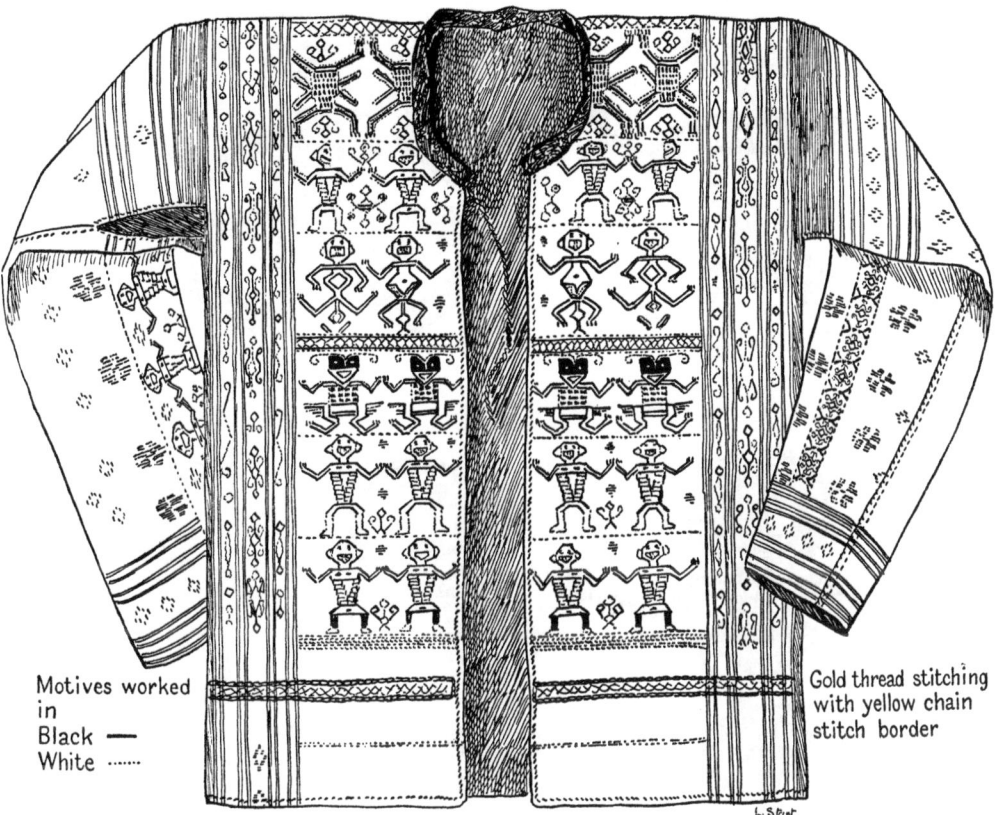

Motives worked in Black ——— White ·······

Gold thread stitching with yellow chain stitch border

Fig. 19. Front of an embroidered *manang bali kalambi* 35.904.

At the bottom of the badge there is a fringe of black and white beads; the beads are threaded on the warp ends, which are then finished off with a knot.

The neck of the jacket is bound by printed cotton of foreign manufacture.

The cloth of which the jacket is made is, as usual, one with a warp surface, in which there are 180 to 204 ends to the inch, grouped in threes. There are

26 to 30 weft picks to the inch, but as three parallel, untwisted threads are carried by the spool, there are really about 90 weft threads to the inch.

The chief interest of the coat, however, lies in the patterns and their meanings.

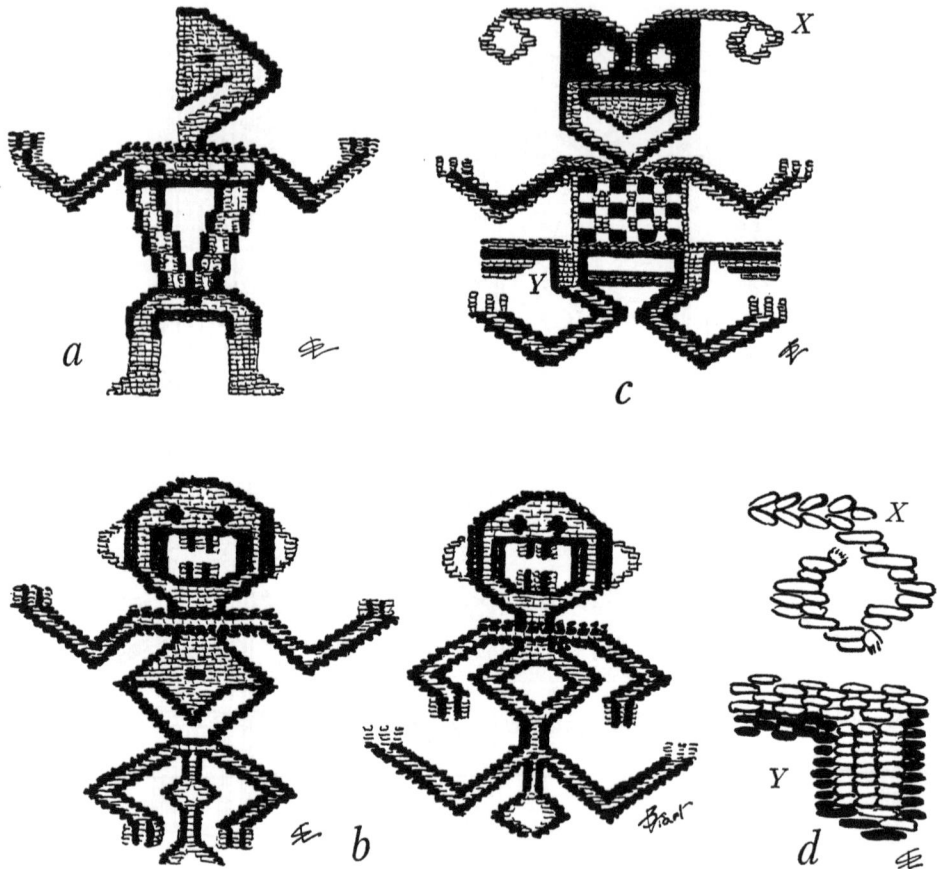

Fig. 20. Anthropomorphic designs on front of *manang bali* jacket 35.904: *a*, second row, figure with half a head and no teeth, see fig. 22 *a*; *b*, third row, presumably these male and female figures are *engkaramba manang bali*, "a *manang* who acts as a woman"; *c*, fourth row, *balu menyagu*, "widower"; *d*, enlargement of parts of *c* showing arrangement of stitches.

The figures in the top row of the front of the coat (fig. 19) are labelled *kengkang kelabong*, this may be translated as striped scorpion. The human figures in the second row (figs. 20, *a*; 22, *a*) are very similar to those in the fifth and sixth rows, except that in the sixth row the legs are blue and not white as in all the others. The figures in the sixth row are labelled *gambar mensia*, representations of a person, or *engkaramba anak orang entepa*, a young man with outstretched arms, and presumably these names also apply to the other two rows. Only half of the face is embroidered in the outer figures of the second row (fig. 20, *a*) and this is labelled *jari engkatak*, hand of frog; probably some mistake has occurred. The human figures in the third row are alternately male and female and are on the whole similar to those in the fourth and sixth rows on the back of the jacket.

A narrow pattern of hexagons divides the third from the fourth row. It is labelled *kembong tikup*, to close a swelling; the stitchery was used to flatten a looseness or crease in the cloth, hence its name.

The figures in the fourth row (fig. 20, *c*) are labelled *engkaramba balu menyagu*, we do not know why they are termed "widower"; they appear to wear a large mask (Hose and McDougall, II, pl. 151, give a photograph of "Kenyah dayongs wearing masks"); the *dayong* of the Kenyah and Kayan are the equivalent of the Iban *manang*, they also are soul-catchers and play a large part in the ceremonies connected with death. We do not know what the wing-like extensions from the waist signify; perhaps they represent the swinging-out of the dress worn owing to a turning movement of the dancer.

Among the numerous designs at the sides of the jacket are: *burong lelayang*, a swallow (pl. IX, *b*); *burong jagi*, which may represent a bird in flight (pl. IX, *i*); *anak burong*, young bird (pl. IX, *j*); *kukut lang*, talon of a kite (pl. X, *h*) (but a somewhat similar device is labelled *daun entibap*, "leaf of the arenga palm", pl. XXII, *e*); other designs are: *burong buah bangkit, burong bekarong, burong sawang prut*, and *lelingkok semberai* (? *semerai*) *sungei*, zigzagging across a river.

There are six rows of human figures on the back of the coat (fig. 21). The first row shows each man (who has no teeth) wearing a chequered coat and carrying something under his flexed arms. The men are labelled *gajah meram engkaramba* (*antu*) and the object under the arm is called *telor gajah* (*telor* is the Malay word for egg) (fig. 22, *b*). There are no elephants in Sarawak, so the Iban are not likely to be acquainted with them, but wild elephants (introduced?) exist in north Borneo. The "egg" is obviously incorrect, but it may be a suggestion of something mysterious and belonging to the spirit-world.

Of great importance, but very rarely observed in modern times, is the *gawai gajah*, "elephant feast", which can only be held by a particularly successful war leader who has obtained a large number of heads. Offerings and incantations are made to Singalang Burong, who is the God of the

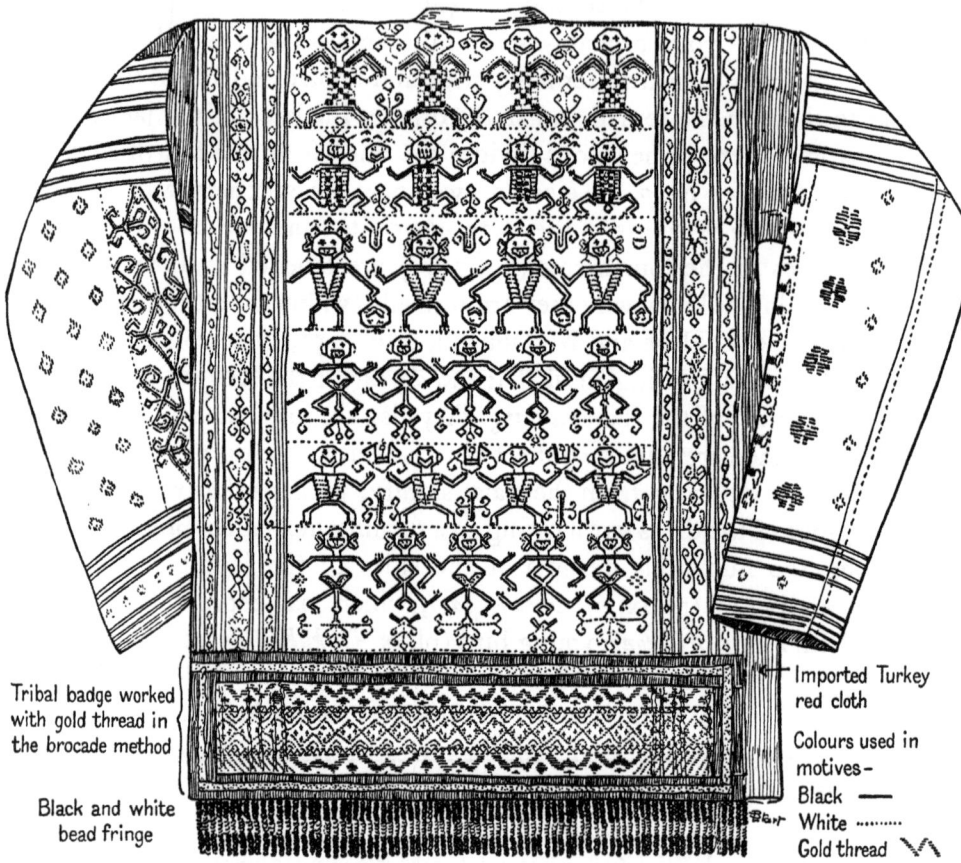

Tribal badge worked with gold thread in the brocade method

Black and white bead fringe

Imported Turkey red cloth

Colours used in motives -
Black ——
White ·········
Gold thread ⋀⋀

Fig. 21. Back of *manang bali kalambi* 35.904. Red cloth embroidered in black, white and orange, with a badge worked in the brocade method.

Heavens and of war. The wooden figure of an elephant is placed on the top of a long pole planted in the ground and to this figure offerings are made (Gomes, 1911, p. 215). It seems probable that the elephant motive is an imperfectly assimilated foreign conception—perhaps of Indian origin. It is, however, possible that it may be reminiscent of a time when their ancestors may have been familiar with elephants. The point requires elucidation by local investigation.

The figures in the second row are also clothed in a chequered garment;

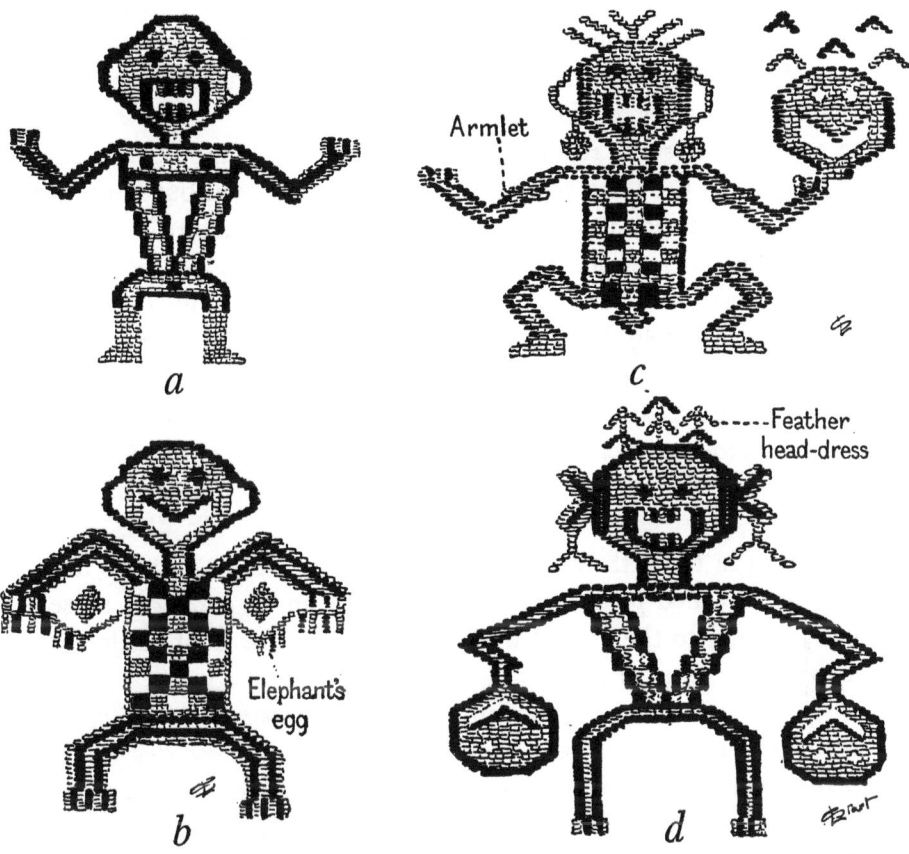

Fig. 22. Anthropomorphic designs on back of *manang bali* jacket 35.904: *a*, inner figure of second row on front of jacket, similar to the figures of rows 5 and 6, and rather similar to those of the fifth row on the back, though these have no teeth; *b*, first row of back, *gajah meram engkaramba* (*antu*), "man's ghost or spirit"; *c*, second row of back, *orang brani*, "brave man"; *d*, third row of back, *engkaramba bekatapu*, man wearing a feathered war-cap and carrying two old human heads, one of which is labelled *minching* (*labu*).

they wear ear-ornaments, perhaps feathers on their heads, and carry heads upright in their left hands (fig. 22, *c*). They are labelled *engkaramba* (*orang brani*), brave men. The possession of trophy heads is doubtless the reason for the adjective *brani*, brave.

43

The third row shows figures, the heads of which are labelled *pala engkaramba bekatapu*, head with war cap, wearing the feathered war cap, *ujok ujok katapu*. One of the carried heads is labelled *minching (labu)*. *Labu* signifies a gourd, and it is possible that it is a gourd with holes for eyes and a slit for the mouth, which is used as a substitute for a head. The attitudes of the figures and the changed position of the heads in the last two rows suggest that they represent a head-hunting dance.

The fourth and sixth rows contain alternate male and female figures similar to those of the third row on the front of the jacket, but in these two rows there is below each figure a *kukut burong*, "claws of a bird". The males have a long line with curled ends passing through the glans penis, which evidently represents a *palang*. According to Brooke Low (Ling Roth, *J.A.I.*, xxii, 1892 (1893), p. 45) the custom of perforating the glans for the permanent insertion of a short rod with a knob at each end, *palang*, was adopted by the Iban from the Kayans. The head of a male figure in the fourth row is labelled *pala engkaramba manang bali*, the head of a *manang bali*, and a male figure in the sixth row is called *engkaramba manang bali*.

The figures in the fifth row are labelled *gambar mensia*, but the head of one of them is called *pala engkaramba*, head of an *engkaramba*; these are essentially similar to the figures in the fifth row on the front of the jacket, except that they have no teeth.

The right sleeve has along its length five *engkaramba anak orang entepa* similar to those on the front and back of the jacket, and also designs: *tabor mata puna*, scattered eyes of pigeons, and *tabor bunga janggat*, scattered flowers of the white pumpkin. The two latter are also scattered over the left sleeve, on which are two other patterns which we do not recall having seen elsewhere.

This is evidently a very special kind of *kalambi*, which we may surmise was worn only on particular occasions. Concerning the human figures it is interesting to find that "only women belonging to ancient and honourable families may make *engkaramba* and even they must begin by making other patterns" (Haddon MS.). The *Sea Dyak Dictionary* gives "*Engkramba*, a representation of anything cut out of wood". They are used to prevent harm from coming to crops, etc.

We suggest that the jacket belonged to a *manang* and more probably to a *manang bali* ("*Bali*, v. to exchange, fade, s. alteration", *S.D.D.*).

The Iban believe that sickness is due to the presence of evil spirits in the patient's body, or to a spirit that has struck him or has enticed his soul out of his body; thus it naturally follows that the medicine men, or *manang*, must be able to charm the evil spirits away and persuade the soul to return to its earthly habitation.

The *manang* is next in importance amongst the Iban to the village chief, and sometimes the office is filled by the same man, especially if he is a faithful interpreter of dreams and successful in exorcizing spirits. The office of *manang* is hereditary, and may be held by either a man or a woman; it is extremely lucrative, as heavy sums are paid for the aid given in performing the ancient rites connected with birth and death, and it is in connection with the latter that three of the most important Iban feasts are held. Charms, which are the personal possession of the *manang*, are frequently used in the case of sickness; sometimes they are rubbed on that part of the body where the pain is felt, at other times they are dipped in water, which the patient afterwards drinks. In serious cases a fowl or a pig may be killed as an offering to the *antu*, or spirit, whose displeasure is the cause of the suffering.

A *manang bali* is the highest rank to which a *manang* can attain and they are infrequent. "They are men who adopt and continuously wear woman's dress and behave in all ways like women, except that they avoid as far as possible taking any part in the domestic labour. They claim to have been told in dreams to adopt this mode of life; they are employed for the same purpose as the more ordinary *manangs*, and they practise similar methods" (Hose and McDougall, II, p. 116). Howell and Bailey say: "Even to the Dyak mind such a process is unnatural, and it is only undergone because of the command of the spirits who must be obeyed." These authors describe the initiation of a *manang bali* and state that after the ceremony "the *Manang Bali* apes the manners of a woman. He does all the work usually done by women. He sometimes even takes a 'husband' who is looked down upon by the community, and whose sole desire is to inherit his 'wife's' property as soon as possible. The *Manang Bali* may be said to have almost ceased to exist, among the down-river Dyaks, but the up-river people possess several recently made specimens!" (*S.D.D.*, 1901, p. 99).

45

E. H. Gomes (1911, p. 37) says *kalambi* "of a particular type can only be worn by men who have succeeded in securing a human head when on the warpath", but, as he does not give particulars, this statement does not help us; perhaps the *kalambi* illustrated by Hose, 1926, pl. p. 170, may be one of this kind—it is ornamented with two feathers of the hornbill, a bird everywhere associated with fighting.

It is somewhat rash to speculate upon what occasions a *kalambi* of this sort would be worn, but some of the embroidered figures seem to indicate that it was associated in some way with head-hunting.

One of the three principal ceremonial feasts of the Iban is *gawai burong* or *gawai pala*, "bird- or head-feast", as described by J. Perham in Ling Roth, I, p. 256; II, pp. 174 ff. When a house has obtained a head a great feast must be made sooner or later; it is not a mere matter of eating and drinking but there is much ceremony of offerings and songs, and Singalang Burong is invoked to attend. Before he can start he must call from the jungle his sons-in-law, who are the sacred birds which the Iban use as omens— hence the term *gawai burong*. The hawk (kite), *lang*, with brown body and white head and breast is a personification of Singalang Burong. The bird-chief and his dependents come from above to give to the men strength and bravery in war, and to the women luck with paddy, cleverness, and beauty. The ceremony is in fact a religious drama.

35.906. An embroidered *kalambi*. This coat is cut in exactly the same way as the others, but has different motives which have been produced by embroidery (fig. 23). Width, $17\frac{1}{2}$ in. (44·4 cm.); length from shoulder to hem, $22\frac{3}{5}$ in. (57·4 cm.).

The body of the cloth is red with warp stripes grouped on the front and back: black, yellow, red, white, black, white, red, yellow, black; these are called *surik ular kendawang*, see pp. 29, 33. The width of these grouped stripes varies, broader bands appearing at the edges of the cloth.

The sleeves, which are made from the full width of the cloth, have no other decoration than the coloured warp stripes.

The edges of the jacket are bound with red flannel and at the neck and round the badge at the back an extra row of yellow flannel with vandyked edges is added.

The number of warp groups to the inch varies from 60–74, averaging

272 ends in all the stripes except the white, where they are in pairs and there are 44 pairs to the inch (88 ends).

The weft is red throughout and consists of a bundle of four, six or eight threads slightly twisted, and there are on an average 22 picks to the inch.

The motives which embellish the garment are embroidered in white and black, with the occasional addition of gold thread, usually in the form of a spot. They are entirely different from those on any other coat in the collection, as can be seen in fig. 23, which shows the front and back of the garment.

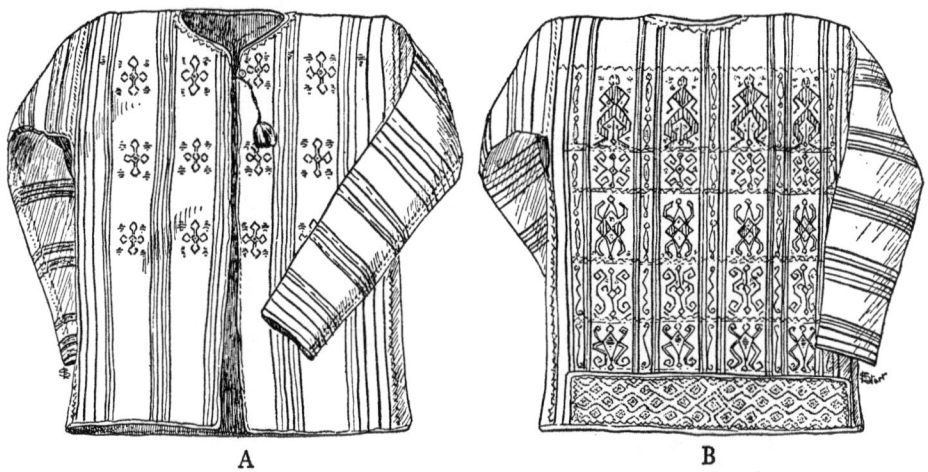

A   B

Fig. 23. A, front and B, back of a *kalambi*, 35.906, with woven stripes and embroidered designs. Fig. 7, p. 15, is an enlargement of a *burong kaki panjai* in the last row of B. The badge (fig. 24) is worked in the brocade method with a gold thread weft.

On the front two isolated, *tabor*, motives appear, the cruciform one representing a flower, *bungai*, rather like pl. xxii, *i*, and, around the flower, four spots, *bintang*, "star", which are worked in gold thread. On the back, taking the figures in the broader stripes in order from top to bottom, the first represents a frog, *engkatak* (pl. xiii, *e*), the second a concealed bird, *burong bekarong*; the third a scorpion, *kala* (pl. xvii, *a*); the fourth a concealed bird slightly different from the previous one (pl. vii, *k*); and the fifth, *burong kaki panjai*, a "bird with long legs" (fig. 7). In the narrow vertical stripes there are three other motives, the upper three of each stripe, the lizard, *lachau* (pl. xii, *a*); the fifth down the stripe is the leech, *lintah* (pl. xvi, *h*), and the last represents ratan leaves, *daun wi*.

The method by which these various devices have been produced is embroidery. If individual threads are followed it will be found that they do not all end at the lowest point of a curve or fret, but sometimes continue round it, which would be impossible if the threads were introduced during the progress of the weaving by free spools. An enlargement of one of the bird motives in which the stitches are clearly indicated is given in fig. 7.

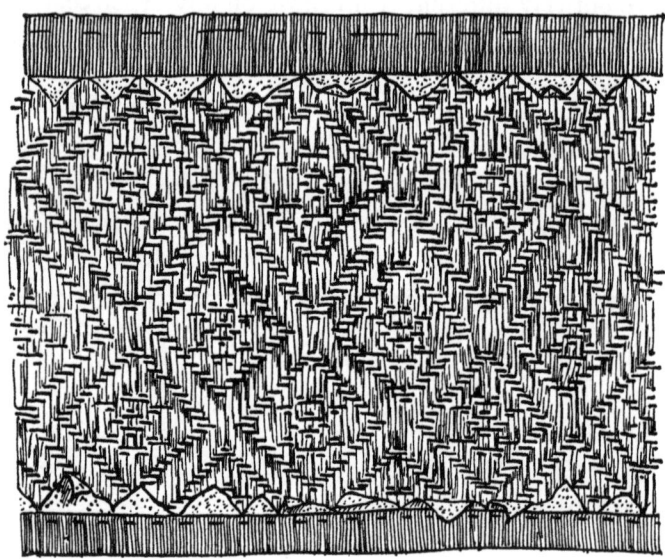

Fig. 24. Badge at the back of *kalambi* 35.906, worked in the brocade method with gold thread weft.

A new embroidery thread is begun in a somewhat unusual manner, being threaded through the cloth singly, then both ends being brought to the front it is worked as a double thread.

The badge at the bottom of the jacket at the back is not a weft-mosaic like the Saribas variety, but is worked like a brocade or damask with a floating weft, the triple gold thread (not twisted) which forms this weft being carried across the back when not needed on the right side. The warps are grouped in fours or sixes and the result is a fabric of very loose texture. Owing to the very loose texture, the coloured warps which form stripes in the cloth are visible in this jacket as a continuation across the badge; these are not shown in figs. 23, *b* and 24.

48

The motives in the badge (fig. 24) represent *lelambak anyam*, a flower similar to that plaited in mats (pl. xxii, *h*), and *dabong lilit*, a dog-tooth pattern in gold thread.

35.901. *Baju sungkit*, an embroidered jacket worn by women; it was made by a Nabai Iban woman.

A plain cloth jacket dyed reddish brown with an applied panel called *tandar* on the upper part of the back, which is much of the same type as the embroidered ends of *sirat*. The white cloth is of coarse texture and the panel is outlined with an inner strip of scarlet flannel and an outer one of yellow flannel. The designs are boldly embroidered in red and blue. A narrow upper border consists of a zigzag, *lelingkok*, with a *pala buntak*, "head of locust", on each apex. The lower border is labelled *pemuchok tubu*, shoot of bamboo. We have no information concerning the design of the broad central band, which is exactly like that on a "little girl's jacket, from Batang Lupar", figured by Ling Roth, ii, p. 33.

35.911. Shell *kalambi*. The jacket in figs. 25, 26 is entirely decorated with *buri* shells (*Nassa* sp.) and is an exceptionally fine example of this method of ornamentation, which is now almost obsolete, European buttons being used instead. An immense amount of labour has been expended on the preparation of the shells, for the spire of each has been ground away, leaving a flat piece about $\frac{1}{10}$ in. in thickness containing the mouth of the shell. A second hole was bored and each shell was then secured to the cloth by two stitches made with strong twine (the fibre of pineapple leaves), one through the aperture and down the drilled hole, the other fastening down the narrow end.

The foundation of the garment is an indigo-dyed cotton cloth backed with a much coarser native cloth in order to give sufficient support for the weight of the shells. The front edges, side seams and armholes are further decorated by being bound with red cloth.

A very primitive and effective method of fastening is provided by means of three roughly shaped flat wooden discs on the right-hand side; each disc has a hole in the centre through which a string is knotted to hold it in place. There are corresponding loops on the left-hand edge made by tying a piece of twine through the back of a few stitches.

This jacket was originally the property of a Baju Bari Dayak from the Baram river, but there is no information whether it was a man's or a woman's

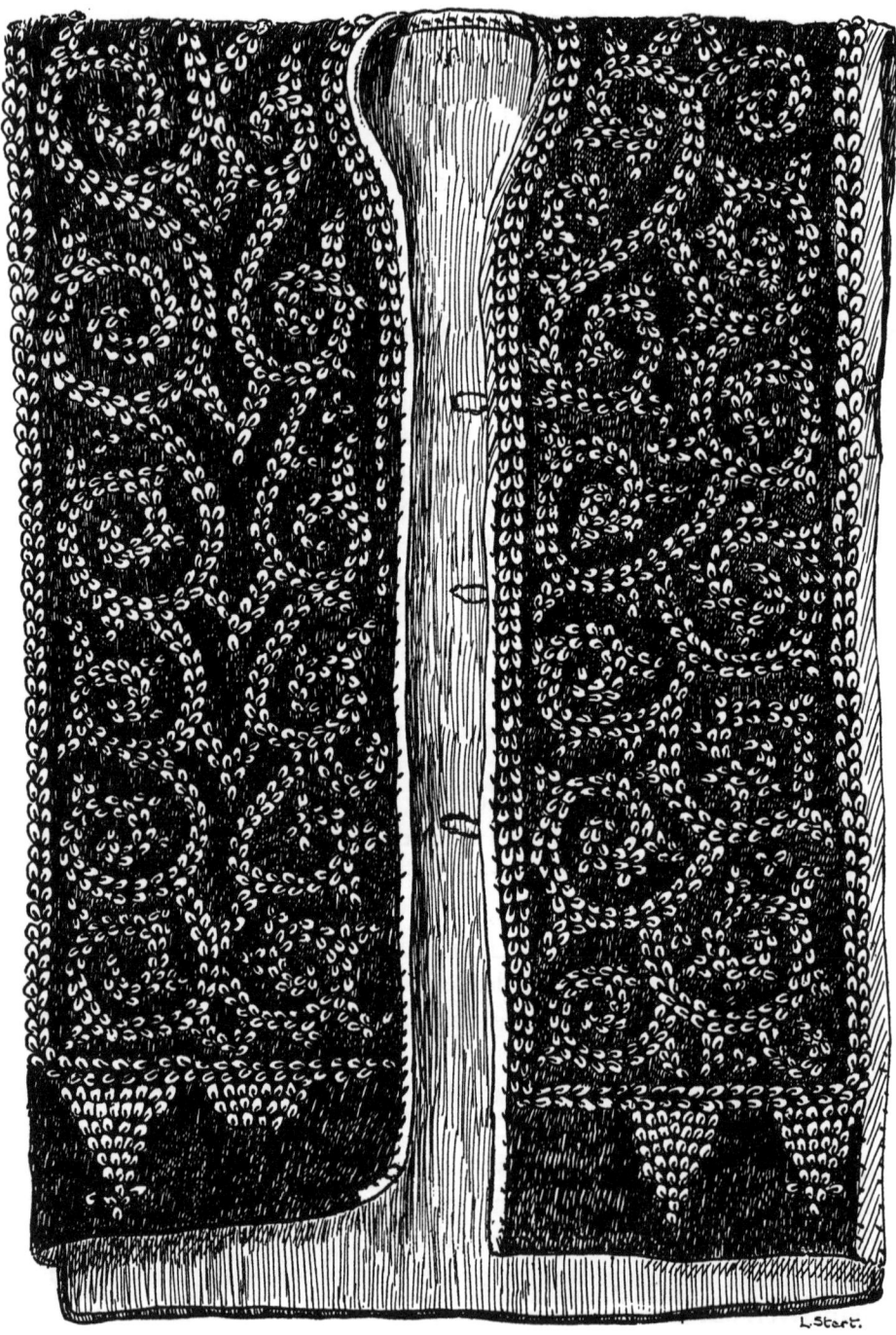

Fig. 25. Front of *kalambi* 35.911, decorated with shells.

Fig. 26. Back of same jacket with a reptilian motive in shells.

4-2

kalambi. Presumably the large reptile that dominates the back is a monitor lizard, *Varanus* sp. The remaining surface is covered with evenly distributed scroll-like designs, which evidently are phyllomorphic; the front of the jacket is ornamented with similar designs. Along the bottom, both back and front, is a pattern of bamboo shoots.

There is a woman's "*kalambi buri*" in the British Museum (1905, 357) very similar to ours; the front is ornamented with "scorpions, crabs, and starfish" and the back with a large "lizard". Another one (1923, 10.18.1) is of particular interest as it is made of bark-cloth; it is ornamented with a lizard, two scorpions, and scrolls also of nassa shells.

An ordinary patterned *bidang* (1905, 393) in the British Museum has a black flounce added to its lower half, which is ornamented with nassa shells arranged in triangles with curves springing from their apices; these are labelled *punchok rebong*, "bamboo shoots".

Hose and McDougall (I, pl. 30) give a photograph of an Iban woman wearing a sleeved *kalambi* decorated with shells; the patterns in front are more open and less complicated than those of our coat. The lower part of the *bidang* she is wearing is also decorated with nassa shells; above the terminal broad band of presumably plant-designs are scorpions or lizards with their long tails interlocked.

The supposition therefore is that our jacket is a woman's *kalambi* and that the reptile on the back is a monitor lizard.

BIDANG, PETTICOATS

The *bidang* or women's petticoats form a particularly interesting group of cloths for study, as almost all are patterned and the patterns comprise a larger and more varied series of motives than are to be found in either the *kalambi* (jackets) or the *pua* (blankets). Each petticoat is made from half a length of cloth as it comes from the loom and therefore exhibits one complete section of the pattern. The cut ends of the cloth are joined together by a rather coarsely sewn counter-hem, such as is often used for the sleeves of the *kalambi* (fig. 12, *c*). The completed garment is pulled on over the head and arranged around the waist, the excess in width being made into a pleat, the top of which is tucked in, to hold the garment firmly to the figure.

The piece of cloth for a *bidang* may vary in width from just over 16 in. to nearly 2 ft. and the length from 3 ft. 6 in. to 4 ft. 3 in. The average length of 30 petticoats taken at random from a group of 40 was 3 ft. 8⅔ in. and their average width just over 20 in.

BIDANG CLOTHS

The cloth used for *bidang* is generally very firm and extremely hard wearing, the yarn used being firmly spun although it varies greatly in thickness, an average section being 0·25 mm.

The yarn used for the warp colour stripes, which form borders at the top and bottom of the petticoat when in wear, but which being warp threads are really parallel with the sides of the cloth, is usually finer in section than that in the patterned part of the web. These coloured yarns are dyed in the hank before being set up in the loom with the patterned warps. The bright reds used by the Saribas Iban are usually the finest, averaging from 0·15 mm. to 0·2 mm. in section, whilst the pure white sometimes used in the border stripes is the coarsest, reaching 0·5 mm.

The white thread is the only yarn in any of the cloths which is used "doubled" in the accepted meaning of that term (i.e. two threads which are twisted upon one another) and for this reason and the fineness of its bleaching one might suspect it to have been an importation, although the twist in the single thread and the quality of the cotton fibre itself indicate native origin. It may be that the fibre is native but has been spun and doubled mechanically, instead of by hand, which would mean that the yarn was not produced by the weaver of the cloth as is usually the case.

The warps in cloths intended for *bidang* are nearly always grouped for the purpose of weaving, being usually arranged in pairs (the threads remaining parallel) or threes, though four in a group occur occasionally in the self-colour stripes, where there are usually a greater number of warp ends to the inch (fig. 27, *a*). Taking a series of 30 cloths it was found that the average number of warp ends to the inch in the self-coloured stripes was 147, whilst in the patterned ones it was only 116; this shows that the fabrics are usually more closely woven at the sides than in the centre. The close weaving of the plain colour stripes enhances their value aesthetically.

In the same set of cloths the grouping of the warps for the borders was

19 pairs, 7 threes, 2 fours and 2 singles; whilst in the patterned portion the grouping was 24 pairs, 4 threes and 2 singles. A detailed analysis of 30 of these cloths is given later.

As the upper and under webs are tied together in arranging the pattern when on the tying frame, this analysis of the grouping of warps means that it is usual to tie up four threads, although on occasions the number may be eight, six or two.

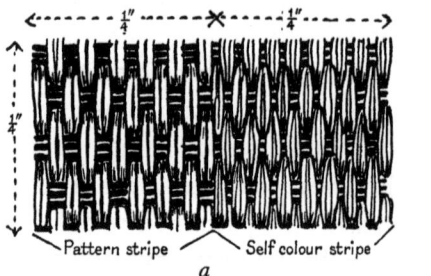

Fig. 27. *a*, Proportions of weft visible when warps are paired and grouped in threes; *b*, three parallel weft threads turned at the edge of the cloth.

The average number of weft picks or shoots to the inch in 30 cloths made for *bidang* and *kalambi* was 21·8, practically 22. In winding the weft on the spools two, three or four threads are wound at the same time and kept quite flat like a ribbon or tape, so that in passing the spool from side to side a series of parallel weft threads is carried across, an arrangement which usually makes the weft broader in section than the warp.

In the group of cloths under consideration 10 had two parallel weft threads in each pick, 11 had three, 4 had four and only 5 were single weft threads. An example with three, showing the crowding of the warps in the plain colour stripes and the turning of the weft threads at the edge of the cloth, is given in fig. 27, *b*.

The weft is usually brown in colour, either reddish or a dull vandyke shade.

The weaving itself is of the simplest type, one group of warp threads being picked up and left down alternately by the spool in passing.

The width of the weft and the large number of warp ends as compared with weft picks result in the production of a cloth with a rep or poplin weave, in which the warp threads form the surface, and as they had been previously dyed after the pattern portion had been reserved by tying up, they produce the desired pattern.

The average width of 30 *bidang* cloths is 1 ft. 8 in. (50·8 cm.) and the average length 3 ft. 10 in. (116·9 cm.), and according to Mr Leggatt it takes several months to dye and weave a piece of cloth 45 in. in circumference, i.e. a length of 3 ft. 9 in. which has been joined by sewing.

ARRANGEMENT OF THE PATTERNS AND GENERAL COLOUR EFFECTS

Most of the *bidang* have a broad central band elaborately decorated with patterns. These patterns appear as designs in stone or buff colour against a background which is a reddish brown in most cases, but occasionally the whole of the warp for the patterned stripe is dyed a light brown first, in which case the patterns appear as light brown.

The reddish-brown ground commonly used is sometimes varied in small patches by being re-dyed in indigo so that it becomes a dark brown, almost vandyke, in those parts. Such variations usually indicate a highly skilled worker. On either side of the broad central pattern is a series of compound stripes, each composed of several narrow warp stripes of different colours. Often a colour consists of only a few warp threads, so producing the effect of a "pin stripe". Narrow patterned stripes are frequently used between these composite ones; three sets of border stripes are illustrated in fig. 28 and it will be noted that the self-colour stripes at the outer edges are often wider. In a large group of cloths (for *bidang*) they vary from half an inch to an inch and a half; sometimes there is one broad one, in other examples there is a series of three or four averaging half an inch each.

These broad self-colour stripes form a strong contrast with the quieter buff and brown pattern in the central band and provide a strong accent which is particularly pleasing in its effect.

One of the most popular arrangements of colour in the composite stripes is scarlet, black, or an indigo so dark that it appears black by contrast, and yellow; or scarlet, black, white and yellow. This arrangement is described as *ara surik kendawang*, "the coloured stripes of a snake", and is derived

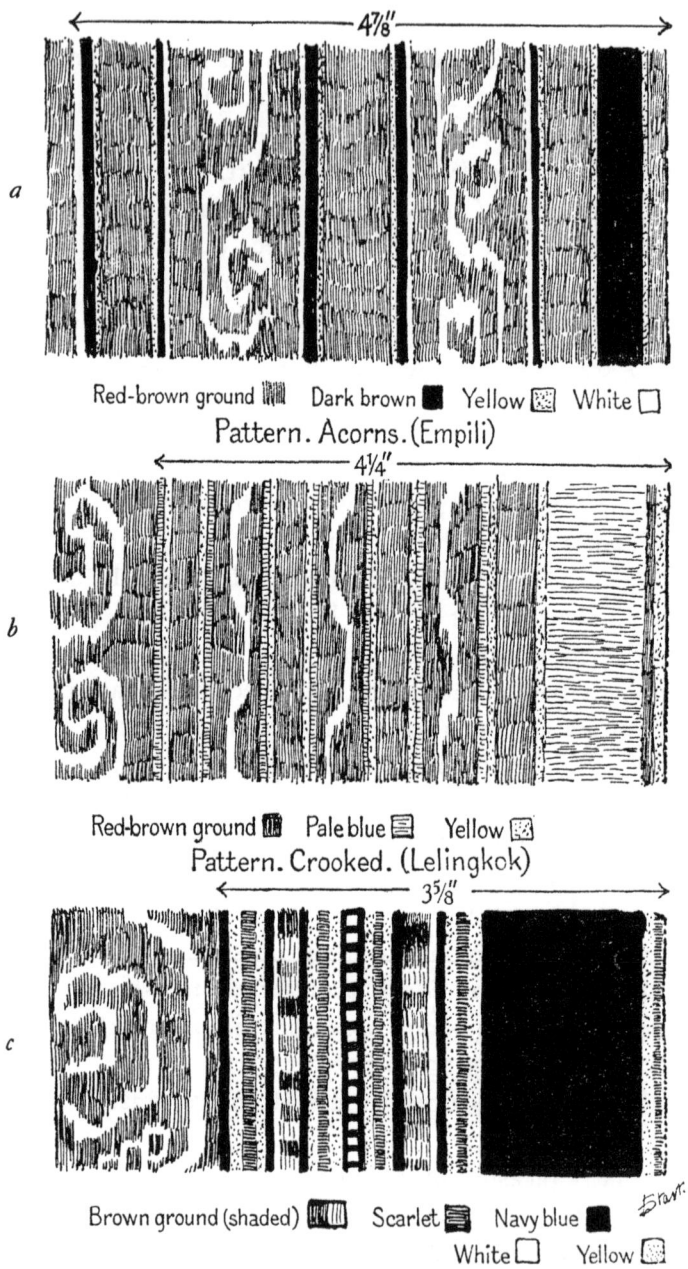

Red-brown ground ▦   Dark brown ■   Yellow ▨   White □

Pattern. Acorns. (Empili)

Red-brown ground ▦   Pale blue ▦   Yellow ▨

Pattern. Crooked. (Lelingkok)

Brown ground (shaded) ▦   Scarlet ▤   Navy blue ■

White □   Yellow ▨

Fig. 28. Various colour arrangements in border stripes: *a, bidang* 35.874, p. 80; *b, bidang* 35.861, p. 71; *c, bidang* 35.878, p. 81.

from the colouring of *Cylindrophis rufus*, a Bornean snake which has a red head, a red tip to its tail and a body striped black, white and red (see p. 33).

Unusual effects are sometimes obtained by dipping the edges of the woven cloth into an indigo dye bath for a short time. This process gives a light-blue pattern on a very dark brown, blue or black ground (according to the strength of the bath or the length of immersion) and alters the coloured border stripes, yellow becoming green, white a pale blue, and scarlet a crimson or magenta tint.

Quieter but good combinations of colour in the compound stripes are black and yellow on a brown ground; buff and dark brown on a red-brown ground; dark brown and pale blue on red-brown; and dark blue, scarlet and white. None of these have any special name but are described as *ara surik*, "a striped pattern", or as *surik anak*, "the child or young stripe", a fanciful designation for the lesser or narrower stripes.

A mourning *bidang* for a widow is obtained by immersing the whole garment in an indigo bath until the pattern appears as light blue on a black ground.

The broad central band of pattern is sometimes replaced by a plain one, and if the border patterns and compound stripes are well spaced this arrangement is sometimes very successful.

A third scheme consists in having a series of narrow patterned stripes, separated by composite colour stripes, right across the width of the cloth. Such arrangements lose a great deal in their general effect.

DESCRIPTION OF INDIVIDUAL *BIDANG*

The patterns of the following *bidang* are described in the position they occupied when being woven on the loom, not as they appear in wear; thus the term "sides" refers to the edges of the cloth running in the direction of the warp. When the petticoat is being worn these edges or "sides" become the top and bottom of the garment.

The native names of the designs are printed in italics; they were obtained when the cloths were obtained. Some *bidang* are only briefly described by us, the designs on which are often insignificant, and as they generally occur more distinctly on those cloths which are more fully treated they have not been described in detail.

An analysis of thirty *bidang*

No. of cloth	Length	Width	No. of warp ends to inch	Description of warp spacing	No. of weft picks to inch	Description of weft	Colour and special notes
35.852	3 ft. 10⅝ in. (118·5 cm.)	1 ft. 9¾ in. (55·5 cm.)	92 (46 groups)	Ends are paired; warp undyed in pattern stripes	20	Three parallel threads; colour brown	Effective, simple. White patterns on brown background. Pin stripes of black and yellow in borders
35.853	3 ft. 7⅞ in. (110 cm.)	1 ft. 7⅒ in. (48 cm.)	72	Single; arranged white and brown alternately to produce stripes; thus 2 w., 3 b., 2 w., 3 b., 6 w., 10 b.	24	Two parallel threads. In part of cloth white —in remainder brown	A simple striped cloth—white and brown
35.854	3 ft. 8½ in. (115·5 cm.)	1 ft. 11⅝ in. (60·4 cm.)	104 ends (52 groups) 128 ends (64 groups)	In main pattern paired Paired in borders	26	Four parallel Brown	Three dyeings required for patterns which have pale-brown outlines—red-brown for the inside of patterns and indigo over red-brown for the background and some spots The edge has been re-dipped in indigo
35.855	3 ft. 7 in. (109·8 cm.)	1 ft. 4⅞ in. (40·5 cm.)	120 ends (60 groups) 112 ends	Paired in pattern stripe Single, in self-colour stripes	24	Single Brown	One dyeing of red-brown on a buff warp
35.856	3 ft. 10 in. (117 cm.)	1 ft. 5½ in. (45 cm.)	56 ends 160 ends (80 groups)	Single, in plain central band Paired in border self-colour stripes	20	Single Brown	Plain central band of greyish black, indigo over red-brown Narrow patterned side borders of white on red-brown, divided by brown stripes with pin stripes of red, yellow and dark blue
35.857	3 ft. 6 in. (106·7 cm.)	1 ft. 6½ in. (47 cm.)	152 ends (76 groups)	Paired throughout, slightly closer in centre of cloth	42	Single. Brown	A finely woven cloth. Patterns, white and brown. Scarlet, black, and yellow self borders
35.858	3 ft. 10 in. (116·9 cm.)	1 ft. 4½ in. (41·9 cm.)	144 ends (72 groups)	Paired except in narrow central stripe, where in threes	28	Two parallel. Brown	Unusual, but ineffective arrangement of narrow striped patterns, divided by pin stripes in colour. There is a narrow, bright red stripe down the centre of the cloth

No.	Length	Width	Ends	Warp	Threads to inch	Weft	Description
35.859	4 ft. (122 cm.)	1 ft. 10 in. (55·9 cm.)	96 ends (48 groups) 152 ends (76 groups)	Paired in pattern stripe. In self-colour border stripes	16–20	Four parallel threads in each pick. Brown	White pattern on brown ground. Second dyeing of indigo in splashes on background. Interesting border stripes in black and white, red, black, yellow
35.860	3 ft. 10 in. (116·9 cm.)	1 ft. 10 in. (55·9 cm.)	96 ends (48 groups) 136 ends (68 groups)	Paired throughout. In self-colour stripes	22	Two parallel in part, four parallel in remainder. Brown	White pattern on brown ground. Dark blue, yellow, scarlet and white self border stripes
35.861	3 ft. 10 in. (116·9 cm.)	1 ft. 10 in. (55·9 cm.)	96 ends (48 groups)	Paired throughout, a good deal of brown background used in border stripes	20–26	Two parallel. Brown	A loosely woven fabric. White pattern on brown ground. Pale blue stripes at edges and in borders
35.862	4 ft. 1¼ in. (125·1 cm.)	1 ft. 8½ in. (52·1 cm.)	104 ends (52 groups) 128 ends (64 groups)	Paired in broad pattern stripe. Paired in black and yellow, threes in scarlet self stripes	26	Two parallel threads in each pick. Brown	White pattern on brown ground. Scarlet, yellow, and black in self-colour border stripes
35.863	4 ft. 1 in. (124·5 cm.)	1 ft. 8½ in. (52·1 cm.)	136 ends (68 groups) 216 ends (72 groups)	Paired in the pattern stripes. Threes in the coloured self stripes	22	Three parallel threads. Brown	White pattern on brown ground. White, black, scarlet, and yellow border stripes
35.865	4 ft. 0½ in. (123·2 cm.)	1 ft. 5¼ in. (43·8 cm.)	144 ends (72 groups)	Paired throughout	24	Two parallel	Evenly woven, brilliant colour. Red and brown background, buff pattern. Interesting border stripes
35.866	3 ft. 10 in. (116·9 cm.)	1 ft. 10¾ in. (57·1 cm.)	136 ends (68 groups) 144 ends (72 groups)	Paired in central band of pattern. Paired in self-colour border stripes	24	Two parallel. Black, may have been brown before second dyeing	A very finely woven cloth. The colour is unusual, the cloth having been dipped in indigo after it had gone through the usual dyeing processes. The result is that the patterns appear as pale blue on a black ground, and in the border stripes red becomes maroon, yellow green, and brown black
35.867	3 ft. 10¾ in. (118·1 cm.)	1 ft. 11 in. (58·4 cm.)	88 ends (44 groups)	Paired throughout.	16–18	Fourfold and parallel. Brown	Pattern white on a vandyke brown ground. A very coarse cloth
35.868	3 ft. 10 in. (116·9 cm.)	1 ft. 6 in. (45·7 cm.)	112–120 (56–60 groups) 228 ends (76 groups)	Paired but not quite evenly spaced in pattern band. Threes in red self stripe	16	Three parallel threads. Light brown	Buff pattern on brown ground. Scarlet, black, and yellow border stripes with a navy blue stripe at the outer edge

An analysis of thirty *bidang*

No. of cloth	Length	Width	No. of warp ends to inch	Description of warp spacing	No. of weft picks to inch	Description of weft	Colour and special notes
35.869	3 ft. 8¾ in. (113·7 cm.)	1 ft. 8½ in. (52·7 cm.)	168 ends (56 groups) 192 ends (48 groups)	Threes in pattern stripe. Fours in self-colour stripes	18	Fourfold and parallel. Dark brown	Strong colour effect as most of the red-brown background has been over-dyed blue, thus giving vandyke brown effect. Red, yellow, blue, and white self-colour border stripes
35.870	3 ft. 8 in. (111·8 cm.)	1 ft. 9 in. (53·4 cm.)	88 ends (44 groups) 108 ends (36 groups)	Paired in pattern bands. Threes in self-colour stripes	24	Three parallel threads. Brown	Background red-brown and black, owing partly to over-dyeing with indigo, the pattern on it in buff and white. Red, yellow, and black self border stripes
35.871	3 ft. 10 in. (116·9 cm.)	1 ft. 7 in. (48·2 cm.)	112 ends (56 groups) 144 ends (72 groups)	Paired throughout in pattern band. In self-colour stripes	23	Three parallel threads. Brown	An evenly woven cloth, of crisp firm texture
35.872	3 ft. 8 in. (111·8 cm.)	1 ft. 7½ in. (49·5 cm.)	128 ends (64 groups)	Paired throughout	20	Single. Brown	Very clear pattern in buff on a reddish brown ground with occasional vandyke spots, also touches of blue in borders. The fineness of the weft produces a fine, soft cloth
35.873	3 ft. 8 in. (111·8 cm.)	1 ft. 9 in. (53·4 cm.)	92 ends (46 groups) 176 ends (88 groups)	Paired in pattern portion and in self-colour stripes	26	Two parallel threads. Brown	Buff pattern on red-brown background
35.874	3 ft. 11 in. (119·4 cm.)	1 ft. 11 in. (58·4 cm.)	80 ends (40 groups)	Paired throughout	16	Four parallel threads. Dark brown	Extra large, coarse cloth. Buff pattern on brown ground. Border stripes and dividing lines in white, yellow, black, and brown
35.875	4 ft. 0½ in. (123·2 cm.)	1 ft. 8¼ in. (51·8 cm.)	96 ends (48 groups)	Paired throughout	20	Single. Brown	Large cloth. Buff on reddish brown ground. Generally of dull appearance. Border stripes black and yellow only

No.	Length	Width	Ends (groups)	Grouping	Picks	Weft	Description
35.877	3 ft. 9½ in. (114·7 cm.)	1 ft. 7⅞ in. (49·3 cm.)	168 ends (56 groups)	Threes practically throughout, one or two fours	20-22	Three parallel. Brown	Very gay in colour in border stripes. Red background to central band, overdyed indigo, the pattern in buff with some parts in red. Red, yellow, blue, and black and white borders
35.878	3 ft. 8 in. (111·8 cm.)	1 ft. 7¾ in. (50·1 cm.)	96 ends (48 groups) 108 ends (36 groups) 192 ends on an average	Curious irregularity in grouping of threads paired for most of pattern stripes, but in threes for 4 in. at left In self-colour stripes, threes and fours indiscriminately	15-16	Three parallel. Brown	Most brilliantly coloured in whole collection although similar to patterns in white, outlined dark brown, on reddish brown background. Narrow border stripes in yellow, scarlet, white, and navy blue, with a black and white horizontally striped border as well
35.879	3 ft. 6½ in. (108 cm.)	1 ft. 8½ in. (52·1 cm.)	132 ends (44 groups) 144 ends (36 groups)	In threes in patterned stripe In fours in red and blue self stripes	20	Two parallel. Brown	Generally dull in tone. Warps of pattern stripe dipped in weak indigo bath, after having been dyed brown. Broad outer stripes of indigo and small border stripes of red, yellow, and black
35.880	3 ft. 9 in. (114·4 cm.)	2 ft. ¾ in. (62·9 cm.)	96 ends (48 groups)	Mostly grouped in twos and threes	26	Two parallel. Brown	Border stripes somewhat unusual in colour, navy blue, scarlet and orange used. The orange, yellow overdyed red. Buff pattern on reddish and black ground
35.883	3 ft. 5 in. (104·2 cm.)	Varies from 1 ft. 5 in. (43·2 cm.) to 1 ft. 3½ in. (39·4 cm.)	120-168 in patterned section 192-280 in finer border stripes	Very uneven spacing. In pattern stripes mostly paired with occasional single warps. Similarly in border stripes	24 of ordinary cloth weft, and in pattern 24 of coloured weft	Two parallel white, right across cloth between each pick; eight parallel strands of red or four of black for pattern picks	Red and black embroidered pattern threads turned back at border stripes. Border stripes of red, yellow, and black enclose three narrow white stripes with embroidery, in black and red on them
35.894	3 ft. 9 in. (114·4 cm.)	1 ft. 7¾ in. (50·1 cm.)	112 ends (56 groups) 144 ends (72 groups)	Paired throughout but closer spacing in dark brown self stripes	20	Three threads parallel	White pattern on brown ground. Dark brown border stripes near outer edge and series of brown and yellow self-colour pin-stripes with two narrow patterned border stripes between
35.882	4 ft. 3 in. (129·6 cm.)	1 ft. 9⅝ in. (53·9 cm.)	108 ends (36 groups)	Grouped in threes throughout	20	Fourfold. Blue	Coarse cloth of firm texture. White pattern on blue background. Border stripes in red, yellow, and white. General colour scheme pleasant

For the sake of convenience for reference the *bidang* are described in the order of their enumeration in the Catalogue of the Museum. The only exceptions we have made are to place the two plain striped cloths, 35.853, 35.876, and the two embroidered cloths, 35.883, 35.886, at the end of the tye-dyed patterned cloths.

35.852. An unmade *bidang* having a length of 3 ft 10⅝ in. (118·4 cm.) and a width 1 ft. 9½ in. (55·5 cm.).

There are 92 warp ends to the inch grouped in pairs and 20 picks of weft. The warp forms the surface of the cloth and there is no variation in the border as regards the number of warp ends. The weft is brown and threefold.

The cloth has a brown background and a broad central band 11⅝ in. (30 cm.) wide having on each side border stripes totalling ½ in. (13 cm.) in width. Some of these stripes are plain brown with a narrow edging of black and yellow, *ara buloh* "bamboo *ara* pattern" (fig. 29, *a*), others are decorated by

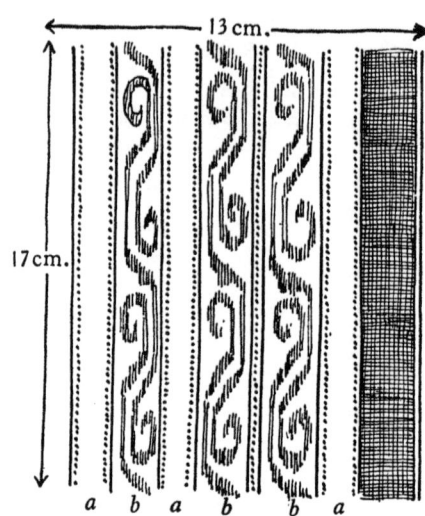

Fig. 29. Border stripes on *bidang* 35.852: *a*, *ara buloh*, "pattern of coloured stripes" (*ara*), "bamboo" (*buloh*); *b*, *empili*, mast.

empili, mast (fig. 29, *b*). There is a slight difference in the arrangement of the two sets of border stripes, for on one side the two patterned ones are only divided by a narrow band (4 cm.) of black, yellow, black, and not by the "bamboo" stripe. At the extreme edge of the cloth on either side is a border approximately black, the warp having been dyed brown and then re-dyed with indigo. This is labelled *ara beranak*, "the *ara* with the smaller ones" ("*beranak*, to give birth to", *S.D.D.*).

The central pattern consists of elongated lozenges, three to the width and four to the length of the cloth. Small spiral hooks decorate both sides of the enclosing lines of the lozenges; the lines represent crossed poles, *penjuang*, or the posts on either side of the staircase supporting the railings (*S.D.D.*). Possibly the hooks may represent the steps cut in the poles which serve as ladders from the ground to the verandah of the house.

One of the terminal lozenges is shown in fig. 30 with a portion of the end border pattern underneath, the uneven zigzag part of which is called "the crooked arm, *lelingkok betayok*" (fig. 30, *d*). The tie, *tikal penjuang*, at the top of the figure (*a*) indicates the method of securing the cross pieces by twisting and knotting ratan, or cord made from palm fibre, round them. Grass lizards (fig. 30, *c*) and heads of birds are used as the motives in the spaces between the lozenges.

35.853. A plain striped *bidang*, see p. 87.

35.854. *Bidang* with *Aki Ungkok*, "the man in the moon" or Grandfather Ungkok. Width, 1 ft. 11⅝ in. (60·4 cm.); length, 3 ft. 8½ in. (113·5 cm.).

The warps are paired or twofold, there are 52 pairs (104 warp ends) in the patterned section and 64 pairs (128 ends) to the inch in the borders. The weft is brown with four parallel threads; there are 26 picks to the inch.

The background is a rich dark brown with lighter reddish-brown spots in some parts and some spaces inside the pattern lines. The pattern appears as biscuit colour, so the warps must have been all slightly coloured in a brown dye before the pattern was tied up.

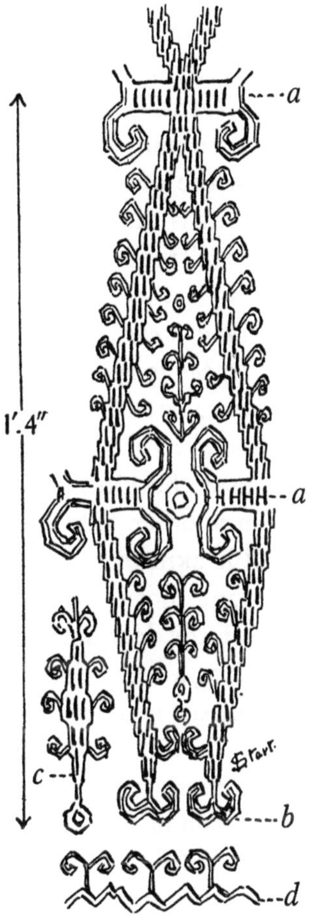

In the borders along the sides there are some light blue stripes which must have been originally white, for this petticoat has had its edges dipped in indigo after it was completed, so that the dark brown in the borders has become black.

The patterns are most interesting. Beginning at the seam is a wavy line,

Fig. 30. Lozenge pattern representing the crossed poles of the house, *bidang* 35.852: *a, tikal penjuang*, "the fold (tie) over two cross-pieces"; *b, kait serepang*, "hook on a split pole"; *c, lachau*, "a grass lizard"; *d, lelingkok betayok*, zigzag and beckoning hand.

lelingkok, connected by uprights, *jaul pempang*, "twisted fence to block the path", to a bold zigzag, *pempang lelingkok* (the upper band of pl. xxiii, *g*). Within the spaces thus formed are *sayap*, "wings". At the other end of the cloth is *pempang lalau lelingkok*, "narrow path (blocked) with a hand rail" (the lower band of pl. xxiii, *g*). The most important row of figures comes next, representing *Aki Ungkok*, Grandfather Ungkok, "the man who lives in the moon and whose face is seen there" (pl. i, *a*). This figure is very similar to the deer, *rusa*, pattern which occupies the central space of the cloth, but it is distinguished from it by the anti-spiral at the head, *sanggol Aki Ungkok*, "the hair of Grandfather Ungkok twisted in a knot at the back of his head", and by his hand, *jari*. His bent back, *bungkok*, rests against a post, *tiang penyadih*, when tired. Another row of similar representations of *Aki Ungkok* is repeated at the other end of the cloth.

In between are two rows of the deer pattern with crossed (or entangled) antlers, *tandok rusa berkaul*. All parts of the animal are definitely named; a hook near the hind legs is the tail, *iko* (pl. iii, *a*); the *kaki*, "feet", are shown in another stag (pl. iii, *b*). The *rusa* is the largest of the Bornean deer and is akin to the Indian deer. The stag has doubly branched antlers and is found mostly in the clearings.

Between the deer figures is a pattern formed by two combs, *sugu* (pl. xxiv, *h*), joined by a wavy line, *lelingkok*, and enclosing a bird, *burong* (pl. vii, *a*).

Some of the smaller spaces are filled by double spirals and are described as *gelong bekait*, "hooks", and *jerit begelong*, "rounds of the pattern", obviously mere space filling.

At both ends near the seam are *gelong paku rĕsam*, "curled tops of the *resam* fern" (pl. xviii, *m*, *n*), and in the narrow border patterns, *empili*, mast (pl. xviii, *a*).

35.855. Width, 1 ft. 4⅘ in. (40·5 cm.); length, 3 ft. 7 in. (109·8 cm.)

The warps are twofold, except in the self-colour stripes at the side where, used singly, they produce a very fine section in the cloth. In the patterned stripes the pairs are 60 to the inch (120 warp ends), whilst the single warps at the sides average 112 to the inch. The weft is brown and single and there are 24 picks to an inch.

The pattern is in biscuit or buff colour on a reddish-brown background with a greyish stripe along the edges, produced by dyeing some light-brown yarn with indigo. This *bidang* has one of the simplest colour schemes and is very pleasant in its general effect.

The motives are mainly derived from plants, but some animals and inanimate objects are shown and the general arrangement is excellent. On the first third of the cloth a lozenge and a half are formed by long crossed bands (like those forming the lozenges of pls. xviii, *i*, xix, *a*, and many others), *tebok tangga pantok*, "holes pecked in a staircase", i.e. notched poles that serve as ladders. Within the frame of the lozenge are two concentric lines with hooks, of which the inner is shown on pl. xix, *a*; this motive is called *jerit tangkai bunga*, "the blossoms completely covering the bunch" (*tangkai*, "fruit stalk"; *jerit*, "in order" or probably may mean "in series"); the lower end of this sketch is called *pala buntak*, "head of locust or grasshopper". In the centre is *jerit buah bangkit*, "a complete bunch of *bangkit* fruit", this is also shown on pl. xviii, *j*. Close by is a design similar to pl. xix, *a*, but the central motive is a bird, *burong buah bangkit* (pl. viii, *b*). Below the lozenge the notched poles are continued as broader bands, *tebok kingking*, "notches cut as on a brass bracelet", bordered on each side by a line, *entali marik*, "string to hold beads". (In another cloth, 35.871, similar bands are called *randau tangkong bi penyuang*, "the lattice-work pattern of the *tangkong* creeper", pl. xx, *a*.) These broader bands at the bottom of the lozenge in the second row turn back on themselves (pl. xx, *c*) and are labelled *tangkong mulai*, "a creeper which bends back from where it starts"; close by it is *rundai bunga tangkong*, "the dangling flower of a creeper" (pl. xix, *c*). At the ends of some of the lozenges is a *pala buntak* (pl. xvii, *h*).

An unusual motive is the framework of a fireplace, *entilang* (pl. xxiii, *h*). An Iban fireplace is like an open cupboard, the lowest shelf rests on the floor and is boarded all round and covered with clay upon which a few stones are placed to support the cooking pots. The shelf above is of lattice-work and is used for smoking fish and meat (in the cloth there is a young bird, *anak burong*, on this shelf); the shelves above this are used for drying firewood. This is the only piece of furniture in the Iban house and is placed at one side of the door that opens into the *tampuan* or *tempuan* or passage that connects all the separate suites of these communal houses.

The last third of the cloth contains three designs, each consisting of two zigzagged bands which form a central lozenge; the spot where these bands meet to form the lozenge is labelled *papan penukoh*, "the plank where the prop is tied" (which is obscure); at the lateral angle of this lozenge is an hexagonal device within which is a motive that elsewhere is called a sleeping cat (cf. pl. xvii, *r–t*). Other *bidang* known to us have these designs. In one the bands are called *papan penukoh* (plank), and the device at the angles *pusat penukoh* (navel or centre), in another simply *penukoh*. In all cases the ends of the bands are prolonged into hooks, in one case termed *bunga penukoh*. Within the lozenges are paddles, *sengayoh*, with curved handles, *ulu* (pl. xxiii, *r*), and nearby are designs of *ulu sengayoh*, which are merely the crutch handles of the paddle (pl. xxiii, *m*); a pair of somewhat similar motives is labelled *spit grama*, "the nippers of a freshwater crab" (pl. xvii, *q*). The spaces between these three designs are occupied by *aji jerit buah bangkit*, "the Gymnura [shrew] with the *bangkit* fruit, the Gymnura has a very unpleasant smell, the *bangkit* a sweet smell" (pl. vi, *d*); *jerit burong buah bangkit* and *kukut bruang*, "the claws of a bear".

At the sides are four "striped" *suriek* bands that form the border; the outer of the enclosed areas have a wavy pattern, *lelingkok semerai sungai*, "the crooked [zigzag] river crossing", and the central pattern is named *entibap*, "the arenga palm".

35.856. Width, 1 ft. 5½ in. (45 cm.); length, 3 ft. 10 in. (117 cm.).

In the coloured border the warps are paired or twofold and are closely arranged, in the self stripes averaging 80 pairs, 160 ends to the inch. In the plain central band single warps of a coarser yarn are used and average 56 to the inch. The weft is brown and single and there are 20 picks to the inch.

The central band is plain and of a greyish black, indigo over brown probably having been used. At the sides there are three narrow patterned borders with designs in buff on brown, divided by shaded brown stripes edged with self-coloured stripes in red which have hair-lines in them of black and yellow. The width of these grouped borders is 4⅛ in. (10·4 cm.).

The patterns are very distinct and show great skill in the tying-up of the warps. The middle patterned stripe contains a series of bird motives: *burong besugu* (pl. vii, *m*), *burong buah bangkit*, *burong jengkuan*, *burong bedayong* (pl. viii, *d, f, j*); *embayer*, "centipedes" (pl. xvi, *a, f*); *entibap*, "arenga palm" (pl. xxii, *c*). The inner and outer pattern stripes contain halves of

66

various birds. Among other designs are *empili*, mast (pl. XVIII, *e*) and *unak wi bekait*, "crossed ratans with thorns" (pl. XXII, *o*). Many of the ratans have very thorny stems which help to make the jungle almost impassable. Beccari (1904, p. 114) describes some with stems as thick as a man's wrist, 200 ft. in length and defended by a formidable array of thorns.

35.857. Width, 1 ft. 6½ in. (47 cm.); length, 3 ft. 6 in. (106·7 cm.).

The warps are twofold throughout the cloth and there is little difference between the borders and the main pattern stripe. An average of 76 pairs (152 ends) to the inch would be accurate if taken throughout the full width. There are 42 weft picks to the inch, which is an unusually high number, and the thread used is single and brown in colour. The resulting cloth is of a very fine, close texture, and as the patterning is also extremely neat and detailed it must have been made by an expert worker.

A light tobacco brown, with buff lines for the patterns, is the colour of the middle section. The wide borders on either side of this are divided again by self-coloured stripes averaging ⅜ in. (0·9 cm.) wide in which the bulk of the warps are red with pin stripes of black and yellow amongst them. At the outer edge there is a ⅝ in. (1·6 cm.) stripe of indigo, followed on its inner side by 1/10 in. (2·5 mm.) yellow and ⅛ in. (0·3 mm.) red.

The patterns are clearly defined and very elaborate. Spiders, *emplawa* (pls. XIV, *b*, *d*; XV, *b*, *c*), form the principal motive on one side of the broad central band, and in two cases other creatures are depicted as if in or on their bodies, a bird (pl. XV, *b*), *burong di tengak tuboh emplawa*, and a grass lizard (pl. XV, *c*), *engkarong empakap di tuboh emplawa*. A superabundance of legs is a feature of spider patterns, which is perhaps due to the fact that the spiders travel very quickly and their legs seem uncountable. At another place in this cloth a more reasonable shaped spider which has only four legs is described as a young one, *anak emplawa* (pl. XIV, *b*).

In the other half of the broad band there is a representation of a hawk, *lang*, (pl. X, *d*) and a tiger cat, *remaung raras* (*Felis marmorata*); portions of these animals help to fill in the remaining space.

An interesting feature of the central pattern stripe in the borders down the side is that of a "centipede crossing the river", *embayar semerai sungai* (pl. XVI, *e*). The stripes on each side represent *lelingkok semerai sungai*, "crossing backwards and forwards across a river" (pl. XXV, *g*).

35.858. Width, 1 ft. 4½ in. (41·9 cm.); length, 3 ft. 10 in. (116·9 cm.).

The warps are paired except in the narrow central stripe of red, where they are grouped in threes, parallel to one another. There is an average of 72 pairs (144 warp ends) to the inch, and the weft, which is brown and twofold, makes 28 picks to the same measurement.

The arrangement of the patterns on this cloth is somewhat unusual, there being a crimson stripe ⅞ in. (22 mm.) wide down the centre, bordered by self stripes in black and yellow, each $\frac{1}{10}$ in. (2·5 mm.) wide. The remainder of the cloth is divided up into narrow pattern stripes separated from each other by a shaded brown edged with pin stripes of yellow, red and black, or brown and yellow. As a design it is ineffective.

The designs are mostly degenerate in the sense that types are mixed or joined together. Birds with netting needles, *burong jengkuan* (pl. VIII, *e*), birds with combs, *burong besugu*, and other variations fill the four widest stripes, whilst young lizards, *anak lachau* (pl. XII, *b*), are the chief motive of the remaining six narrower pattern stripes.

35.859. Width, 1 ft. 10 in. (55·9 cm.); length, 4 ft. (122 cm.). Pl. XXVIII, A.

The warps are paired or twofold throughout most of the cloth, but there is some variation in the red stripes. In the patterned portion there are 48 pairs (96 ends) to the inch and in the self-colour stripes 76 pairs (152 ends). The weft is fourfold, the threads lying side by side like a tape, and as a consequence of this width there are on an average only 18 picks to the inch.

The broad patterned band has figures in buff on a shaded ground of deep red and dark brown. The border stripes are particularly gay and show refinement in their treatment.

Two narrow $\frac{3}{10}$ in. (7·5 mm.) shaded borders with a "crossing the river" pattern are divided and edged by a composite stripe arranged as follows: 5 red warp groups (12 ends), 5 yellow (10 ends), 3 black (6 ends), 5 yellow (10 ends), 10 red (20 ends) and then 5 white pairs and 4 black ones alternately, which in weaving produces the effect of horizontal stripes of black and white. This completes half of the composite stripe, the remainder being the reverse of the first part.

The red, black and yellow lines of the composite stripe are labelled *ara surik kendawang* as they are like the markings on the "*kendawang* snake (*Callophis flaviceps*)". The complete group of five borders occupies 3 in.

(7·6 cm.) and is finished off on the outer edge by a ⅝ in. (1·6 cm.) self border in dark brown edged with a narrow coloured one in white, red and yellow. The general effect is rich, with accented interest in the striped border.

The patterns are unusual and interesting. At one end of the cloth (the right in the photograph) there are representations of "clouds in steps", *miga dudok* (pls. xxviii, A; xxv, *i*, *j*), against which a bird is flying; it is labelled *burong berayah*, "bird with outstretched wings" (pl. viii, *l*). Below the clouds are their feet or base, *kaki miga dudok*. Between the clouds are designs called *betayok*, "to beckon with the hand" (pl. ii, *k*), but these are very like the *rayot miga dudok*. Above the big clouds, which possibly represent a cumulus, are two smaller clouds, *rayok miga dudok* (pl. xxv, *k*), which make a very fair suggestion of smaller floating clouds.

In the next row are two large designs labelled *remaung*, "the tiger-cat, *Felis nebulosa*, or possibly the real tiger" (pls. xxviii, A; iv, *e*). They face the "clouds", but in pl. iv the head is downwards. These "tigers" are not very characteristic and in fact they suggest the usual hawk motive (cf. pl. x).

On the other side of the cloth (not shown in pl. xxviii) is an elaborate and inconclusive design (pl. xxv, *e*); on each side is a *padong remaung*, "ledge or sleeping place [lair] of the tiger; tigers are supposed to live in holes in the rocks". The curved elements above and below the centre are labelled *kaki padong remaung*, "the foot of the tiger's ledge"; but it looks more like the foot of the tiger on the ledge. The remainder of the pattern, as far as the joining, is made up of two complete and two half shrews, *aji*, of the usual conventional type.

The border contains two zigzags, *legingkok semerai sungai*, "crossing the river backwards and forwards" or "again and again", and three black and white stripes, *surik gran permalu tekalong*, the ridges on the mallet used for beating the bark of the *tekalong* tree into bark-cloth.

35.860. *Bidang* with *beringin* fruit in bunches. Width, 1 ft. 10 in. (55·9 cm.); length 3 ft. 10 in. (116·9 cm.).

In the patterned stripe down the centre the warps are twofold or paired, there being 48 pairs (96 ends) to the inch, whilst in the self-coloured stripes down the sides there are 68 pairs (136 ends) in the same space. The weft is twofold for part of the cloth and fourfold in the remainder. All of it is brown and there are 22 picks to the inch.

The design in the wide central band is in pale buff on a background of red-brown. Three narrow patterned stripes at the side have the same colour scheme and are divided by ½ in. (13 mm.) compound stripes made up of red, navy blue, yellow, red, yellow, navy blue and red. There is an outer border just over half an inch in width of the dark navy finished off by very narrow ones of yellow and red.

The patterns are of a different type from those in the cloths already considered, as the chief motive is the *beringin* tree. The first big pattern is made up of three branches of the fruit, *upong buah beringin* (or *berangin*) (pl. xviii, *l*); immediately below these are *gelong paku*, "fern tops" (pl. xviii, *o*). These are followed by *batang beringin*, "the trunk of the *beringin* tree"; its many branches have projections described as *tangkin berangin*. One of two very similar projections at the end of the pattern is labelled *tangkin berangin*, "to put on a parang",[1] [sword], and the other *tangkin mulai*, "the sword swinging back as the man walks". Slightly different projections are called *lintah*, "leeches" (pl. xvi, *i*).

The narrower patterned borders down the sides contain *empili*, mast (pl. xviii, *n*), *entibap*, "arenga palm" (pl. xxii, *b*), and *serok genok*, "a gourd with a long twisted stalk" (pl. xxii, *f*). "The fruit is used by the Dayaks to rub their bodies in the place of soap." The dried gourd is used as a water-vessel. The broader border contains *entibap* and various birds: *burong burak prut*, "bird with a white breast" (pl. vii, *e*), *burong sawang prut*, "bird with an opening in its breast" (pl. vii, *h*), *burong besugu*, "bird with a comb" (pl. vii, *n*), and *burong bedayong*, "bird rowing" (or paddling) (pl. viii, *h*).

35.861. Unmade *bidang*. Width, 1 ft. 10 in. (55·9 cm.); length, 3 ft. 10 in. (116·9 cm.).

This is a rather loosely woven fabric in which the warps are paired and number 48 pairs (96 ends) to the inch and there are 26 picks of a twofold brown weft.

A brown background with biscuit-coloured designs forms the pattern stripe, but a successful note of colour is introduced by several pairs of narrow yellow and bright blue stripes used in the border, and by a broad band of light blue, ⅝ in. (1·6 cm.) wide, at the outer edge.

[1] Dr Hose added to this label: "The lines of a Dayak song are: *Tangkin berangin pedang soran, igi kabu kabu kakambu bulu duam* = The sword is put on, the sheath of which is covered with fluttering hornbill feathers."

The general effect is simple; there are, as the most important feature, four repeats of a pattern, composed of a pair of crossed poles, *penjuang*, in the width of the cloth. This design is repeated three times in the length of the cloth. Filling the acute angle at either end of the crossed poles is a *pasak serpang*, "the wedge of the fork" (pl. XXIII, *r*); and between each pair of poles at the ends of the cloth is a large representation of a lizard (skink), *engkarong* (pl. XII, *j*). Between the crossed poles in the centre of the cloth are *bubul kukut burong*, filling up with claws of birds; the middle one also has *igi brass*, "rice grains". There is some obscurity about the *engkarong* designs as in some cases the double-hooked ends are labelled *serpang jengkuan*, "the slit in the weaving needle" (spool) (pl. XXIV, *e*), but it is probably a netting needle used for making fishing nets, see Long Roth, I, p. 454; *S.D.D.* gives "*jengkuan*, a netting needle". It appears to us that the lizard is resting on a netting needle.

The border patterns are shown in fig. 28, *b*: at the extreme edge is a narrow red-brown and yellow stripe called *ara beranak*, "the child of the *ara*" (as in 35.852), there are three *lelingkok* zigzags and between them are *surik*, "stripes".

35.862. Tiger cloth. Width, 1 ft. 8½ in. (52·1 cm.); length, 4 ft. 1¼ in. (125 cm.).

In the self-coloured stripes of the border the red warps are grouped in threes and the rest are paired; the whole averages 128 warp ends to the inch. In the broad patterned stripe the warps are also paired and number 52 (104 ends) to the inch. In the same measurement there are 26 picks of weft, which is twofold and brown.

The broad band of pattern in the centre is in buff on a brown background. On either side of this there are three narrow patterned borders in the same colouring divided by composite warp stripes, the first two being yellow, brown and black, and the two outer ones red, yellow and black. A broad black stripe edged with red comes nearest to the outside.

Palm, *entibap*, "arenga palm", motives (pl. XXII, *a*) and birds, *burong* (pl. VII, *d*), fill the narrow pattern stripes at the sides, but the chief interest in this cloth centres in the use of the "tiger", *remaung*, doubtless the tiger-cat; other designs are shrews and spiders. One end of the cloth consists almost entirely of "tigers", one being recognizable (pl. IV, *a*), and parts of

71

tigers, the paws and legs of which occur many times separately and fill in awkward spaces.

In the remaining part of the central band are the spider, *emplawa*, in several variations (pl. xiv, *a*, *c*), and the white shrew, *aji*; *aji bulan* is shown in pl. v, *f*, and *aji bulan bangkit*, "the [moon] *aji* in the *bangkit* fruit", pl. vi, *a*. The stepped pattern of the lozenge (which represents the *bangkit* fruit) is called *tebok tangga pantok*, "notched steps", *pantok* means to peck as a fowl and the scrolls are labelled *jerit nyangking*, "a pattern of itself". The white shrew (*Gymnura rafflesi*) is peculiar to Borneo and is often called the "moon rat", *aji bulan*, by the Iban, because of its nocturnal habits. The general aspect of these two patterns is certainly different from the one of the tiger and a slight resemblance to the original creatures can be traced.

As all the animals on this cloth are inimical to human beings, it may have been intended to protect the wearer from them.

35.863. Plant forms. Width 1 ft. 8½ in. (52·1 cm.); length, 4 ft. 1 in. (124·5 cm.) Pl. XXVIII, B.

In the patterned stripes the warps are twofold or paired, and in the self-coloured border stripes of red and orange they are grouped in threes; 68 pairs or 136 ends go to the inch in the former and 72 groups of 3 (216 ends) in the latter. The weft is brown and threefold and there are 22 picks to the inch.

The background is reddish brown and the patterns upon it are in buff. The self-coloured stripes in the borders are less striking than in most of the cloths, although the colour scheme used is much the same. Three patterned stripes are divided and edged by composite stripes in which the colours are red, white, black, orange, red, orange, black, white and red and there is a very dark brown, almost black, border near the outer edge which is ½ in. (1·3 cm.) wide.

The patterns are interesting and some are unusual; most of them are derived from plants.

Near the joining is a design called *kait betulak*, "a hook pushing another back" (pl. xxiii, *p*).

Two-thirds of the length of the cloth is mainly occupied by a lozenge-shaped arrangement of the branches of the *tangkong* with *bunga tangkong*, "flowers" (pl. xx, *b*, and near the upper left corner of pl. xxviii, B); below

72

this in the photograph is *pating betula*, "branches pushing one another back" (pl. xxi, *a*). Near the middle line of pl. xxviii, B are three *dawn tangkong mulai*, "leaf of the *tangkong* twisted back", part of which is shown in pl. xx, *d*. In one place the blossom of the creeper is shown enclosed in its sheath (technically the spathe of the spadix) *upong bunga tangkong* (pl. xx, *e*). A triangular space (bottom of pl. xxviii, B), is filled (*jerit*) with *bingka lia*, "root of ginger" (pl. xix, *d*; this appears reversed, as it was drawn from the other side of the cloth to that photographed).

The last third of the cloth has a somewhat degenerate deer pattern, but the antlers of the deer are strikingly developed and are labelled *ujong tandok rusa bekaul*, "the tips of the antlers twisted over one another"; evidently two stags are butting each other, one is shown in pl. iii, *g*.

In the border are two stripes of *daun wi*, "tendrils of ratan" (pl. xxii, *k*), and one of *entibap*, "arenga palm" (cf. pl. xxii). The blank space in all the stripes almost certainly is *kengkang lang* (see p. 33), although the zigzag in the central stripe is labelled *dabong pemuchok nyemberai sungai*, "the notches of the river crossing".

35.864. This *bidang* has a general resemblance to 35.852. The pattern consists mainly of *bua bangkit* with enclosed *burong*; the borders contain *empili*.

35.865. Width 1 ft. 5¼ in. (43·8 cm.); length 4 ft. 0½ in. (123·2 cm.). Pl. xxix.

This cloth is very evenly woven throughout and both warp and weft are two-fold. There are 72 pairs of warps (144 ends) and 24 picks of weft to the inch.

The dyeing is the work of an expert, for the pattern lines are quite clear although the ground has been dyed twice, first red and then blue on top to produce a brown and so give a shaded effect. The spots along the inside of the long pattern lines are also alternately coloured red and brown.

The border stripes down the side are important and measure as a whole 4¾ in. (12 cm.). They are gay in colour: at one edge there are four stripes, yellow, red, white and dark navy blue, averaging ⅝ in. (1·6 cm.) in width, called *ara belambang*; at the other edge is a stripe of red and indigo. Inside this group are six multicoloured strips, *surik*, of yellow, red, black and white dividing five pattern stripes. These many-coloured stripes, like some in previous examples, may represent the markings of a snake.

Two-thirds of the central band is occupied by representations of shrews, *aji*, Gymnura. Near one end is *aji bua bangkit bekarong*, shrew hidden in a *bangkit* fruit (pl. VI, *e* and top of pl. XXIX). In the middle of the photograph is an *aji* (pl. VI, *c*): at its upper end is the snout, *junggur*, at the lower end the testes, *plir*; the stomach, *prut*, encloses white spots, and the four clawed feet, *kaki*, are clearly seen. Below this (pls. XXIX and V, *g*) are *aji beradap*, two shrews facing one another in what appear to be fighting attitudes, a good indication of the pugnacity of these animals. Beside these is what is probably a young shrew (pl. V, *b*). The three small rings seen at the top of the photograph are labelled "*pantak penandok*" (pl. XVII, *d*); this can be translated as "the wound caused by the sting of a wasp" (see p. 132). The remainder of the cloth includes some conventional patterns which are difficult to understand. The last pattern is a row of sigmoid designs, labelled "*tayok gasing*" (pl. XXIV, *a*), each of which appears to be a hooked piece of wood used for winding thread from the spinning wheel, but it is also very like the handle of a *gasing* (fig. 3).

The patterned border stripes consist of *lelingkok*, "zigzags", *empetut* (alternate red, dark and white squares) and a central one of *entibap*, "arenga". The blank space in all the stripes is not labelled, it is like *kengkang lang* (see p. 34).

35.866. Width, 1 ft. 10½ in. (57·1 cm.); length, 3 ft. 10 in. (116·9 cm.).

Parallel pairs are used in both warp and weft. In the central band there are 68 pairs (136 ends) and in the borders 72 pairs or 144 warp ends to the inch. The black weft picks number 24 to the inch and the resulting cloth has a fine even texture. Black is an unusual colour for weft; it may be the result of the second dyeing.

The colour is unusual, because although originally a brown and white central band with the usual red and yellow self stripes in the border, the whole cloth has been re-dipped in an indigo bath, which has resulted in the central band having a pale blue pattern on a black ground and the outer stripes being dull green and reddish purple.

The designs are very interesting and represent shrews, spiders and a tiger-cat. Certain distinctive features can be recognized in each motive, e.g. the long snout of the shrew, its stomach and its claws (pl. V, *c*); the powerful legs of the tiger-cat (pl. IV, *c*); and the approximately round body of the

74

spider with many legs (pl. xv, *a*). In each outer border are two *lelingkok semberai sungai* and one *entibap* patterns.

The blue dyeing of the skirt was probably done so that it might be worn by a widow.

35.867. Unmade *bidang*. Similar to 35.861. The cloth is labelled "*kain serpang buah pedalai—serpang samoa subuka*". Width, 1 ft. 11 in. (58·4 cm.); length, 3 ft. 10½ in. (118·1 cm.).

The warps are paired or twofold and are 44 (88 ends) to the inch, the weft is brown used fourfold and makes only 16–18 picks to the inch on account of its width.

The colour is generally quiet in effect, a light pattern upon a dark brown background with border pattern lines in dull yellow brown. The yellow is probably obtained from jack-wood (*Artocarpus integrifolia*), the term *pedalai* on the label refers to that tree.

This cloth is similar in every respect to 35.874 and is very like 35.861. It is an example of a simple and effective arrangement of a few units; there are four repeats of the pattern in the width and also in the length of the cloth. It consists of crossed poles of *pedalai* with the lozenge-shaped space between filled with a motive, *bubul lapang*, "fill up space", of no particular form, and between the acute angles of the poles is a *pasak serpang*, "wedge of the fork" (pl. xxiii, *s*). Two of the narrow border patterns consist of mast, *empili* (pl. xviii, *c*), and *daun wi*.

35.868. Unmade *bidang*. Width, 1 ft. 6 in. (45·7 cm.); length, 3 ft. 10 in. (116·9 cm.).

The warps are paired, except in the bright red self stripes of the border, where they are grouped in threes, thus producing a more solid colour effect. On an average there are 56 pairs (112 warp ends) to the inch, the weft being of three parallel brown threads and making 16 picks to the inch.

The central band has a stone colour pattern on a brown background, but the whole cloth is enlivened by three scarlet stripes averaging ⅝ in. (1·5 cm.) wide which divide up the patterns down the sides. Each of these red stripes is edged with a narrow band of yellow, black, yellow, which occupies about ⅛ in. (0·3 cm.) on either side of the red. Near to the outer edge of the cloth is a very dark-brown stripe about ½ in. (1·2 cm.) in width which adds character to the whole.

The chief motive is the tiger-cat (pl. IV, *b*, *d*), but a frog, *pamā* (pl. XIII, *f*), also occurs in one place. There are many meaningless space-filling patterns. The two narrow border patterns are arenga palms (pl. XXII, *d*), ratans, *daun wi*, and mast, *empili* (pl. XVIII, *b*), with a centipede, *embayer* (pl. XVI, *b*), at one end of the cloth.

35.869. Spider cloth. Width, 1 ft. $8\frac{3}{4}$ in. (52·7 cm.); length, 3 ft. $8\frac{3}{4}$ in. (113·7 cm.).

In the broad central band and the narrow border pattern stripes the warps are grouped in threes and in the black and red self-colour stripes in fours. In the latter there are 48 groups (192 ends) and in the former 56 (168 ends) to the inch. The weft is dark brown, is used fourfold, and there are 18 picks to the inch.

The background of the central band is dark brown with patterns in reddish brown outlined with buff, and there are rectangular spots of reddish brown used to fill the larger spaces of the ground.

The border stripe has a yellow and red edge $\frac{1}{4}$ in. (0·7 cm.), then a broad indigo stripe $1\frac{3}{8}$ in. (3·5 cm.), followed by three red, black and yellow stripes averaging $\frac{7}{12}$ in. (1·5 cm.) in width which are separated from one another by the two narrow zigzag-patterned stripes of $\frac{1}{4}$ in. (6 mm.) width.

The principal motives are spiders, one and a half occupying the full width of the broad central band. Elaborate filling-in patterns decorate the spaces between the spiders and intermingle with them. One of the spider motives, with birds' heads inside, is very similar to one on cloth 35.879, which is figured at *d* on pl. XV and like that has fanciful legs which merge at either side into other filling-in devices.

The only other pattern of interest on the cloth is the occurrence in two rows of a representation of the piece of wood upon which the thread from the spinning wheel is wound, *tayok gasing* (pl. XXIV, *b*), see p. 74.

35.870. A deer cloth with hinds only. Width, 1 ft. 9 in. (53·4 cm.); length, 3 ft. 8 in. (111·8 cm.).

The warps are paired, except in the self-coloured border stripes, where they are grouped in threes. The paired warps number 44 groups to the inch (88 ends), the border ones 108 ends in 36 groups. The weft is threefold, dyed brown, and, on an average there are 24 picks to the inch.

The colour is arranged in a somewhat unusual manner. The background is a reddish brown with all the patterns outlined in black, the patterns themselves being a light stone colour with a reddish-brown filling and occasional black spots. The whole effect is rich. Border stripes of scarlet, with yellow and black narrower borders, ornament the sides of the cloth, the extreme edges having a wide black stripe edged with yellow and red.

The pattern is extremely interesting; deer, *rusa*, form the chief motive, although apparently only hinds are represented (pl. III, *d*).

At the end of the cloth the hind is coiled up, or at least has its head turned back towards the under side of its body; the Λ-shaped object on the head is called *tandok*, "antler" in two places, and *tanggi*, "sun-hat", in another. There are certainly no recognizable antlers in these figures (pl. III, *e*).

In the two central rows the figure of the deer is still more coiled up, and the last row is similar to the first. Some of the spaces are filled by bird motives, one of which is a young bird, perhaps a swallow (pl. IX, *n*). One figure (pl. XXI, *b*) described as *patieng*, "branches", may be part of two deer. To fill up spaces there are *tunku asi*, "a tripod for cooking rice" (pl. XXIV, *f*), and *terabai bungkok*, "a shield" (pl. XXIII, *a*).

35.871. Unmade *bidang*. Creepers and hanging blossoms. Width, 1 ft. 7 in. (48·2 cm.); length, 3 ft. 10 in. (116·9 cm.).

The warps are paired throughout and average 56 pairs to the inch in the pattern stripes and 72 pairs (144 ends) in the self-colour stripes. The weft is threefold without twist and there are 23 picks to the inch. The whole cloth is very evenly woven and has a crisp, firm texture.

The pattern is of the natural cotton colour on a red-brown background and the grouped stripes of bright red, yellow and a very dark brown, giving the effect of black in the borders, indicates Seribas Iban work. There are two narrow bands of colour at the outer edges, red and yellow, then a broad stripe of dark brown, followed by three compound stripes of narrow red, yellow, brown, yellow, red, yellow, brown, yellow, red, divided by slightly wider pattern stripes.

The broad central band is very interesting; it is covered completely by a lattice work or lozenge pattern, in a half-drop style, the lozenges being 7½ in. by 3½ in. (19 cm. by 8·9 cm.). The lines forming the lozenges are described as *randau tangkong bi penyuang*, "the lattice work pattern of the *tangkong* creeper", and hanging from the upper corner of each diamond and within it is the flower, *bunga tangkong*, whilst from the two lower sides what appear to be leaves project (pl. xx, *a*). The flowers vary slightly in different rows. In three lozenges are *gelang terabai*, "the handle of a shield" (pl. xxiii, *b*).

The narrow patterned borders at the sides are ornamented with a *engkarong kejong*, "stiff lizard, skink", *S.D.D.* (pl. xii, *f*), "*entibap*" but actually *empili* (cf. pl. xviii, *d*), a palm pattern, and at one end, *semerai sungai*, "crossing the river".

35.872. Width, 1 ft. 7½ in. (49·5 cm.); length, 3 ft. 8 in. (111·8 cm.). Pl. xxx, A.

One unusual feature in the making of this cloth is that the weft, which is brown, is a single thread making 20 picks to the inch. There are 128 paired warp ends to the inch, making 64 pairs. The thinness in quality of the weft and the closeness of the warps has resulted in a fine, soft cloth.

The colour is much lighter than in the average *bidang*, the pattern being in buff on a warm Indian red ground with touches of dark brown. There are one or two touches of pale blue in the main pattern and in the narrow side borders; these are unusual and very effective, the dark brown spots being probably due to over-dyeing the brown with the light-blue colour. The bordering stripes at the sides are narrow lines of buff and black or very dark brown.

The patterns are very elaborate in form but excellently spaced as decoration and clearly defined; their accuracy has been made possible by the closeness of the warp and the fine weft.

Included amongst the motives are degenerate, but elaborate, forms of the tiger-cat, *remaung*, and white shrew, *aji bulan*. The most interesting feature of this cloth is the decorative use of the "box for padi husking", *entilang plangka* (a *plangka* may be an oblong wooden frame about 6 ft. by 3 ft. enclosing ratan work which is used for threshing paddy, or a propitiatory offering on behalf of a sick person in the *saut* ceremony. The *plangka* used in the ceremony is a plate or an oblong wooden box, without a cover, standing upon four ornamental legs about 6 in. from the ground). A large one labelled "*pelangka (manang besaut)*", is shown on pl. xxiv, *i* and in the lower centre of pl. xxx, A, and a smaller one, within which is a shrew, *aji*, on pl. vi, *b* and in the upper centre of pl. xxx, A. The representation of the larger *plangka* is very elaborate. Beyond the right-hand end of it, at the edge of the photograph, is a small design, *spit kala*, "nippers of a scorpion" (pl. xvii, *b*).

In the borders at the edges are *embayer*, "centipedes" (pl. xvi, *c*), and birds. Among the latter are *burong besugu*, "bird with comb" (pl. vii, *o*), and a *lelayang*, "swallow" (pl. ix, *c*), of which the tail is somewhat like that of the argus pheasant.

35.873. Unmade *bidang*. Width, 1 ft. 9 in. (53·4 cm.); length 3 ft. 8 in. (111·8 cm.).

Both the warp and weft threads have been used in pairs or sisters of even thickness, the slackness of the warp during the process of weaving resulting in a cloth having a warp surface. There are 46 pairs of warp threads to the inch in the patterned stripe and 88 pairs (176 ends) in the self-colour stripes. There are 26 picks of sistered weft, brown in colour.

The background of the patterned portion has been dyed a reddish brown, leaving the pattern in the natural colour of unbleached cotton.

The central band is decorated with tiger-cats, *remaung* (pl. iv, *f*), white shrews, *aji bulan*, and parts of these animals, with, in a few places, patterns devised purely to fill up an empty space. The shrews are represented in two attitudes, one in which they are facing one another or facing the border—these are distinctly pugnacious (cf. pl. v, *g*), and the other (cf. pl. v, *g*) in a resting attitude, showing the long body and snout (as in pl. v, *e*). The tiger pattern is more purely decorative and is chiefly recognizable by the arrangement of paws in a form fairly constant in patterns bearing this name.

The wider of the narrow borders at the side represents *tangkai buah wi*, "the stalk of a ratan with fruit", and at one end *anak burong*, "a young bird" (pl. ix, *m*). On either side of this is a narrower border with a *lelingkok* or zigzag pattern.

35.874. Unmade *bidang*. An exceptionally wide cloth: width, 1 ft. 11 in. (58·4 cm.); length, 3 ft. 11 in. (119·4 cm.)

Paired warps, 40 to the inch (80 ends), and four parallel threads as weft, dyed brown, 16 picks to the inch, have made a coarse cloth.

Buff patterns on a brown ground fill the central panel and three simple self stripes of brown edged with fine lines of white, yellow and black are divided by two patterned stripes to form the border.

The patterns are very simple; there are four repeats in the width and four in the length. Each repeat consists of crossed poles of *pedalai*, "bread-fruit tree", with hooks, *kayit srepang*, at the end, a *pasak*, "wedge", fills in the acute angle outside whilst a filling-in pattern, *jerit bubul*, adorns the lozenge shape.

This cloth is similar to 35.861, but lacks the charm of colour produced by the light-blue border in the latter, and is a duplicate of 35.867 and like it has a *lelingkok* pattern at one end and at the other end, *jerit bubul*, a pattern to fill a space; in this case it is paired scrolls.

The border patterns are shown in fig. 28, *a*.

35.875. Unmade *bidang*. Width, 1 ft. 8⅖ in. (51·8 cm.); length, 4 ft. ½ in. (123·2 cm.).

The warps are paired, 48 pairs occurring in the inch, and the weft is single, brown in colour, and averages 20 picks to the inch.

In this cloth the colour is dull and does not enhance the pattern, which is in buff on a reddish brown ground. At the sides there are three narrow patterned stripes edged by self-colour stripes of yellow, black and brown, with a broad black stripe on either side near the edge.

The patterns are interesting; the broad central band has designs based upon the shrew and a *sampan* or canoe with its distinctive platforms at the ends and paddles, *dayong*, projecting from the sides (pl. xxiii, *c*). The shrew patterns vary somewhat from those in the cloths previously described. At one end is a row of *tebok leka labu*, "gourd seeds with holes" (pl. xix, *f*).

The border patterns are various kinds of *burong* and some *empili*.

35.876. A plain striped *bidang*, see p. 87.

35.877. Width, 1 ft. 7⅖ in. (49·4 cm.); length, 3 ft. 9⅕ in. (114·7 cm.).

There are 56 warp groups of threes (168 ends) to the inch in the bright-coloured stripes and also in the central band. The weft is brown, consists of three parallel threads, and makes 20–22 picks to the inch.

The gaiety of colour in the side borders of this cloth is its most noticeable feature and forms a strong contrast to the background of red in the central band, which has been over-dyed with indigo leaving the patterns in buff, with some parts still red.

Hawk designs prevail in the central band (pl. x, *c*); smaller designs include a young shrew, *anak aji* (pl. v, *a*), and a "leech on a creeping plant", *randau lintah* (pl. XVI, *j*). One of the border patterns is described as *tangkal tangga*, "the notched steps of a ladder", i.e. a notched pole that serves as a ladder. The horizontal black and white stripes (perhaps suggesting the notched steps of a ladder) are produced by groups of warps in threes arranged alternately in black and white. As the cloth has a warp surface, in the weaving the groups of white come to the surface when one pick is made and black when the next pick goes through a shed formed of the alternate groups.

35.878. The deer family. Width, 1 ft. 7¾ in. (50·1 cm.); length, 3 ft. 8 in. (111·8 cm.). **Pl. XXX, B.**

A curious variation occurs in the warping of this cloth, the brilliant red, yellow and white self stripes and the narrow shaded borders between them have warps indiscriminately grouped in threes and fours but averaging 192 ends to the inch. The bulk of the patterned central stripe has paired warps of 48 to the inch (96 ends), but for 4 in. from the border on the left side the warps are in groups of three and average 36 groups to the inch (108 ends). The firmness and thickness of the cloth varies with the number of warps to the inch, and the different grouping influences the pattern to the extent of making it lighter where the warps are in threes than where they are only paired. There is a triple brown weft (used as parallel threads) averaging 16 picks to the inch.

This *bidang* is one of the most brilliantly coloured in the collection, and is even more distinctive than 35.870, which is similar in both colour and pattern.

The patterns are white, outlined with very dark brown on a rich reddish brown background. Occasionally dark spots are used effectively inside the pattern lines. The well-proportioned narrow border stripes (fig. 28, *c*) are of light yellow, centred with scarlet and edged with navy blue. There are four of these *surik*, the outer ones enclosing shaded stripes of pattern *empetut* and having a pin stripe of white in addition, and the central one, *gigi rinik*, "steps of a ladder", a black and white band horizontally striped. Between the outermost of these narrow stripes and the edge is a solid stripe of indigo 1⅜ in. wide, which has a very rich effect, and this has a narrow bordering, *surik beranak*, at the extreme edge of the cloth of red and yellow measuring ⅖ in.

The deer patterns are clearly defined and fill the central band of the cloth. The spaces between the animals in the first and second rows are filled by a representation of a frame for winding cotton upon, *tukal jengkuan*; the curved ends are called *brang tukal* ("*brang* = the upper arm", *S.D.D.*), "*tukal*, a wooden frame about three feet long upon which cotton thread is strung for weaving" (*S.D.D.*), pl. xxiv, *d*, and to the left in pl. xxx, B. Three deer in the second row are hornless and are described as *anak rusa*, "young deer" (pl. iii, *h*); three others can be seen on pl. xxx, B. The second row of animals must be male, as they possess a feature elsewhere described as "crossed horns", *tandok berkaul* (cf. pl. iii, *a*, *b*). In the third row of animals (not shown in the photograph) the hind is the motive; no antlers are shown, but the breasts, *tusu rusa*, are indicated (pl. iii, *c*). The head appears as an anti-spiral, and in this and other respects it is very like *Aki Ungkok* in cloth 35.854, pl. i, *a*. The tail is realistic. The last row represents three stags (pl. iii, *f*) with more imposing antlers entangled, *balut*, but although the parts representing the antlers, snout, body and tail are definitely named it is not easy to decide the real position of these animals, for with the usual desire for bi-symmetry and the dislike of an empty space, the artist has duplicated the tails and added bits of pattern to the antlers, which are elsewhere described as "crossed horns"; perhaps a neat way of suggesting a fight. The "notched hole", *tebok kengking*, pattern on the "body of the deer", *tuboh rusa*, has no obvious significance other than being decorative.

35.879. Spider cloth. Width, 1 ft. 8½ in. (52·1 cm.); length, 3 ft. 6½ in. (108 cm.).

The warps are arranged in groups of threes in the patterned stripes, and in the red and blue self stripes at the sides in fours. In the former there are 44 groups to the inch and in the latter 36. The brown weft is double (sisters or parallel) and there are 20 picks to the inch.

The colour is generally of a dull tone, the warps of the pattern stripe having apparently been dipped in a weak indigo bath after the previous dyeing of the background of dark brown. The small border stripes are mostly red with narrow edgings of yellow and black. A broad band of deep indigo, almost black in effect, about an inch and a quarter in width, finishes off the striped border on each side.

Three rows of spider, *emplawa*, patterns are begun by a row of half spiders and the spaces between contain indeterminate filling-in patterns, *bubul lapang*. The spiders in the second row, which are the largest, have two birds' heads, *pala burong*, inside their stomachs, *prut emplawa* (pl. xv, *d*); in other respects the designs are of the usual type.

35.880. Width, 2 ft. ¾ in. (62·9 cm.); length 3 ft. 9 in. (114·4 cm.).

The warps are paired except in the wide navy-blue stripes at the sides and the red and yellow warp stripes, where they are in threes. The weft is brown and twofold. There are 48 pairs (96 ends) of warps and 26 picks of weft to the inch.

This unusually wide cloth has broad navy-blue stripes at the sides with composite ones of warp stripes enclosing an *empili*, mast, stripe between the navy-blue and the broad central pattern. The patterns are very clear and are white on a reddish brown background with darker lines around them produced by over-dyeing the brown with blue.

Near the joining of the cloth is a transverse broad white zigzag with dark vertical lines; this is labelled *leku sawa*, "the twisting of the python", which is something like the lower zigzag of *g*, pl. xxiii. Below this and occupying about one-third of the length of the cloth are four lizards, *engkarong* (pl. xii, *i*). Next comes a very pronounced zigzag, *leku sawa*, with a filling-in pattern of hooks, and then four deer, *rusa*, fill up another third of the cloth. The remaining portion is occupied by rather indefinite patterns except in the centre, where there is an interesting figure with hooks described as *jengku ruyit*, "a curved barb" (pl. xxiii, *q*).

35.881. The purple colour of this *bidang* is due to its having had all parts, except the outlines of the patterns and the orange and red self stripes, over-dyed in a light indigo bath. The wider of the borders at the side are each filled by two centipedes (pl. xvi, *d*) and the narrow ones by grubs, *empetut* (pl. xvii, *g*). The central band has two large hawk designs, one of which has a distinct head with a beak, *patok* (pl. x, *a*), and a second in which a figure like the previous head appears as the body of the bird (pl. x, *b*); the *patok* is at the top and the *plir* at the bottom of this drawing. Just above the tail of the first of these two hawks is a young bird (pl. ix, *k*) and on a level with the body of the hawk a knot of wood, *tangkong bara* (pl. xxi, *g*). At one end of the cloth are leeches; one, *bungai lintah* (pl. xvi, *k*), is attached to flowers of the *tangkong*.

35.882. *Kain selam*, "diving cloth"; "pattern *kara*". Width, 1 ft. 9⅖ in. (53·9 cm.); length, 4 ft. 3 in. (129·6 cm.). **Pl. XXXI, A.**

The warps are grouped in threes throughout the whole width of this cloth, and except in the red stripes, where they are a little closer, the general number of groups to the inch is 36, i.e. 108 ends. The weft is fourfold, untwisted, and blue in colour and there are 20 picks to the inch. The resulting cloth has a coarse but very firm texture.

This is the only cloth in the collection with bright blue as a background to the central band, which measures 14½ in. in width. There are some coloured border stripes in blue, red, yellow and white and the general effect of the colour scheme is pleasant.

This is the only *bidang* in our collection with "diving", *selam*, figures which may be human (pl. 11, *j*). A somewhat similar figure on a cloth in the Sarawak Museum is drawn on pl. 11, *l*. Ordeal by diving is practised by the Iban (Ling Roth, 1, p. 236; see *S.D.D.* Appendix, p. 11). We cannot identify the patterns which fill in the spaces between them. The two narrow pattern borders at the sides are filled with the "crossing the river" design.

35.883. An embroidered *bidang*, see pp. 87–89.

35.884. This cloth has had its edges dipped in indigo. The narrow borders at the side contain arenga palm (cf. pl. xxii, *b, c*) and "crossing the river" designs; the central band is filled with various hawk figures, including *kengkang lang*. Inside a pattern which is somewhat like the beetle on cloth 35.928 figured on pl. xvii, *c*, is a "wedge" (cf. pl. xxiii, *r, s*).

35.885. A cloth of the usual reddish brown colour covered with numerous patterns in a paler tone. Most of the designs are degenerate in form, although a "wedge" (cf. pl. xxiii, *r*) and a young bird (cf. pl. ix, *k*) occur several times and are quite clear. One figure in a hexagon with scrolls is called *aji bata bras* and another larger figure is called *janga buan*; *janga* is an angle, the forked branch of a tree. The scrolls around it may be *buan* flowers ("*Buan*, a small shrub whose fruit and flowers are the favourite food of the mouse-deer (*plandok*)", *S.D.D.*). The border patterns are *empetut* and ratan.

35.886. An embroidered *bidang*, see pp. 89–91.

35.887. The three narrow border patterns at the side of this clearly patterned cloth consist of a central one with centipedes (cf. pl. xvi) alternating with a *tayok gasing*, "hand spinning wheel", and *ruit gansai*, "a spear with one barb" (pl. xxii, *p*); a "crossing the river" pattern occurs in the narrow stripes on each side (cf. pl. xxv, *g*). The designs in the middle of the cloth are described as *tangkong lumbong*, "the *tangkong* creeper" (cf. pl. xx, *a*).

35.888. A "*serundam* cloth". This is a very gaily coloured cloth, it has a broad blue band down the centre and three sets of compound stripes in white, red, yellow and blue divided by two patterned stripes on either side. The patterned stripes are filled by representations of centipedes (cf. pl. xvi, *d, e, f*) on one side and arenga palms (cf. pl. xxii, *a, c*) on the other.

35.889. *Kain engkudu.* ("*Engkudu*, a plant of which the skin of the root produces a red dye", *S.D.D.*) A cloth of a bright red colour with a broad central band of poor patterns in which a design called *lang*, "kite", is much more like the spider designs on other cloths (cf. pl. xv, *b, d*). Other patterns recall the simpler shrew types and shrews facing (cf. pl. v, *g*).

35.890. *Kain maba.* This cloth has narrow borders at the sides with well-defined arenga palms (cf. pl. xxii, *a*) and ratan. The broad central band has recognizable deer forms (cf. pl. iii), and here and there young birds filling in the spaces (cf. pl. ix, *k, m*).

35.891. *Kain pampul*, "covered cloth"; "*penukoh* pattern". This cloth has brightly coloured self stripes at the sides and in the centre two rows of crossed poles (fig. 30), with knots, *penukoh*, resembling sleeping cats (cf. pl. xvii, *t, u*). Well-defined wedges (cf. pl. xxiii, *r*) appear between the crossed poles and at the other end of the cloth are some deer figures. *Empili* and *empetut* in the borders.

35.892. *Kain maba.* A cloth with narrow borders at the sides filled with patterns based on the arenga palm (cf. pl. xxii, *b*), centipede (cf. pl. xvi, *d*) and ratan (cf. pl. xxii, *l, m*). The central band has shrew patterns which can be compared with pl. v, *a, g*, and a more elaborate form compounded of shrew and spider which may be compared with pls. v, *f*; xiv, *d* and xv, *b*.

35.893. *Kain maba—Buah bungai.* This cloth has a narrow border on each side filled with a mast design (cf. pl. xviii, *d*) and a broad central band filled with rather confused shrew patterns. Near the joining of the cloth there is a branch with fruit (*buah*) and flowers (*bungai*), which can be compared with pl. xx, *b*.

35.894. A cloth with some narrow composite borders at the sides of bright yellow and brown which enclose a "crossing the river" motive (cf.

pl. xxv, g). The main designs in the centre of the cloth consist of various shrew patterns; one of rather unusual type is simplified in a figure (pl. v, e).

35.895. Three narrow border patterns decorate the sides of the cloth and are filled with *empili* and "crossing the river" patterns. Rather more than half of the central pattern is filled with shrews, one variant of the motive is unusual (pl. v, d); on each side of it are designs like pl. v, g. The rest of the cloth is filled with ginger root patterns (cf. pl. xix, d).

35.896. The main design of this cloth is unusual because it is a regular half drop pattern of hexagons filled with rather poor bird motives, some of which resemble the bird dancing (cf. pl. viii, k). This geometrical arrangement suggests an outside influence. The *bidang* is labelled "pattern *bunkang*". The narrow borders at the side have indistinct patterns.

35.897. The pattern of this cloth seems to be named inaccurately as *bali* (perhaps because the colour fades). The main pattern is a bold but poor deer design.

35.898. A cloth with a reddish brown background, which has again been dipped in brown dye after the pattern had been reserved. There is a broad green stripe at the edges. The central pattern is entirely made up of long and elegant *puchok tubu*, "bamboo shoots", and the arenga palm (cf. pl. xxii, a) fills up the widest of the outer stripes, the narrowest being *empetut*.

35.899. A cloth with bright self stripes in red, yellow, black and white down the sides and a central band of confused patterns with two lozenges described as *pandin*, "buckle". The pattern is called *tukuyo*.

35.900. A very clearly patterned *bidang* with intricate patterns at the ends. The centre of the cloth is taken up by three pairs of bands united in two places; the central lozenge thus formed encloses two *burong* with wedge-shaped bodies. The bands are labelled *papan penokoh*, "board of the *penokoh*"; in the centre of each is a *pusat penokoh*, "centre (or navel) of the *penokoh*"; this design is similar to the "sleeping cat" (pl. xvii, r, u). At the ends of the "boards" (which are evidently branches) are *bungai penokoh*, "flower of the *penokoh*". Dr Hose says on a label: "The meaning of *penokoh* is uncertain, it may mean holding", and he suggests that the central design, *pusat*, may be "the real *penokoh*, as it appears to hold the *papan* together". At one end of the cloth is an *aji*, decorated with many spirals; it is labelled *aji besumpiang*, "the filled up *aji*", referring to the spirals in the pattern; *besumpiang* also means to complete or finish off.

The border patterns consist of two stripes of unnamed simple designs and three stripes containing a continuous series of small white, red, white, black squares; this is labelled *urar empatut*, "the *empatut* snake (*Tropidonotus petersii*)"; it should be *empetut*.

35.853. A *bidang* extremely simple in its design, the pattern consisting of cream-coloured warp stripes on a brown ground. It is 3 ft. 7⅘ in. (110 cm.) in length and 1 ft. 7$\frac{1}{10}$ in. (48 cm.) in width.

The warps are arranged singly and there are 72 ends to an inch. The weft is twofold (i.e. two parallel threads form each pick), and in part of the cloth it is white, in the remainder brown. There are 24 picks of weft to the inch. The white stripes of the pattern are regular, the arrangement of the warps being 2 white, 3 brown, 2 white, 3 brown, 6 white, 10 brown repeated. This pattern is labelled *ara rinik anak udun*, "close lines called after a young fish named *udun*".

At the edge there is a plain brown stripe, 2 cm. wide, labelled *kain baloi*, "cloth striped like the *baloi* bamboo". This evidently refers to the cloth as a whole, the reference to "bamboo" is not evident.

35.876. This *bidang* is similar to the previous one, but has been dyed in a different way.

Originally it was striped white and light brown in the warp, which was paired and arranged in a repeating pattern thus: 2 white pairs (4 warp ends), 3 brown pairs, 3 white pairs, 6 brown pairs, 2 white pairs, across the entire width except for one wider brown stripe near each edge.

The cloth is described as *Kain baloi udah di karam*, "*baloi* cloth which has been put (*karam*) into a pot with water and *tarum*" (indigo); this was done after it had been made up and it shows pale blue stripes on a black ground (*udah*, finish).

The pattern is termed *ara besurik*, and if the latter is a form of *suri* (*besuri*) then it means stripes like ripples on the surface of the water. *Bidang* dyed with blue in this way are usually worn by widows.

35.883. *Kain sunkit.* An embroidered cloth. Width at centre, 1 ft. 5 in. (43·2 cm.); length, 3 ft. 5 in. (104·2 cm.).

This is a plain piece of rather loosely woven tabby cloth, measuring

1 ft. 6 in. (45·7 cm.) at one end and narrowing to 1 ft. 3½ in. (39·4 cm.) at the other. The spacing of the warp threads varies from 120 ends to a crowded 168 ends to the inch; in the middle of the cloth most of the warps are paired.

The patterns are embroidered with a bone needle called *sunkit*, from which the term *kain sunkit* is derived. The threads are carried nearly across the cloth in working the pattern, just as if a pick of weft had been used. A lattice design with horizontal lozenges at alternate crossings of the ground lines occupies the centre of the cloth for just over a foot in width, and the pattern has been produced by two needles, *sunkit*, one carrying red, the other black threads. In the case of the red the needle carries eight threads, which are worked across the cloth as far as the pattern extends as a flat series of strands between two picks of weft. The black is made up of four coarser threads carried by a second needle and used in the same manner. There are three rows of red stitching and three rows of black alternating with one shoot of plain white weft between each row. The needle is turned back at the edge of the pattern and is not carried right across the cloth.

Down the sides there are three narrow embroidered borders divided by narrow composite colour stripes a quarter of an inch wide, and there is a black stripe half an inch wide nearer to the outer edge.

The red warps in the self-colour stripes are much finer than the white used in the body of the cloth, and in these coloured border stripes the warp ends vary in number from 192 to 280 in an inch.

There are 24 picks of the white cloth weft taken right across the web and 24 coloured rows of stitching between them in the patterned section. The introduction of the coloured threads makes this part of the cloth much thicker and heavier than that between the border stripes at the sides, where it is rather open in texture. The loose weave is necessary for such a form of embroidery.

The background of the cloth is white and the central pattern is striped horizontally red and black alternately, and measures 12½ in. (31·8 cm.) across.

The embroidered patterned stripes at the sides are divided by composite stripes of black, red, yellow, black, and still nearer the outer edge is a half-inch black stripe. Pin stripes of white and red finish off the actual edges.

No descriptive labels were attached to the pattern, which is planned out geometrically all over the surface. It consists of diagonally crossing lines forming lozenges, averaging $2\frac{1}{2}$ in. by 1 in.

Horizontal diamonds, about 2 in. by $\frac{3}{4}$ in. across and more solidly coloured, occur at the alternate crossings of the lines.

The two narrowest embroidered side borders have only alternate squares of red and black as pattern with a rather longer space left between them than their own widths; this is probably the *empetut* pattern, p. 87.

The central border pattern, also needle worked, begins experimentally, settles down to a zigzag stripe in red and black, and before it completes half the length of the cloth changes first to two zigzags meeting diamond-wise, one side red and the other black, and then to a much better design of two zigzag lines crossing one another, one of the lines being red and the other black. The first of the patterns in the stripe may have been suggested by the "crossing the river" design, *semerai sungai*, so often used on the warp-dyed cloths.

The same pattern occurs in the badge of Saribas Iban *kalambi*, photo-graphed at Limbang by Haddon, Mus. photo. 403 (pl. XVII, *m*), and as a band pattern on a *kalambi* and a shawl photographed by Haddon at Kuching, where the lozenges were identified as *mata puna*, "eye of green pigeon", Mus. photos. 397, 398.

35.886. An embroidered *bidang* from the Upper Rejang river. Width, 1 ft. $6\frac{1}{4}$ in. (45·8 cm.); length, 2 ft. $4\frac{1}{4}$ in. (86·5 cm.). **Pl. XXXI, B.**

This is an evenly woven cloth with both warp and weft threefold. There are 60 groups of warps (180 ends) and 20 picks of weft to the inch. The resulting cloth is less like a rep than a fine canvas and this quality has been very useful in the working of the elaborate embroidered patterns. In the self-coloured stripes down the sides of the cloth there are, on an average, 48 groups of warp (144 ends) to the inch. This cloth has an extremely rich effect, produced by embroidered pattern lines of thick red and black wool, and is the only example we have found that has any wool in it. When woven the cloth was white bordered by two composite self-coloured stripes with a narrow white stripe between them. The whole of the white portion has been covered by embroidered patterns. The inner composite stripe, part of which has been stitched over, measures $1\frac{3}{4}$ in. (4·2 cm.) in width and is made up of the following warp groups: 3 red, 3 white, 3 black, 3 yellow, 3 red and 5 white, and 4 black arranged alternately, then 3 red, 3 yellow, 3 black, 3 white, 6 red, and then the whole repeated. The outer stripe is $1\frac{5}{8}$ in. (5·3 cm.) and is similarly arranged, except that at the selvedge there is a solid red stripe measuring $\frac{1}{8}$ in. in width with a solid black stripe inside it of the same size. The threefold weft is white, except for about $3\frac{1}{2}$ in. near the seam, where a threefold red weft has been used. It is interesting to note that these few inches are less brilliant in their colour effect.

At one end and extending to one-third of the cloth are three zigzag branches; from the upper end and middle of each projects a squared fret and from the lower end an hexagonal fret; these evidently represent the spirals of the usual tie-dye technique. The lozenge-shaped spaces between the branches enclose various devices; two look as if they might be winged insects and one seems to be a squared version of the *bunga* design of pl. XIX, *a*. The main portion of the cloth is occupied by leeches and they may be intentionally depicted as on the creeper since the pattern is continuous. There are three sets of two leeches which have their mouths interlocked (pls. XVI, *a*; XXXI, B); their tails are coiled, but in two (shown on the right side of the photograph) the coiled tails are discontinuous from their bodies. Another set of incomplete and irregular leeches complete the main pattern. All the spaces contain bird and other motives.

The border pattern begins with an experimental zigzag and develops into a series of lozenges with a central spot resembling the eye of the green pigeon, *mata puna* (cf. pl. XVII, *l*, *m*).

It might be thought that a series of pattern heddles had been used to produce this design, but the constant change of motives which in their lines do not correspond to any re-grouping in the use of a set of heddles and the very short lengths of wool used, just a comfortable needle-full, are two of the proofs against the employment of pattern heddles or that of free spools.

The pattern has been produced in the same way as damask darning; a needle carrying either black or red wool picks up just as much of the cloth as is required for the white outline, passes over the surface of the fabric until the next group of warps is picked up for the next bit of pattern. This process is continued right across the pattern; then one pick of weft being left in between, the needle is turned so as to work back along the width of the central stripe, picking up each bit of the pattern on the way. Three rows of black darning are followed by three rows of red alternately, and as only the outlines of the pattern or some spots between them are picked up on the needle the result is a white pattern on a background of black and red horizontal stripes. The patterned border stripes are worked separately.

This cloth was given to the Museum by A. E. Lawrence.

SIRAT, LOIN-CLOTHS

The *sirat*, called a *chawat* by the Malays, is a strip of cloth generally 6 yd. in length, and may be as much as a yard wide, but more often about 15 in. It is wound round the loins and between the thighs with great precision; the ends are sometimes elaborately decorated by coloured strips of cloth and embroidery. According to Brooke Low "a *klapong sirat*, or tail flap, is often worn by the elder men of the latter tribes [Lamanaks and Sakarang tribes] ...it is prettily and fancifully embroidered with coloured thread and is sewn on to either end of the *sirat* to hang before and behind" (Ling Roth, II, p. 55). The way in which a waist-cloth is wound on, its colour and the fashion of its decoration are indications as to what tribe the wearer belongs. Dark-blue cotton cloth is the material most commonly used, but white is worn in mourning or during outdoor labour.

The only whole *sirat* we have is 35.915; its ends are not very elaborately embroidered and the same applies to the whole *sirat* in the British Museum (1905, 400).

Judging from two specimens in the British Museum (1905, 396, 397), the *klapong sirat* or ends of the loin-cloth are woven as one piece of cloth and are embroidered in the characteristic manner, one being very different from the other. Subsequently they are severed and sewn on to the ends of a *sirat*. All the other specimens we have seen have evidently been cut off from loin cloths, as they are soiled from being worn.

One type of *klapong sirat* has an elaborate embroidered panel, the central portion of which appears to portray cultivated swamp-land. The designs are very much alike in our three specimens (35.913, 35.917 and Z.2344) and in those in the British Museum and the Sarawak Museum. A careful study of all the available material of this motive would be of considerable

91

interest, but this would have to be undertaken by someone having local knowledge.

The second type of *klapong sirat* is decorated with horizontal bands. This is represented in our collection by 35.912, Z.2345, and 35.916.

As we have no information as to whether one type is worn in front and the other behind, we are obliged to refer to them as type 1 and type 2 respectively.

The *sirat* are described in the following order:

| 35.915 | 35.917 | 35.912 | 35.916 |
| 35.913 | Z.2344 | Z.2345 | |

35.915. A complete *sirat* or loin-cloth. Width varies from 1 ft. to 1 ft. $\frac{1}{4}$ in. (30·5–31·1 cm.); length, including fringe, 15 ft. (4·572 metres).

The cloth is of native weaving with decorated ends, and is a simple tabby, or alternately one up, one down weave; the warp and weft are both single, although the warp varies greatly in thickness. There are on an average 48 warp ends and 16 picks to the inch, few enough to produce a cloth into which extra threads in the direction of the weft can easily be introduced. This is an old dirty specimen.

The fringe has been produced by working with a needle over groups of warps whilst still on the loom, each group of about 24 ends being arranged in eights, and a darning or weaving stitch has been worked backwards and forwards over each set of three eights with thick red thread for half an inch and then with thick yellow thread for another half inch. The warps have then been freed from the loom, twisted together in threes or fours, and the twisted strands from each strip of needle-weaving divided so as to form three-stranded plaits about 1½ in. long. To complete the fringe each strand from the plait has been tied round a bunch of short cotton strands to form a tassel; in this way are produced two or three tassels to each plait, usually of different colours, white, red and blue; these are described as *kelapong iko* (fig. 31).

There are patterns at both ends; the one without the fringe has the more elaborate and certainly embroidered designs; those at the fringed end are all worked in lines right across the cloth and were probably darned or woven in with a needle; the same result could, however, be obtained by picking up the warps with small free spools to form the pattern, one throw of ordinary weaving being made between each pick of the pattern. In the latter case the shed stick or a heddle would group the warps in threes. Either of the methods would produce a reversible pattern, owing to the passing of the floating threads. The very thick coloured weft, used for working the patterns,

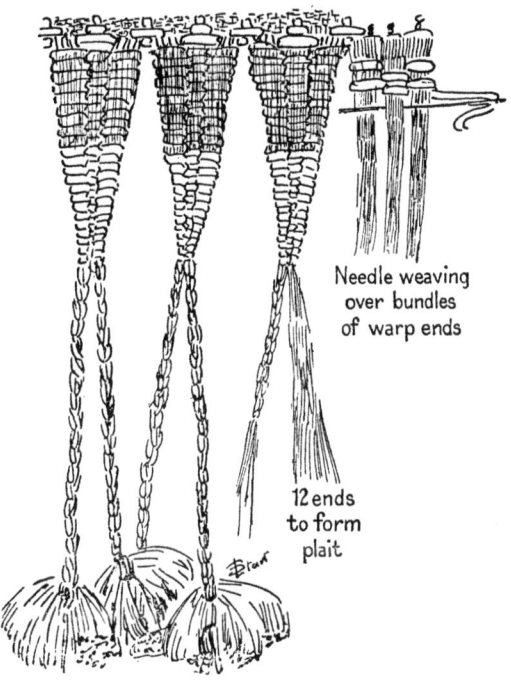

Needle weaving
over bundles
of warp ends

12 ends
to form
plait

Fig. 31. Method of making the fringe at the end of *sirat* 35.915.

is made up of a number of fine threads used parallel to one another, as many as 12 being used in the red and yellow and six or eight slightly coarser ones in the blue.

Unbleached cotton provides the stone colour of the background, and the patterns at the fringed end are worked on it in pale blue and in what has been a beautiful bright red. Some yellow is introduced in the heading of the fringe. At the other end all three colours are used.

At the fringed end half-inch bands of plain cloth separate a wide central from two narrow embroidered bands; the whole occupies a depth of $4\frac{2}{5}$ in.

93

(11·1 cm.). The upper and lower narrow bands consists of a zigzag with chevrons in the angles and is called *lelingkok mata puna* (zigzag, eye, pigeon). The broadest central band contains a complicated pattern of *kukut burong*, "birds' claws", one element of which is shown in pl. x, g. Above this is a stitchery band labelled *penuri pakan belebas*; this is a needle-weaving where some weft threads have been drawn out, and above it is a narrow blue band with a central white zigzag, *dabong lelingkok*.

The patterns at the other end of the *sirat* (which is probably the front flap) occupy a rather longer space. Three bands of 1¾ in., 1¾ in. and 2 in. (4·4, 4·4 and 5·1 cm.) in width are separated from one another by quarter-inch bands of plain cloth which are bordered by a blue band also called *dabong lelingkok*. The central band labelled *bengka senggang* (pl. xxv, d) is the counterpart of two transverse bands in the panel of the front flap of a *sirat* in the Sarawak Museum, no. 262, where it is called *tutup long*, which signifies the cover of a Kayan bark basket. The bands above and below this are very effective arrangements in red and blue and represent *pala buntak* and *kukut burong*, "heads of locusts" and "claws of birds". Above and below these three bands is a half-inch band of plain cloth and beyond this a half-inch embroidered band of *lelingkok mata puna*.

35.913. *Klapong sirat*, type A. "*Tanda sirat slampor*" (*?selampur*). Pl. XXXII, A.

The embroidered portion has a width of 11½ in. (29·2 cm.) and a length of 1 ft. 5½ in. (44·4 cm.). It has been joined, like *sirat* 35.912, to the main part of the waist-cloth by some horizontal bands of navy and yellow imported cotton cloth. The whole of the embroidered portion is edged with a binding, *lilit*, of scarlet flannel. On three sides, where it folds over the edge, its folded width varies from ⅝ in. to 1 in. (1·6–2·5 cm.), and on the fourth side, where it is joined to a strip of yellow cotton, there is a flat band of the scarlet flannel 1¼ in. (3·1 cm.) wide.

The weave is simple, one up and one down, both warp and weft being single, but of greatly varying thickness. There are on an average 68 warp ends and 26 picks of weft to the inch.

Two strips of scarlet flannel ¼ in. (0·6 cm.) wide divide an upper and a lower band from the main design. Each band consists of two needle-woven stripes, *pakan belebas* (pl. xix, g), of three rows of red and black weft.

94

Above and below the stripes are alternate red and black triangles embroidered with the same yarn as that of the needle-weaving. The triangles are labelled *dabong mayang* (dog-tooth, blossom of a palm); the central zigzag, judging from a similar *sirat* in the Sarawak Museum, no. 263, is merely incidental to the disposition of the triangles.

The main design is a rectangular area, $10\frac{1}{4}$ in. by 12 in. (26 cm. by 30·5 cm.), and is treated as a panel; in the centre is a rectangle, 6 in. by $8\frac{1}{4}$ in. This central portion is outlined by very narrow borders, the top and bottom are particularly interesting, as weft threads have been cut and withdrawn and a needle-woven weft inserted in their place. This is called *pakan belebas*. The side stripes are called *penuri daun resam*.

At the top and bottom of the panel is an elaborate pattern of *pala buntak*, "heads of locusts" (pls. XXXII, A; XVII, *i*). Immediately above and below the central rectangle is a border of *mayau tindok*, "sleeping cats" (pl. XVII, *u*), and at the sides is a pattern of hexagons, as also occurs in a *sirat* in the Sarawak Museum, no. 263, and in cloth 35.917 is termed *lalat tampok panggal*, "fly resting on a fruit stalk".

The central rectangle is filled with embroidered patterns worked in red and black thread; the position of the black stitches is indicated in the diagram (pl. XXV, *a*), by solid black lines, the enclosed spaces being filled in with red. The area is covered with designs called *tabor paya*, "sown swamp-land" (pl. XXV, *b*); the lozenges between the X-elements are called (in the Sarawak cloth, no. 262) *urat kaia*, "the root of a tree". The two lateral vertical designs (pls. XXXII, A; XXV, *a*) are called *paya bepadong* or *padong paya* and have been translated as "rocky ledges in the swamp-land".

The whole embroidery, with its neat, detailed, and evenly distributed patterns in dull red and black and chevrons of blue in the spaces between the sleeping cats and between the hexagons, produces a handsome effect.

35.917. *Klapong sirat*, type A, labelled *slampur*. Width, 1 ft. $1\frac{3}{4}$ in. (34·9 cm.); length, 1 ft. $4\frac{1}{2}$ in. (41·9 cm.).

As is usual in cloths which are to be embroidered, a plain tabby weave, one up and one down, is used; the yarn is of uneven thickness and the resulting cloth is strong but sufficiently loose to permit of the needle working the pattern. There are 56 warp ends and 18 picks of weft to the inch and both are single throughout.

An interesting variation of the weaving method is provided by four narrow horizontal borders occurring near the top and bottom of the piece. After a row of twining in red, which partly helps to group the warps in sixes, the ordinary weft alternates with three rows of stitchery-like weaving in black, red and black. A twofold thread is used and the whole is finished by a second row of twining. This pattern is called *gran pemalu*, "marks made by the bark-cloth beater", and is also described in other *sirat* (35.913) as *pakan belebas*, "made in weaving", but in that case weft threads are withdrawn and the little pattern is really needle-woven.

The cloth is in the natural unbleached colour of cotton, and the embroidery is worked in dull crimson and a greyish black; the figures are mostly outlined in black and filled in with crimson. A rather short fringe finishes off the bottom edge and is made by winding some of the red thread round a flat piece of cane about ¾ in. (1·9 cm.) in width about a dozen times, then slipping it off and tying it tightly in the middle with four of the warp ends. This fringe of tassels is described as *tanda kelapong bungai rambu*, "an embroidered flower fringed end", a far more picturesque name than it warrants.

The embroidery is very similar to that of 35.913, except that the upper and lower bands are wanting. The top and bottom borders of the panel contain a fringed zigzag motive labelled *lelingkok kaki embayer*, which represents a zigzagging centipede and its legs; on the apices are the heads (only) of locusts, *pala buntak*, and within the angles are more typical *pala buntak*. Between these bands and the central rectangle are two stripes of *gran pemalu* that stretch right across the cloth and enclose a pattern called *lalat tampok panggal*, which we translate as "fly resting on a fruit stalk". This is the same pattern as that on the vertical borders of the central rectangle of 35.913 (pl. xxxii, A). The same pattern occurs at the sides of the cloth and is bounded on each side by a vertical stripe called *tulang ikan*, "fish bones". An identical stripe is found on 35.913 in the same position, where it is called *penuri daun resam*.

The main patterns of the central rectangle are labelled *paya betabor*, and the *urat kaiku*, "roots of trees", are also indicated, but not labelled. The [-shaped elements are here called *entada paya*. The two lateral vertical designs are labelled *padong paya*, "cleared swamp-land" (pl. xxv, c).

96

Immediately above the fringe is a horizontal pattern, *mata ulat*, which consists of alternate blue and white rectangles; a red thread is sewn across their centres so as to form irregular spots, the white rectangles are probably the "grub's eyes".

Z.2344. *Klapong sirat*, type 1, labelled *tanda chawat*. The embroidery is in red and grey on a rather fine native cloth. The bright-red cotton fringe at the end is constructed in the same manner as that of 35.917, which *sirat* it resembles in many details.

At the top is a *pakan belebas* with alternate red and blue triangles on each side, which are labelled *dabong mayang*, "notched spathe of the areca palm". It corresponds to one-half of the double row in 35.913 (pl. XXXII, A). The bottom row is like that of 35.913, except that the central white zigzag is embroidered with a red zigzag.

The panel is bordered above with *kukut burong*, "birds' claws", and below with a more complicated pattern of the same type, and is identical with that in a similar position in 35.913, where, and in other cloths, it is termed *pala buntak*, "head of locust". Between this border pattern and the central rectangle are two stripes of *gran pemalu* that stretch right across the cloth and enclose an unnamed pattern similar to one on a *sirat* in the Sarawak Museum, no. 263; most of the small lozenges of the pattern have a yellow centre. Below the central rectangle the *gran pemalu* enclose *mayau tindok*, "cats asleep". On the lateral borders of the cloth is a series of lozenges containing four spots, named *buah bangkit*, "fruit of the wild mango". Between these and the central rectangle is a stripe of a squared zigzag or fret.

The central rectangle has four vertical rows of X-designs resembling those of other *sirat*, except that they are enclosed in hexagons (as in the Sarawak cloth, no. 263); parts of the hexagons appear to be related to the [-elements of other *sirat*. In this cloth there is a central as well as two lateral vertical designs, which are very similar to those of 35.913.

35.912. *Klapong sirat*, type 2, with a fringed end. This is an exceedingly interesting example of an embroidered and pattern-darned end to a man's waist-cloth, *sirat paya*. The decorated portion, which is of native manufacture, is $10\frac{1}{2}$ in. (26·7 cm.) in width and 1 ft. $8\frac{1}{2}$ in. (52·1 cm.) long, including the bead fringe. It is attached, under a strip of red flannel $2\frac{1}{4}$ in. (5·7 cm.) wide, by a row of running stitches to a band of navy-blue cotton cloth 3½ in. (8·9 cm.) wide, which is one of a series of five horizontal bands of navy blue and yellow, used alternately and varying in width from 2 in. (5·1 cm.) to 3½ in. (8·9 cm.). All this material is imported and the strips are joined by a running stitch, except the last navy-blue band at the top, which is of double material for strength and is joined to its yellow neighbour by a run and fell, also for strength. This navy-blue band was probably part of the main length of the *sirat*. The edges of this striped portion, as well as of the decorated end, are bound with red flannel (fig. 32, *a*).

The native cloth which forms the end is a plain tabby weave, of one up and one down, both warp and weft being used singly. The warp is generally coarser in section than the weft, but both vary considerably; there are on an average 88 warp ends and 24 picks of weft to an inch.

The ornamentation is divided into five horizontal panels by strips of fine scarlet flannel. The four upper panels are simply and very effectively decorated with horizontal bands—two in each panel, except the uppermost. Each band is composed of darning and embroidery, the first four stripes being practically alike in design although varying in width, and the last three being similar to one another and differing only slightly from the first group. The motive in all seven is the same; the central portion of each, which is darned and edged top and bottom by a row of twining, represents the eye of a green pigeon in a *bangkit* fruit, *mata puna buah bangkit* (pl. XVII, *k*). This part (fig. 32, *b*) is darned with twofold weft, sometimes red, sometimes black, each being used alternately for a few rows, e.g. in the fourth stripe from the top the red and black is used as follows: a row of black twining, four rows of red darning, seven black, four red and then a row of twining again. Outside the rows of twining in each case is a series of small triangles embroidered in red and black alternately and described as *dabong mayang*, a dog tooth, blossom of a palm.

The lowest division is the most interesting; it has two embroidered borders, the chief feature of each being a row of "*burong*", but they are not like any of our bird designs. These figures are partly outlined in black; the remaining portion is red with the exception of a spot in the head and end, where a yellow grass-like fibre has been introduced (fig. 32, *c*).

Immediately above and below the two bands of *burong* is a zigzag with spots in the angles, which is called *lelingkok mata puna*.

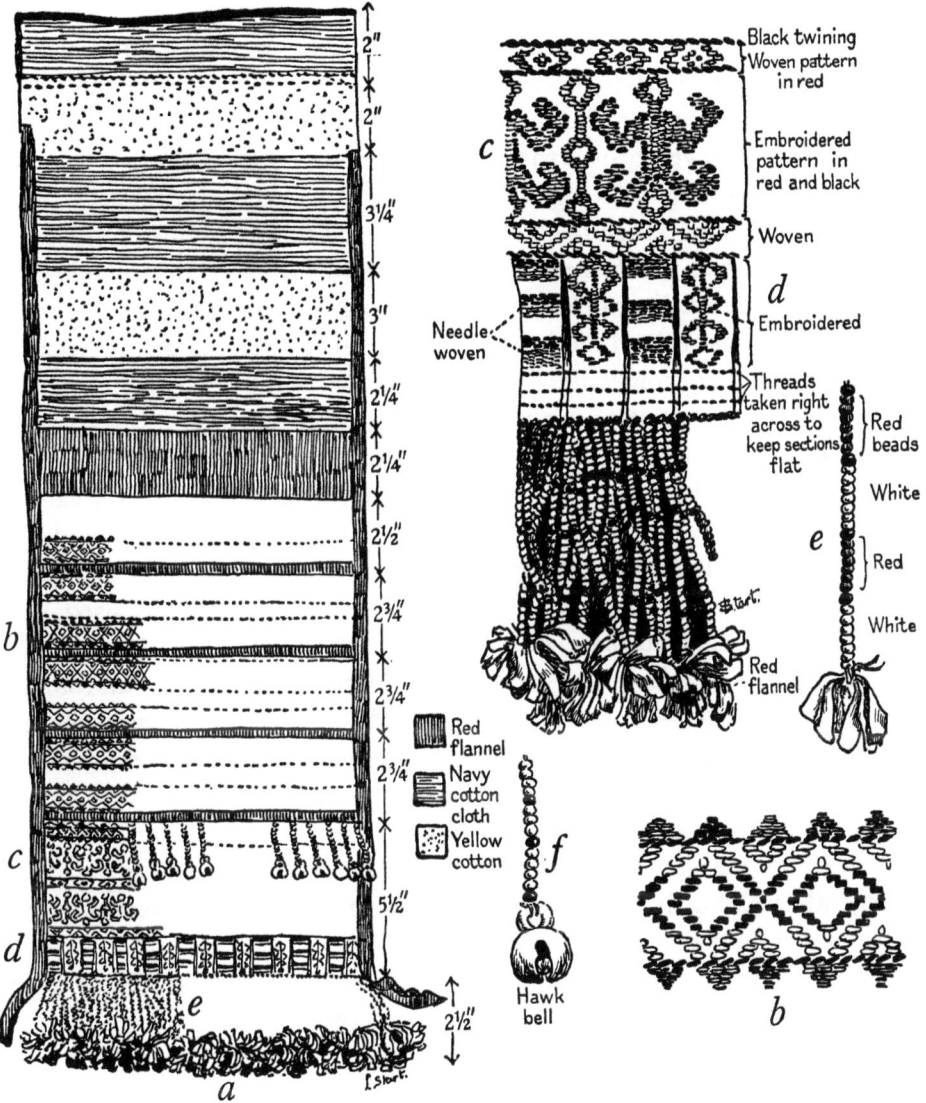

Fig. 32. *a*, End of *sirat* 35.912, with embroidered and darned patterns and a bead fringe; *b*, detail of the patterns, *mata puna*, *buah bangkit*, and *dabong mayang* of the first four bands; *c*, detail of one of the two *burong bands*; *d*, *e*, details of the fringe; *f*, detail of a fringe of hawk bells which is immediately below the lowermost strip of scarlet flannel as indicated in *a*.

99

The mixture of darning and embroidery is noticeable, and one is at first tempted to think that the embroidered figures have been woven by a brocade method with free shuttles, because there is so much flushing of the thread and it is used twofold in the red parts and threefold in the black. Careful examination, however, proves the work to have been done with the needle, for in the black outlining of the figures, the thread is worked continuously round them, stitches being taken back into the finished fabric, a course impossible with a free shuttle. The few ends in each motive do not occur at the highest point of a downwardly worked line, which would also have to be the case if free shuttles were used, and there are no threads passing at the back.

Below the *burong* comes the fringe, which has two distinct sections and is perhaps, from the point of view of its novelty and the skill necessary in its production, the most interesting part of this example of Iban work.

The upper portion consists of a series of eighteen strips of cloth, varying from ½ in. to ¾ in. (1·3–1·9 cm.) in width and 1½ in. (3·8 cm.) in depth. Each of these little tabs is a complete piece of weaving and must have been executed separately; it is probable that for this a needle was used. The patterns on the tabs alternate, one set have needle-woven horizontal stripes, *kengkang aning*, of black and red and the other set have an embroidered motive representing *pala burong*, "bird's head" (fig. 32, *d*). (These two types of tabs, and the two rows of *burong*, can be perfectly matched on a *sirat* in the Sarawak Museum, no. 263.) Three rows of running stitches are carried across the ends of these woven tabs to keep them flat, and then their warp ends are grouped in threes and fours and threaded through a series of red, white and black beads, each strand being finished off with a tassel of narrow strips of red flannel (fig. 32, *e*).

The beads and tassels form a heavy fringe, which has most weight at the sides where the bead fringe is thicker. The actual number of strands to the individual tabs beginning from the left are: 7, 12, 8, 12, 8, 12, 8, 7, 2, 4, 5, 8, 6, 9, 2, 11, 8, 12, 8 and 11.

At the top of the bottom panel there was originally a second fringe of beads finished off with little bronze hawk-bells (fig. 32, *f*), a considerable portion of which still remains.

Z.2345. *Klapong sirat*, type 2. This *sirat* is made of native cloth with both warp and weft used singly. There are 92–100 warp ends and 28 weft picks to the inch; the warps vary greatly in thickness but the resulting cloth is firm and has a fine texture. It is neatly embroidered in red and black and has an interesting fringe at the end of plaited warp ends with five red cotton balls tied on at the end of each plait.

The pattern (pl. xxxii, b) consists of six rows of lozenges varying slightly in size, they are labelled *mata puna*, "eye of pigeon (*Treson* sp.)", and of two rows of what are probably birds. At the lower end are two rows of simple designs, of which the solid triangles represent *dabong mayang*, "notched spathe of the areca palm".

35.916. *Klapong sirat*, type 2. Width, 11 in. (27·9 cm.); length, 1 ft. 2½ in. (36·8 cm.).

The weave is a plain one, one up and down, and there are 72 warp ends and 20 picks of weft to an inch, both warp and weft being single.

The piece of native weaving is joined to a bit of imported black cotton cloth by a counter hem with hemming stitches that meet in the middle of the fold and so are both strong and decorative. The end of the cloth appears at one time to have been bound by a native-made braid, but there are only a few fragments left.

The unbleached colour of the cotton forms the background to embroidered patterns in dull crimson and black.

Seven horizontal band patterns of widths varying from $\frac{3}{4}$ in. to $2\frac{3}{10}$ in. (1·9–5·9 cm.) are divided from one another by plain bands half an inch in width (1·3 cm.). Occurring as narrow bands above and below the three middle patterns and singly in the others are one or two picks of black weft or needle-weaving taken through a shed in which the warps are grouped as three up and three down. This is described as *gran pemalu tekalong*, "the mallet used for beating out bark cloth". A little more elaborate pattern produced in the same way is described for cloth 35.917. The second and sixth bands are described as *pala buntak balang*, "head of the big yellow grasshopper"; the pattern is the usual one called elsewhere *pala buntak*; the third and fifth borders are of *buah anyam*, "woven or plaited fruit" (pl. xxi, *f*). The repeated element of the central pattern is labelled *mayau tindok*, "sleeping cat", but this must be a mistake; it appears to be a *burong*, perhaps a variety of *burong besugu*.

BEDONG, WOMAN'S GIRDLE

35.914. *Dilak bedong,* a narrow girdle for a woman. Width averages 6¾ in. (17·1 cm.); length, including a 4½ in. (11·4 cm.) fringe at each end, 5 ft. 7 in. (170·2 cm.).

The cloth is of an unusually fine, close texture, having paired red warps, which form the 4-in. (10·1 cm.) central stripe, and the narrow stripes at the extreme edges, there being 80 pairs (160 ends) to the inch. The yellow stripes are coarser and have paired warps averaging 50 pairs to the inch, and in the black and white stripes an imported doubled yarn has been used, which has 120 fine single warps to the inch in the black and 88 single, but coarser in section, in the white stripe. The weft is fourfold in some parts, and threefold in others; the strands are always parallel or tape-wise. The picks average 25 to the inch. The weft is dark grey in colour for two-thirds of the length of the cloth and a threefold red weft is used for the remaining third, which is the part with the principal decoration.

This decoration is worked in silk and, although it appears to have been embroidered, may have been worked with a tiny free shuttle or a needle left hanging from the web when not in use. The description of one motive of concentric triangles as *pemuchok anyam,* "a woven shoot", seems to indicate the latter method. The use of silk and imported yarn shows a more intimate knowledge of other forms of weaving than most of the other cloths indicate, and judging from the colour and the quality of the workmanship it is probable that the girdle is of Saribas origin.

The girdle has a broad bright-red central band bordered on either side by narrower bands of white, black, yellow and red. The patterns are worked in rows, black and white silk being used more or less alternately; there are dividing lines between some of the patterns, which are in most cases made by two shoots of yellow weft, but in three of the lines thus formed the white silk has been used instead. To introduce these lines it appears as if two weft threads have been withdrawn in some places and the new ones darned in, rather than that they have been introduced during the ordinary weaving process. In one case the line is called *anyam belebas,* "the long stitch", in the other *pakan belebas,* or "made in the weaving", so that both processes may have been used. The small patterns produced are described as *gran pemalu tekalong*, "marks like the ridges on a bark cloth beater".

The motives used are few and not very interesting; one end is decorated for about a foot and the other has a single band of triangles, $1\frac{1}{4}$ in. (3·1 cm.) wide. The same shaded or concentric triangles occur as bands in three places at the end of the girdle and are described as *pemuchok*, "shoots". The small lozenge set corner-wise at the apex is described as *pemuchok pala buntak*, "a grasshopper's head on a shoot". Lozenges, with a central spot like the grasshopper's head, are the only other motives.

The warps are twisted together to form the fringes at the ends, and where two colours come together at the junction of the stripes, a thicker strand of the two colours is twisted and adds some interest to the general effect.

DANGDONG, SHAWLS

35.918. This is probably a *dangdong* or shawl, or it may have been used as a small coverlet. The width of the woven section is 1 ft. $11\frac{3}{4}$ in. (60·3 cm.) and the length 3 ft. $3\frac{1}{2}$ in. (100·4 cm.). It has coloured ends of strips of imported cotton cloth, white, red and yellow, measuring $1\frac{1}{4}$ in. and $\frac{3}{4}$ in. respectively at either end, neither being complete.

This is an extremely finely woven cloth; the skill shown in the actual cloth making, the fine red colour and the very accurate stitching in the embroidered patterns indicate Saribas origin.

The warp is red in the main part of the cloth and there are from 136 to 152 ends to the inch, which are paired; there are 26 weft picks to the inch.

At either side of the cloth there is a broad greyish black stripe, $1\frac{3}{4}$ in. wide, then a series of narrow coloured stripes, white, red, yellow, pale green and black, measuring three-quarters of an inch over all. Between these stripes and the embroidered central portion there are four narrow embroidered stripes divided by narrow compound stripes of white, black, yellow, red, and a horizontal black and white, each totalling about a quarter of an inch in width.

The white and black warps used in the stripes also provide the thread for the embroidery and are much thicker in section than the other colours; they appear to be mechanically twisted threads and are used singly. The red and yellow are of native hand-spun yarn and are paired.

The bright red background provided by the red warp forms a splendid contrast to the patterns, which are embroidered in black and outlined with white and occasional touches of yellow. The narrow embroidered border stripes are worked in black and white only and are separated by the composite colour stripes described in the previous paragraph.

There are eight horizontal rows of patterns across the cloth. The first row consists of two broad zigzags between which is a series of hexagonal panels filled in with *lelambak*, "a wasp and flower design plaited in mats" (pl. xxii, *i*). The second, fourth and fifth are alike and have representations of *biyak*, "the monitor lizard (*Varanus* sp.)" (pl. xii, *l*). The design in the third and sixth rows is the most elaborate, two repeats almost fill the width; they are described as *taio gasieng*, "thread driving the spinning wheel" (pl. xxiv, *c*). The two dark bands are apparently the vertical supports of the wheel, but the whole design is inconclusive. Between these motives is *buah bunut*, "the horse mango (*Mangifera* sp.)"; the label, which also says "fruit and root", is attached to the central portion (pl. xxii, *r*) of a larger design comprising a diamond decorated with squared scrolls; the label may apply to the whole pattern. In the sixth row one of the dark vertical bands is labelled *nemaiar*, "centipede" (pl. xvi, *g*), which adds to the confusion.

The seventh row consists of two white and two black rows of lozenges representing *buah angkong*, "fruit of a species of *Mangifera* (mango)" (pl. xxii, *s*). Above and below is a white zigzag edged by a pick of white weft. The last pattern is worked in chain-stitch and is the only example of chain-stitch in the collection; it is labelled *tankei marau*, "bundles of *marau* cane (*Calamus* sp.)"; *tangkai* in the *S.D.D.* is translated as a fruit stalk, but evidently it may mean other kinds of stalk.

The border patterns are very simple.

35.926. A shawl, *dangdong*, or a coverlet. Width, 1 ft. 6½ in. (47 cm.); length, with fringe, 7 ft. (213·4 cm.).

A label said the name of this cloth is *kumbu*. The *S.D.D.* gives "*kumbu* or *pua kumbu*, a Dyak-made blanket or coverlet". This cloth is too narrow to serve as a blanket or coverlet, so we can only regard it as a shawl. Ling Roth (ii, p. 42), on the authority of Brooke Low, says a *dangdong* or shawl is part

104

of the full dress of an Iban man and the garment under consideration is decorated in such a manner as to suggest that it was worn on a very special occasion.

This cloth has an average of 120 warp ends to the inch throughout its width. The border stripes, which are less important in effect than usual, have, at one side only, some red self-colour stripes in which four warp ends are grouped together. This number is, however, counterbalanced by the use of single warps in the black and white stripes, whilst in the rest of the cloth they are paired. At each end the warps are twisted together and knotted to form a fringe, which appears at one time to have had a knotted heading also.

The rather coarse, bluish-grey weft is used singly and there are 24 picks to the inch.

Dull Indian red forms the background to the pale buff patterns, which have touches of a darker brown. At the sides there are three patterned stripes, divided by composite ones, in which pin-stripes of white, red, black, yellow, red, a horizontally striped black and white, red, yellow, black and white are arranged in the width of half an inch. Near the edge of the cloth there are five wider solid colour stripes, totalling $\frac{7}{8}$ in. and consisting of black, white, red, yellow and blue, the last being at the actual edge.

The wide central band has a blank space about $2\frac{1}{4}$ in. wide across its middle. The designs of one-half of the cloth duplicate those of the other; they are disposed in 14 transverse rows and all are well arranged and clearly defined human figures, which are termed *engkaramba*, that ward off evil and prevent harm coming to crops. For the sake of convenience only one-half of the *kumbu* need be described; the first row is that nearest to the middle and the seventh is close to the fringe.

Row 1: *Engkaramba gajai* (pl. XIII, *i*). "The *gajai* figure. The *gajai* is said to be an animal. It comes into the Dayak songs but it is not known what it is like. *Ningal n'obat pandai, ambi timbai, lau nyapai gajai ambi perambai manoh menang*, '(I) leave the drug (to make you) skilful and able to work the *gajai*, like those who take the feathers of the winning fighting cock', i.e. better than anyone else. Said to a girl to make her skilful in making cloths. The drug is a pig's tusk or some such thing, but generally it is only a blessing from *Petara* that is asked" (C. Hose MS.). *Petara* is alluded to on pp. 142, 144: "*Engkramba*, a representation of anything cut out of wood", *S.D.D.* "*Gajai*, as *kalambi gajai*, a jacket with a frog pattern", *S.D.D.* We cannot add any further information about this figure.

Rows 2 and 5: *Engkaramba*, figure used to keep off harm, etc. Rows 3 and 6: *Engkaramba engkatak*, "the frog figure, the *engkaramba* part is the head only, the body is that of a frog" (pl. XIII, *h*). Rows 4 and 7: *Engkaramba besuga*, "a female figure with a comb in the hair. The Dayak comb is ornamented with silver" (pl. I, *i*, the rest of the figure is like that of *h*).

There are five variously coloured longitudinal stripes in the border, the outermost, *ara surik betong*, "the striped *betong* bamboo pattern", is a large kind of bamboo used for carrying water; the colours are indigo, yellow, red, white, indigo. Two of the others are *ara buloh bala*, "the yellow bamboo *ara* pattern", and the other two, with a black and white central stripe, *ara rinik*, "close (rainbow) pattern". Two patterned stripes are *daun wi*, "ratan leaf" and the central contains numerous birds, among which are: *burong berdayong*, "bird paddling (or rowing)" (pl. VIII, *i*), *burong besugu*, "bird with a comb" (pl. VII, *l*), *burong berspit*, "bird grasping (with its claws)", *burong surong dayong*, "bird pushing the oar".

PUA, BLANKETS

The blankets always consist of two pieces of cloth joined down the centre, usually by a lacing stitch, similar to that used for joining the side seams of the *kalambi*. The two pieces of cloth are the upper and lower webs from a loom. The web threads which have been tied together in the dyeing process, have patterns alike, but reversed, so that if half a motive comes to the edge of the cloth its other half completes it when the central joining is made. The *pua* are usually fringed at both ends, and to make this possible a gap must be left in the weaving between the upper and lower webs; it is not continuously woven like the cloth for a *kalambi*, which has only a fringe at the lower edge, if at all. There are generally one or two rows of coarse twining at the ends of a *pua*, which help to give firmness and a good wearing quality to those edges. According to the Catalogue of the Lady Brooke collection in the British Museum, *pua* with anthropomorphic patterns are used at the Dayak feasts.

The *pua* are described in the following order:

35.930	35.925	35.920	35.927
35.929	35.923	35.922	35.921
35.931	35.924	35.928	

35.930. *Pua* with human figures. Width, 3 ft. 9½ in. (115·6 cm.); length, 6 ft. 4 in. (193·1 cm.).

In the body of the cloth the warps are generally paired and average 52 pairs or 104 ends to the inch; but in the self-coloured stripes at the side, whilst paired in the white and blue stripes, they are arranged in threes, parallel, in the red stripes and average 128 ends to the inch. The weft is threefold, brown in colour and there are 20 picks to the inch.

The pattern is in buff colour, in which there are spots of dark purplish brown, on a ground of Indian red. At the extreme edge of the cloth is a red and white strip an inch in width, and inside this a series of composite stripes edging a pattern stripe 1⅝ in. (4·1 cm.) wide and two narrower ones just over a quarter of an inch wide (6 mm.). The composite stripes are made up of a red stripe, a horizontally banded one of indigo and white, another red, then blue, white, blue and red, the whole measuring ⅞ in. (2·2 cm.).

This is one of the cloths in which the middle is quite plain and the ends are patterned and alike.

A geometrically arranged motive which produces the effect of three rows of elongated hexagons is the terminal pattern; it has not been identified. A dark brown band of irregular outline on a white ground separates this design from a row of six male anthropomorphs, which are divided by pairs of bird motives. The human motives show the lobes of the ears distended (pl. II, *c*).

The two narrow patterned borders at each side are ornamented entirely with young grass lizards, *anak lachau*, and the wider one has two types of human figures (pl II, *d*, *e*) and some curiously mixed motives.

35.929. *Kalaka Dyak pua*. Width, 3 ft. 8¼ in. (112·4 cm.); length, 6 ft. 7 in. (200·7 cm.), including fringe. **Pl. XXXIII.**

This is one of the rougher fabrics in which a thick, coarse yarn is used. In the central band the warps are paired, 30 pairs or 60 warp ends being the average to an inch. In the self-colour stripes down the sides the red remain in the same proportion to the main part of the cloth, 60 ends to an inch, but the greyish and purple stripes are very fine yarn and are grouped in fours, whilst the white is thicker and paired. The average warp ends to an inch, taking the self-colour stripes without the red is 168, rising to 192 in the purple stripe which has the finest yarn. The weft is brown, single and of very uneven thickness, sometimes very coarse and at other times quite fine and so producing an uneven rib in the cloth. There are on an average only 12 picks to the inch. The cloth is a very heavy one and has short warp fringes.

The wide central stripe and the patterned border stripes have dull Indian red backgrounds with buff patterns accentuated in places by spots of a dark purplish brown. At the edge there is a series of solid colour stripes which total 3¾ in. (9·5 cm.) in width. Beginning at the outer edge the colour order is white, dull red, green, dull red, white, violet and white. Next to the white row come two narrow patterned stripes divided by composite stripes of green, red, white, red and green, making a total of ½ in. (1·3 cm.) in width.

At the upper end is a row of six human figures wearing masks and elaborate head-dresses; they have distended ear-lobes (pl. II, g), between which are probably long-tailed *burong* in an inverted position. A simple buff linear design separates this border from the main pattern. In this are two rows of six *baia*, "crocodiles" (pl. XI, b); the remainder of the surface is covered with varied human figures, some like those at the top; one type is shown on pl. II, f, and on the second row from the bottom are three headless corpses (pl. II, h). One form (pl. XIII, g) is labelled "*pama*, frog, Dayak; *katak* Malay"; it evidently is a man-frog, the original is spotted.

A buff line separates the foregoing from the lower border pattern, which is 1 ft. 5 in. (43·2 cm.) in depth. We have no names for the designs, the character of which can best be ascertained from the photograph (pl. XXXIII).

The narrow border patterns running lengthways are in some cases confused by the coarseness of the fabric blurring the outline, but they appear to be ratan leaves, *daun wi*, and young grass lizards, *anak lachau*. Both stripes are alike. The bold self-coloured stripes at the edge are labelled *pamanyar*, the colours are white, red, green, red, white, mauve, white. Probably the informant said *pama nya*, "good (are) those".

The end of the cloth is finished by a fringe of warp ends and about half an inch above the fringe there is a row of twining in white and mauve.

35.931. Crocodile pattern *pua*. Width 3 ft. 3½ in. (100·4 cm.); length 4 ft. 1 in. (124·5 cm.).

The warps are paired throughout except in the red border stripes, where the much finer yarn necessitates grouping in threes. There are 52 pairs or 104 warp ends to the inch in the main body of the cloth. The weft is pale blue, coarse, and three parallel threads are used, resulting in a heavier cloth than is found in the majority of the finer quality blankets. There are 24 weft picks to the inch.

The thick blue weft used has sufficient value in the surface colour to give the otherwise dull Indian red background a purplish tone upon which the pattern appears in pale buff with black lines and dots and touches of red.

The outer edges of the blanket have wide border stripes of red, white and dark indigo on one side and of red, white, red, white and indigo on the other, totalling 1¼ in. (3·1 cm.). Inside there are four composite stripes dividing three very narrow patterned ones. The composite stripes are made up of a blue centre with four or five pin stripes of white, the whole being edged with bright red on either side and the entire stripe measuring ½ in. (1·3 cm.) in width.

The upper and lower halves of the cloth are precisely alike and therefore only one-half need be described. The main design consists of twelve crocodiles, six of which (pl. XI, *a*) differ slightly from the other six (pl. XI, *c*). We identified these as crocodiles, as the cloth was labelled a crocodile cloth, but they may represent monitor lizards. There is an upper row of three men (pl. II, *a*) between the "crocodiles" and a lower row of three men with feathers in their hair; owing to the constricted space these men have no arms.

A line, elsewhere identified as *resam* leaves, divides the main pattern from the border pattern; these are alike at both ends, which is an unusual feature. Three very large toothed lozenges occupy the whole width of the cloth, except the lateral borders, and each lozenge contains two standing men (pl. II, *b*); a grass lizard is placed between the heads of the men and a white bird between their bodies and two white birds on either side.

In the spaces between the lozenges and the *resam* line is a triangular figure (pl. XXIII, *e*), which, except for the lateral scrolls, resembles that called *ladang*, "a farm", or ridge of earth round a paddy farm, on cloth 35.927 (pl. XXIII, *f*), on either side of it is what appears to be a swift or swallow (cf. pl. IX, *a*). Round the apex of the "farm" are some spots resembling those often called "rice grains" and have been so named by us in our sketch. Is it possible that the whole border pattern may be regarded as an invocation to success in the cultivation of paddy? The necessary good omen birds are represented around the men.

35.925. This is a blanket cloth just as it is taken from the loom, with some of the heading rods made of bamboo leaves still in place. The cloth is extremely coarse, and there is just enough material to make a blanket by cutting the strip in two and joining up two of the long sides. The width is 1 ft. 7½ in. (49·5 cm.) and the length 13 ft. 6 in. (411·4 cm.).

A very coarse, thick but tightly twisted yarn is used for the warp, which is paired in the central part of the cloth, there being 26 pairs or 52 ends to the inch.

In the self-coloured stripes at the one side the grouping of the warps varies, the red-brown ground colour is used singly, the white double, the yellow fourfold, and taking an average between these groupings the warp ends are 100 to the inch, the high number being entirely due to the fine yarn used in the yellow stripes, where four parallel warps are grouped as one. The weft is double and very coarse in most of the cloth, averaging only nine picks to the inch, but in another section where a single weft has been used the number of picks rises to 12.

The tightly twisted coarse yarn produces a cloth which is strong but very harsh to the touch.

The colour is a dull red with patterns in half in the main portion of the cloth, and at one side there is a series of solid colour stripes, beginning at the edge with red and following on with yellow, black, white, red, yellow, then very narrow stripes of white, yellow, red, yellow, white. The whole group is about 4 in. (10·1 cm.) in width. When the blanket is made up the stripes will appear at both the long edges.

The horizontal border pattern at one end is described as a frog pattern, but it is more like a human figure and there is also a very indistinct bird motive called *burong semalau* (a species of thrush, *Copsychus amaenus*).

The border pattern at the other end consists of two rows of hexagons with a buff spot in the centre of each; they are labelled *sempong*.

Owing to the coarse texture of the material all the patterns are very indistinct, but the main pattern between the borders appears to consist of plant motives, resembling the arrangement of the *tangkong* creeper pattern on other cloths.

There are no subsidiary pattern stripes at the side of the cloth.

35.923. *Engkaramba pua.* Width, 3 ft. (91·5 cm.); length, 6 ft. 10 in. (208·4 cm.), including fringe. **Pl. XXXIV.**

The warps are twofold (paired) throughout and there is little difference between the weaving of the coloured self stripes at the sides and the main pattern. The yarn used for this cloth is a fine one and there are 60 pairs of warps or 120 ends to the inch. A twofold blue weft is used and there are 18 picks to the inch.

A central band nearly 2 ft. (61 cm.) wide of buff-coloured figures with touches of a deep purplish brown on a red background has its general effect enhanced by a group of very distinctive border stripes. Three of these on each side are patterned and coloured similarly to the main pattern. They are separated from one another by composite stripes, averaging $\frac{5}{8}$ in. (1·6 cm.) in width, consisting of a central pale gold stripe edged with white and light red. Beyond these and towards the outer edge of the cloth solid colour stripes make an effective finish. Beginning at the outer edge there is a red stripe $\frac{5}{8}$ in. wide (1·6 cm.), then white, blue, red, white and yellow, each about $\frac{3}{8}$ in. (0·9 mm.). It is labelled *dilah kendawang*, "tongue of the snake" (pp. 29, 112); but an informant in Sarawak called it *sulor nyang* and said it was the four colours in the sky at dawn ("*nyang*, sunset", *S.D.D.*). The general effect is excellent.

The border of the photographed end of the cloth (pl. XXXIV) consists of lozenge-shaped *papan sengayoh*, blades of paddles, with their W-shaped handles *ulu sengayoh* below (pl. XXIII, *l*). At the apex of the blade is a *pala buntak*, "head of locust", and the fringe of hooks is labelled *kukut burong*, "claws of bird". Within the lozenge is an *anak engkatak*, "young frog" (pl. XIII, *a*). The transverse black band on a white ground is *slaku*, a ratan used as a rope; there is another at the other end of the main pattern.

The central portion of the *pua* is entirely covered by finely drawn rows of *engkaramba*; there are eight figures in each row. There are nine rows, and in every third row there is a change in the appearance of the figures (pl. I, *c*), the body is spotted and the legs turned down as in representations of frogs and in an *engkaramba engkatak* (pl. xiii, *h*). All the other figures (pl. i, *b*) have elongated ear-lobes and feathers (?) in the hair and all but the first row have tall head-dresses that vary from row to row. The first row is labelled *zanggoi langgeng*, for which we cannot find a translation. The small spaces between the figures are filled very skilfully with frogs, lizards, etc., one between the heads of the sixth row is called *bubul pantak*, space-filling wasp; in the first row the banded fillings are kites' feathers (cf. pl. x, *e*, *f*).

The other border of the cloth, below the *slaku*, consists of light *engkaramba* with large white triangular body and without legs, separated by ratan leaves.

The outer of the three patterned stripes at the sides have *anak lachau*, "young lizards" (pl. xii, *c*); one of them is wrongly labelled as *burong andin* (pl. ix, *f*). The central stripe contains various birds, including birds with white breasts and *burong jengkuan*, "bird on a spool" (pl. viii, *g*).

35.924. Width, 2 ft. 10 in. (86·4 cm.); length, 6 ft. 3 in. (190·5 cm.). The *pua* is, as usual, made of two strips of cloth joined by a fish-bone stitch down the centre.

The yarn is rather coarse and the warps are paired throughout except in the yellow self stripes of the border, where three parallel warps are treated as one. There are 56 pairs or 112 ends to the inch in the cloth, but in the yellow stripes there are 48 groups of threes or 144 ends to the inch, the yarn used in these stripes being of a much finer quality. The weft averages 20 picks to the inch throughout the whole length, is of a dull brown, not the reddish tone of the background, and is coarse and therefore used singly.

The central pattern band has a reddish brown background with a buff-coloured pattern, sometimes strengthened by lines and patches of black, produced by dyeing with indigo over the brown. An interesting feature, which makes this one of the most charmingly coloured of the blankets, is the use of touches of pale blue as emphasis for the main lines of the design.

The self-coloured border stripes of yellow, dark indigo, yellow, dark indigo, white and dull red are of a more even width than is usual, the group being 2 in. across, and their colour being very distinctive adds charm to the whole scheme. They are labelled *ara dilah kendawang*, the different coloured stripes of the tongue of the *kendawang* snake.

The pattern, which has a main central portion with important borders above and below, is very beautiful from the purely aesthetic point of view. The spacing out, which is chiefly done by the bluer parts of the pattern, is very interesting in shape and well distributed, the lines forming a pleasing contrast with the curved forms used as motives for filling in the spaces.

An inch from both the edges two rows of twining, described as *kelalin lantai* (interlaced bamboo), strengthens the fabric. Just below is the first row of patterns representing *pemuchok tubu bekengkang*, "striped bamboo shoots"; these are hollow triangles between every two of which is a solid white triangle below which and connected with it by a thin line is a *burong burak*, "white bird": it has no head. Below the *burong* is a widely spaced irregular double zigzag *lelingkok tebok igi bras*, "zigzag with rice grains"; its internal projections are called *dabong beserang*. The interior space contains *pantak penandok iku ruai* (pl. XVII, *e*), which may mean the wound caused by the sting of a wasp or a cupping scarification (resembling the ocelli on the) tail (wing, not tail, feathers of the) argus pheasant; but *ruai* also means the verandah of a long house (see p. 132). Below the lower zigzag are curious little designs, *gari enk* (*engku*), my clothes (pl. II, *i*). A wide horizontal stripe of white, black, white *kengkang slaku*, "striped ratan", divides these patterns and the precisely similar patterns at the other end of the cloth from the main central pattern.

In the central pattern is a framework (as in pl. XXXV, though very different from it) which is difficult to interpret, and the names for various parts are obscure and vary in spelling. In the interspaces are *engkaramba*, *engkatak*, etc. About 2 ft. 3 in. (68·6 cm.) from the upper end of the blanket are five prominent *kengkang bulu lang*, "striped feathers of the kite" (pl. X, *e*), coloured white, red and black. Above them are three *bukang engkaramba* (pl. I, *d*), but these "headless *engkaramba*" seem to possess heads!

Three long spaces about the middle of the cloth are filled by an *anak engkaramba*, "young *engkaramba*" (pl. I, *e*), who does not wear a head-dress, and by what is apparently a frog (pl. XIII, *c*). Lower down are some *engkaramba mensia*, *engkaramba* people (pl. I, *f*). In the next row are some good frogs (pl. XIII, *b*), and between them is what are described as *ruyit*, "the barb of a fish-spear" (pl. XXIV, *j*), and *serpang pala tangga beji* (pl. XXIV, *k*), which may mean forks or hooks at the top of the ladder of a house; for barbed spears see Ling Roth, II, p. 108.

The lower border consists of *bukang*, "headless corpse" (pl. i, *g*). Near the fringed end are two rows of twining, *kelalin lantai*.

At the sides of the blanket are three patterned vertical stripes. The middle and wider one is decorated with *burong buah bangkit*, *burong jengkuan* and *burong bedayong* (cf. pl. viii). On either side the stripe contains *lachau*, "green grass lizards" (pl. xii, *h*), alternating with *kengkang bulu lang*, "striped feather of the kite", similar to pl. x, *f*.

35.920. This is a *pua gajai burong*, blanket with omen *gajai*. Width, 2 ft. 10½ in. (87·7 cm.); length 6 ft. 5 in. (1·956 m.) with a fringe at one end.

The warps are paired except in the black and white border stripes, where they are coarser and used singly. There are 52 pairs (104 ends) of warp to the inch in the main body of the cloth and 54 warp ends in the self borders where the yarn is coarser. The brown weft is used singly and there are 20 picks to the inch. Instead of the more usual row of twining, near the ends there is some rough stitching called *kelalin gelegar*, to interlace ratan, etc. for the flooring of a house. One end is fringed, and where the self-colour stripes occur, the warp ends are twisted and knotted to form the fringe.

The general effect is quiet, the narrow self borders at the sides being black and white and the remainder of the cloth dull red with patterns in pale buff and a dull purplish brown, probably produced by using weak indigo dye over the red.

The patterns are unusually interesting and include fanciful designs resembling frogs.

The elements *ras* of the horizontal border pattern at the fringed end are something like handled vases in form. A *ras* is found in cloth 35.922 (at the top of pl. xxxv), and it occurs on other cloths not in the collection; we think this signifies a plot of land. Between the *ras* are unnamed designs. The row of *ras* is divided from the main pattern by a *slaku*, a dark line on a white ground.

Six *entilang gajai* form the first row of the main pattern; they have four-pronged projections from the head labelled *perambai gajai* and fringes on the fore-legs (pl. xiii, *k*). The next row consists of *gagai burong*, omen *gajai* (pl. viii, *n*). Below it are two rows of *entilang gajai*, figures something like those of the first row but with two curled projections from the head (pl. xiii, *j*).

There is a row of unnamed figures between the legs of one row and the heads of the next. These are followed by a row of *tuboh gajai*, *gajai* person, these are somewhat similar to the *gajai burong*. From this point, which is halfway down the cloth, the figures are reversed so as to face the opposite end. Those of the first row are similar to pl. XIII, *k* and the head projections are labelled *perambai*. Then follows a row of very simple *tuboh gajai*, succeeded by a row of *gajai* something like pl. XIII, *j*. This is followed by a row of another kind of *tuboh gajai* alternating with *bubul lapang*, "design to fill a space". The last row consists of six *entilang gajai* with two pairs of hind legs (pl. VIII, *o*), and on both sides of the body of each is a white disc with black spots, *telu gajai*, spawn or eggs of the *gajai*, pl. XIII, *l*.

A transverse band of white, red, white, black, white named *kengkang kelikut*, striped — ?, separates the central patterns from the elaborate border pattern at the non-fringed end. This has a row of *entilang gajai*, something like pl. XIII, *k*; there is a vertical line from each head which passes through a *burong burak* and ends in a *lancham pemuchok*, "pointed shoot", a solid white triangle with two streamers. Alternating with the *entilang gajai* is another type of *gajai burong* (pl. VIII, *m*), and alternating with the *burong burak* are *jengam jengkuan tali*, solid white triangles with lateral scrolls and convergent projections at each end, which seems to signify a forked spool.

Of the three patterned stripes at the side the central one is nearly an inch wide and is ornamented with various kinds of *burong*: bird on spool, bird dancing, bird with comb, etc. divided by portions of kite feathers. The two narrower stripes are filled with *unak wi*, thorn of ratan (pl. XXII, *l*), alternating with kite feathers.

Most of the figures on this cloth are fabulous creatures which appear to be more frog-like than human, and some of them may represent *Salampandai*, who in unseen regions hammers out children as they are born into the world. She makes people either by her independent power as a *petara* or by command of *Petara*. She is never visible in her own person but is supposed to have a visible manifestation in a creature something like a frog, which is also called *Salampandai*. "This creature is regarded with reverence and must not be killed. It if goes up into a Dayak house, they offer it sacrifice, and let it go again, but it is very seldom seen.... The noise it makes is said to be the sound of the spirit's hammer, as she works at her anvil" (Perham in Ling Roth, 1, pp. 176, 177). This blanket should be a sure shield against evil for the beneficent *gajai* are equivalent to a blessing from *Petara*.

35·922. This cloth, Pl. xxxv, as is usual with the blanket type, consists of two strips of material joined by a lacing stitch, *kelalin lambai*, down the centre; including the fringe it is 2 ft. 10 in. (86·4 cm.) wide and 6 ft. 8 in. (203·2 cm.) long.

This is an evenly woven cloth of medium texture, the warps in the main body of the cloth average 26 pairs (52 ends) to the inch and there are 22 picks of weft to the inch. The weft is single and light blue in colour, a pale tint of indigo. In the border stripes the arrangement of the warps varies, those in the yellow bands are grouped in threes and are of a much finer yarn, whilst the white and pale blue are each single warp strands. There are 88 ends to the inch in the border. Two horizontal stripes of twining in white and blue, each consisting of three rows, are used to strengthen the ends of the blanket; they are ⅜ in. (9 mm.) apart and the first is 2 in. from the end of the cloth.

This beautiful blanket owes its great charm to well-arranged patterns and the very effective use of a limited range of colours. The background of the broad central band is a ruddy brown, almost Indian red in tone, and on it the patterns are clearly outlined in pale buff. Between the lines enclosing the pattern effective use is made of a very dark filling, varied by lines and spots of the buff or stone colour. This dark tone is obtained by a second dyeing of indigo over the reddish brown, and the accuracy of workmanship combined with a skilful use of dye stuffs indicates a Saribas origin.

The upper border of the main pattern consists of two patterned rows, the upper a series of *ras* alternating with *anak lachau*, "young grass lizards" (pl. xii, *d*). A white line separates these from a row of *burong burak prut*, "birds with a white breast"; the dark interspaces are *petik igi bras*, "spotted with rice grains". Then follows a transverse band, *kengkang selaku*, "striped ratan", which divides the border from the main pattern.

The handsome central pattern is most unusual, consisting chiefly of trunks, *batang*, and branches, *dan*, of trees arranged to form elongated polygonal spaces which are filled with leaves and pendant branches with blossoms (pl. xxi, *c*). The trunks and branches are outlined by a pale buff edge, and spots of this pale colour occur regularly between the outlines. This bright outline is described as being caused by the light of the fireflies, *sepepat* (*selempepat*), with which the tree is covered, and it is not unusual for these insects to settle all over a tree or shrub so that it looks as if on fire. In speaking of these insects Beccari says (p. 75): "The intense darkness was lit up from time to time by brilliant intermittent flashes—the love-lights of enormous fireflies!" At least six species of firefly have been observed in Sarawak, some as large as 21 mm. by 9 mm., that is, fully three-quarters of an inch in length. Trees entirely illuminated by innumerable fireflies which emit their light in rhythmic pulsations of intensity are well known in New Guinea and elsewhere.

The central lozenge of pl. xxi, *c* is a *buah bangkit*, "*bangkit* fruit", the second fork or branch below it is labelled *batang sepepat tebok igi bras*; the white spots are here referred to as rice grains, *igi bras*, which seems improbable. From these branches depend *tangkai sepepat*, "branch with fireflies".

At the top, in each of the two bays of the branches is an inverted triangular design with bent projections which enclose two hooks labelled *jangkam spit*, "to squeeze with pincers", and immediately below this is a large design, *jerit bubul indu buyah*, "filling pattern like the insect which eats honey"; in cloth 39.928 (pl. xvii, *c*) the same figure is called *buyah*, "beetle", but in *S.D.D.* "*buyah* a species of moth often seen round lamps"—*indu* signifies female. In the same row and between these insects are three smaller designs, *jerit bubul mata lungu*, "filling-in design, blade of spear". The three white spots below the spears are the bodies of *burong berayah*, bird dancing with extended wings (pl. viii, *k*). "*Berayah*, a ceremonious dance performed by chiefs leaping up with their arms extended in imitation of a soaring kite...[it] is an imitation of the soaring of the *menaul* [hawk, kite], the spirit representative of *Singalang Burong*....(One of three ancient Dayak dances.) All these dances are of a processional character" (*S.D.D.*). Lower down are two white spots with four projections called *ketam*, "crab" (pl. xvii, *p*); crabs are frequently found on the mud banks of rivers and are used for food. The scrolls on the three cross bars close to the crabs are labelled *spit api behilak*, "fire-tongs?" The three lozenges near the bottom are *buah bangkit*, and below them are striped feathers of the kite; the white triangles with converging projections are *spit*, "pincers".

The lower border begins with a white, black, white, red band, *kengkang slaku*, "striped ratan"; the six double hooks on it are *kait slaku*, "slaku hooks". A *slaku* is a ratan which is used for climbing down trees. The triangles are called *dilah munsang*, "the tongue of a wild animal", but similar designs on other cloths are *pemuchok tubu*, "shoots of bamboo".

There are three narrow patterned borders at the outer edges, divided by plain reddish brown ones which have a fine yellow line down their centres and are bordered on either side by narrow white, blue and white stripes. At the selvedge there is a reddish-brown stripe, next to it a yellow band with white and blue striped edges, this combination of white, blue, yellow and red is known as "break of day", *sulor nyang*, as it represents the four colours of the eastern sky at dawn ("*nyang*, sunset", *S.D.D.*). The patterned stripes contain *lachau*, "lizard", alternating with *kengkang lang*, "striped feather of kite" (pl. x, *f*).

35.928. Width, 3 ft. 1½ in. (95·3 cm.); length, 7 ft. 1 in. (215·9 cm.).

The major portion of this cloth has its warps paired; they number 48 pairs or 96 warp ends to the inch, but in the narrow pale blue and white stripes of the border, which appear to be more closely woven, the warps are single and there are only 60 ends to an inch.

The weft is brown in colour and single, which makes the resulting fabric much softer to handle. There are 20 picks to the inch.

The background to the central band of pattern is a dull Indian red, the pattern itself is outlined in buff, with spots of pale buff and streaks of dark brown accentuating certain portions of the design. The outer borders are narrow, only one is patterned and this has a composite stripe on either side of pale blue, red, pale blue divided by pin stripes of white. At the edge there are two broader self stripes, totalling ⅞ in. (22 mm.), of which the outer is red and the inner white.

The elaborate transverse band at the upper end of the cloth consists of a folded zigzag, in the band of which are *tebok igi bras*, "holes like the rice grains". The zigzag encloses two rows of lozenges; each upper lozenge contains *pantak penandok*, which may signify the wound caused by the sting of a wasp (see p. 132 and Vocabulary). The lower lozenges contain *sesimpong*, "a creeper cut off its stem". On the apices of the upper row are *sanggul sesimpong*, "tendrils of a creeper which has been cut in two" (pl. xix, *b*);

on the top of these is a *pala burong*, "bird's head". Below the lozenges are *pemuchok bubul lapang*, "a shoot filling up a space"; they stand on a transverse band, *penuri daun resam*, "the spiky leaf of the *resam*", a species of fern, *Pteris arachnoiden*, which usually grows in secondary jungle where the primaeval forest has been destroyed.

The central space of the cloth is almost a duplicate of that of 35.922 and like it is divided by trunks and branches of the *bangkit* tree; the fruit, *buah*, and flowers, *bunga*, are shown in pl. xxi, *e*. The branches divide and unite in regular order, but some of the junctions are labelled *entilang dapur*, "fire hearth" (pl. xxiii, *j*, *k*). The scrolls at these places are called *spit*, which judging from cloth 35.922 are fire-tongs. Here also, fireflies, *sepepat*, are noted as being on forks, *spit*, twigs, *pating*, tendrils, *sanggul*, etc., all being outlined with their light.

The two *buyah*, "beetle", designs (pl. xvii, *c*) occupy the same position as the "insect which eats honey" on cloth 35.922. The *burong berayah* of that cloth are here ignominiously called *bubul lapang*, "space-filling". Two crabs, *ketam* (pl. xvii, *n*), occupy the same position as in the former cloth and three crabs (pl. xvii, *o*) occur near the bottom.

The border at the lower end is separated from the main pattern by a *penuri daun resam*; it has two zigzagged bands, *lelingkok tebok igi bras*, "zigzag with holes (like) rice grains". In the lozenges thus formed are diamonds, which are the ocelli of the tail feathers of the argus pheasant, *tugang langgai burong ruai*, as the whole pattern is called. In the lower angles of the zigzag are *burong* (pl. vii, *c*). Finally there is a row of alternate white and speckled *pemuchok tubu*, "bamboo shoots" (pl. xviii, *h*).

There is only one patterned border at the sides of the cloth; it contains rather indistinct birds: *burong buah bangkit* (pl. xviii, *i*), *burong lelayang* (pl. ix, *a*) and *burong entepa*, "bird with outstretched wings".

The whole blanket is most decorative and shows a highly developed sense of appreciation in the placing of regular pattern over a large surface; the same applies to 35.922, which, however, has more brilliant coloration.

35.927. This is only one-half of a blanket and is very much soiled so that its colour is faded. Width 1 ft. 10½ in. (57·1 cm.); length, 6 ft. 6 in. (198·1 cm.) with the fringe.

The workmanship in this cloth is inferior and the weaving is very irregular and coarse. The warps are paired and there are 36 pairs (72 ends) to the inch in the central part and 60 ends to the inch in the coloured border stripes, where they are woven singly.

The weft varies in colour, without any attempt at regularity; it is sometimes red and at others a dull stone colour. On the spool it has been wound sometimes singly and sometimes twofold; this also helps to produce irregular weaving.

The colour has been mostly lost through use and soiling, but originally the pattern was in buff and dark indigo on a reddish background, and apparently there have been pale blue and white stripes enclosing a narrow border down the sides.

The middle of the blanket is plain, and at each end there are three rows of somewhat unusual designs.

At one end a squat lozenge-like form represents *sanggul simpong*, "tendrils of a creeper cut off" (pl. xxi, *d*). This is divided from the next pattern by a horizontal line of *daun resam*, "*resam* fern leaves" (pl. xviii, *p*). The second band consists of *sarong kris*, "dagger sheaths" (pl. xxiii, *d*), and one *ladang* (pl. xxiii, *f*), a bank surrounding a paddy field, a farm, or a division of land. Compare with pl. xxiii, *e*, which has a similar form but with what we take to be rice grains. The third row represents *mayau tindok*, "sleeping cats" (pl. xvii, *s*), enclosed between two stripes of *kengkang slaku*, "ratan used for climbing".

At the other end of the cloth are two rows of sleeping cats, though they are labelled *chayam*, "pig's whiskers" (pl. xvii, *t*). They are divided by a row of *resam* fern leaves from two rows of larger representations of sleeping cats (pl. xvii, *r*) provided with what apparently are whiskers; the spots on the bodies of the cats are *mata ulat*, "eye of grub". Another row of *resam* leaves divides these cats from a row of *tubu*, "bamboo shoots".

The border pattern at the side has designs only at the ends; these are: *burong jengkuan*, here termed a kingfisher, though elsewhere "bird and spool", and *burong entepa*, "bird with outstretched wings" (cf. pl. vii, *r*).

35.921. *Pua bulan menyembang.* Saribas. A moon cloth. Width 2 ft. 7½ in. (80 cm.); length, 7 ft. ½ in. (214·7 cm.).

The cloth has a coarsely woven effect in the main pattern, partly due to the irregular grouping of the warps in twos and threes, without apparent plan, but averaging 40 groups with approximately 116 warp ends to the inch. In the self-coloured borders at the sides the warps are arranged in threes, with 44 groups and 132 ends to an inch.

The weft is threefold and there are 22 picks to the inch; the thickness of the weft is a contributary cause to the coarse texture of the fabric. In colour the weft is unusual, being blue.

The cloth is fringed at the ends to a depth of $\frac{3}{4}$ in. (1·9 cm.) and then $\frac{1}{2}$ in. (1·3 cm.) further in it has a series of three very coarse twined patterns, one single in white, one double in dark blue and white and then another single in white.

The colour is simple and effective because it is more massed than usual, partly owing to the fact that one simple motive recurs again and again. This motive appears as light stone colour with indigo lines in it on a background of dull light red. The border stripes, which provide the strongest colour in the cloth, have a total width of $4\frac{1}{4}$ in. (10·7 cm.) and consist of four half-inch stripes beginning with red at the outer edge, then yellow, black and white; this composite stripe is called *ara belampang*; this is followed by a $\frac{1}{4}$ in. (0·6 mm.) stripe of horizontally banded black and white, *ara rinik*, and black, and yellow and red stripes, *surik*, each $\frac{1}{8}$ in. (0·3 mm.) in width. A patterned stripe $\frac{5}{8}$ in. (1·3 cm.) wide comes next and its edge nearest the centre of the cloth is bordered by a composite stripe of red, yellow, black, black and white horizontally banded, black, yellow and red, of a total width of 1 in. (2·5 cm.).

At each end of the cloth is a line of black and white twined weaving, *ungki*, "edge of pattern", below this a row of *pemuchok pala burong*, "shoots with head of a bird" (pl. xviii, *f*), and below this a dark blue line on a white background, *ladi burak unggo chilom*, which at the other end of the cloth is called *kengkang slaku*.

At the ends of the main series of designs is a row of simple triangular motives called *burong lelayang*, "swallows (without heads)" or *bulan*, "moon" (pl. xxv, *h*); these do not look like other swallow designs, nor do they look like the moon. The next row consists of diamonds with converging arms and a central solid red oblong.

The rest of the cloth is covered with groups of four of these devices arranged to form a large lozenge (pl. 1, *j*), in the centre of which is a simple design; in one it is *buah angkong*, "fruit of the horse-mango", in another *buah bangkit*, "*bangkit* fruit". In this cloth the two lateral devices of each lozenge have a red oblong with a white spot with a black clot in the middle —doubtless an eye spot; one of these lateral devices is named *Bulan menimbang*, "name of a god in the heavens", and another *Bulan menyembang*. There is nothing to identify this personage with Grandfather Ungkok, the man in the moon, cf. *bidang* 35.854 (pl. I, *a*). In the section on Religion it is stated on the authority of Perham that the moon is not regarded as a divinity, but merely that it is the seat of a *Petara*. We have not been able to find a meaning for *menyembang* and its variants. In this cloth the upper and lower devices of each lozenge have red and black comb-like designs, which may possibly represent closed eyes and eyelashes, except the terminal ones at both ends, which have a solid red oblong, but this regularity does not occur on a cloth in the Sarawak Museum, no. 257; Camb. Mus. photo. Indon. Born. 374, on which there are only eyes and solid red oblongs. In this *pua* the pattern is labelled *simpang taribang*, and an Iban gave the name of *simang taraba* for the same pattern on another *pua*. In the *S.D.D.* *simpang* is given as "branch of a path or river, a junction"; the other word is not given. This evidently refers to the red background, which has the appearance of narrow branched bands which join one another; these bands are outlined by white lines in no. 257, but not in our *pua*. The lateral devices are connected with the central *buah* design by a broad horizontal white line. This device seems to have a special significance as it is found on other *pua* (cf. Sarawak Museum, no. 257; Camb. Mus. photo. 374) and it occurs in two rows on the upper part of the back of an Iban "priest's coat" from the Batang Lupar (*Verslag Mus. voor Land- en Volkenkunde en Marit. Mus.*, Rotterdam, 1925, pl. I).

There is a central transverse band across the main field of the cloth consisting of narrow acute lozenges, *lancham puchok*, "sharpened points", and fringed oblongs, *dabong penuri*, "serrated"; *S.D.D.* gives "*penuri*, pressed down, hole made with the fingers". Down the sides of the cloth is a narrow patterned stripe of what we identify as intercrossing ratan (pl. XXII, *n*), at each end of which is an *engkarong*, "the green lizard", but it closely resembles the *lachau* figured on pl. XII, *g*.

AN ANALYSIS OF THE PATTERNS

The particular fascination of a study of the woven textiles of the Iban lies in their patterns. These are traditional and hereditary, being handed down from mother to daughter, and we have already stated (p. 44) that the *engkaramba* figures may be made only by women belonging to ancient and honourable families.

The motives employed on the cloths include human and fabulous forms, zoomorphs (mammals, birds, reptiles, insects, etc.), phyllomorphs (trunks, branches, tendrils, leaves, flowers, fruit, etc.), material culture (hooks, spools, boats, paddles, ladders, fences, etc.) and finally natural phenomena (clouds, rivers, and the moon), but examples of this group are rare.

Some of the designs are fairly realistic, but most of them are highly conventionalized, so much so that it would be impossible to recognize what they were intended to represent were local information not forthcoming. We have referred in the Introduction to the difficulties we have experienced in the identification of some of the designs.

Hose and McDougall (1, pp. 242–244) state that: "In wealth of decorative designs the Ibans surpass all the other tribes. These designs are displayed most abundantly in the decoration of bamboo surfaces and in the dyeing of cloths. The designs on bamboo surfaces are largely foliate scrolls, especially the yam-leaf, but also occasionally animal derivatives.

"The designs dyed upon the cloths (fig. 61) are largely animal derivatives; but the artists themselves seldom are aware of the derivation, even when the pattern bears the name of its animal origin; and as to the names of all, except the most obvious animal derivatives, even experts will differ. The frog, the young bird, the human form, and the lizard are the originals most frequently claimed. Parts of the animal, such as the head or eye, are commonly repeated in serial fashion detached from the rest of its form. And in many cases it is, of course, impossible to identify the parts of the pattern, although it may show a general affinity with unmistakable animal patterns. One such pattern very commonly used in dyeing is named after *Agi bulan*, the large shrew (*Gymnura*); but we have not been able to trace the slightest resemblance to the animal in any of the various examples we have seen (pls. 131, 132)."

123

Two plates, I and II, are devoted to the representation of human figures, *engkaramba*, and another set is drawn in connection with the *manang bali* jacket referred to on pp. 37–46. The *S.D.D.* defines an *engkaramba* as "a representation of anything cut out of wood"; labels on cloth 35.926 state, "figure used to keep off harm", "*engkarambas* are used to prevent harm coming to crops, etc." We have failed to find any reference to *engkaramba* in the literature dealing with the Iban (see Vocabulary).

These designs occur chiefly on blankets, *pua*, and jackets, *kalambi*, and may be made only by the wives and daughters of chiefs, and even they must begin by making other patterns. They have a protective and beneficent influence, except in the case of headless corpses, *bukang* (pls. I, *d*, *g*; II, *h*), which may only be made in the *pua* by old women, as sickness is feared if this pattern is produced; it is *mali* (tabooed, forbidden) for young people to make it.

In a fairly large number of examples the legs are turned up, probably because in this way the figure fits better into the horizontal band of pattern of which it is a motive (pl. I, *b*, *e*, *f*, *h*). A "female figure" *engkaramba besugu* is depicted on a shawl (p. 106; pl. I, *i*) but the design is the same as that for a man, except for the "comb" in the hair. "Feathers" are shown in the hair of men in fig. 22, *c*, *d*. The only other representations of women are found in a jacket (pp. 41, 44 and figs. 19, 20, 21) where they alternate with men.

In addition to the typical *engkaramba*, *Aki Ungkok*, grandfather Ungkok who lives in the moon and whose face is seen there, is figured in pl. I, *a*. One label refers to his *bungkok*, "bent back" (it also signifies "hunchbacked") and another label to *tiang penyandih*, "the post against which he leans when tired". This design is quite unlike the other anthropomorphic figures, but has great similarity to the deer patterns. An unusual figure (pl. I, *j*) (could it be a stooping figure making obeisance to the moon?) occurs as an all-over pattern on the *pua* called a moon cloth (pp. 120–122). A similar *pua* is seen in Camb. Mus. photo. Indon. Born. no. 374.

On pl. II all the figures from *a* to *g* are merely entitled human figures, *engkaramba*; that at *j* is named a "diving pattern" and is the only anthropomorph (if it be one) on a *bidang*. The attitude of this figure is quite realistic.

One other very interesting little detail occurs on cloth 35.924 and is figured on pl. II, *i*; this is called *gari enk* [*engku*], my clothes; perhaps it is a private mark or a mark of possession.

Further details of the meaning of some anthropomorphs are given at length in the note on the *manang bali* jacket, pp. 40–46.

ZOOMORPHS

VERTEBRATES

Deer

Three kinds of animals are usually termed "deer" by most authors on Bornean ethnography. These are *rusa*, a true deer (*Cervus equinus*)—this is a variety of the sambar which is widely distributed in the East—*kijang*, the barking deer (*Cervulus muntjac*) and *plandok*, the diminutive mouse-deer (*Tragulus*, two sp.), which is not really a deer; this inhabits the jungle, whereas the two former are generally found in clearings.

The patterns in the deer cloths are particularly interesting but difficult to follow. When, however, they are carefully traced out, representations of the stag have "branching" or "crossed antlers", the doe is hornless and the udder is represented; on one cloth where both sexes occur another pattern, a "young deer", *anak rusa*, is also shown (pl. III, *h*). All the deer patterns have a line of darker spots down the centre of the form, but the deer have a uniform brown colour without any markings; this type of decoration is used in some other patterns.

The muntjac is very important as an omen to all Bornean peoples, but least so to the Iban. The bark of the deer prevents people from continuing their journey, and even divorces people who are newly married. The little chevrotains, *plandok*, have the same function so far as a journey is concerned, but otherwise they are not very important. Sir Spencer St John says (1, p. 64): "To hear the cry of a deer is at all times unlucky"; we cannot find any specific mention of the *rusa* as being an omen animal apart from the general statement that the noises made by all "deer" are bad omens. If, as we suppose, the patterns on the cloths act largely as talismans or as amulets, it seems rather strange that the *kijang* and *plandok* are entirely unrepresented so far as we are aware, whereas the *rusa*, which apparently is the least important in this respect, is frequently represented. It may be that the decorative branching antlers, which this species alone possesses, appeal strongly to these artistic women. Deer are regularly hunted with dogs for food, and perhaps success in the chase may be the underlying idea of these representations on the cloths.

Tigers

Highly conventionalized tiger, *remaung*, patterns are frequent on cloths (pl. IV), and in basketry the foot of a *remaung* is sometimes represented. As the true tiger, *remaung bendar*, does not inhabit Borneo, it can be known to the Iban only by repute. Of the six species of *Felis* in Sarawak, by far the most important is the clouded tiger-cat or clouded tree-leopard, *engkuli*, *Felis nebulosa*, and it is the *remaung* most frequently depicted. *F. planiceps*, *jelu mayau*, is often very destructive in the gardens, as it is very fond of fruit, and digs up and eats sweet potatoes. *F. bengalensis*, *mayau kuching bata*, is about the size of a domestic cat and steals fowls; it lives in rocks (*batu*). *F. marmorata*, *remaung raras*, the marbled cat, is larger than a domestic cat and is very fierce. The other two species are very rare.

The supernumerary legs and paws which appear in many designs, as in pl. IV, may be suggestive of the agility and ferocity of these animals. The large size of the paws is especially noticeable in most of the designs.

It might be supposed that the patterns were intended to confer strength, agility and fierceness on the wearers, but as the designs are almost confined to the *bidang* of the woman the idea of protection seems here to be indicated, not only of the woman herself but of her crops and fowls.

Interesting designs are the sleeping cats, *mayau tindok*, represented on pl. XVII, *r–u*.

Shrews

The *Gymnura rafflesi*, *aji*, *aji bulan* (*tikus bulan*, "moon rat"; *tikus antu*, "spirit rat", Malay) is the survivor of a Tertiary group of Insectivora. It is not unlike a large rough-haired shrew and it has some affinities with hedgehogs; for convenience it may be termed a shrew. It is mainly white in colour. It is purely nocturnal and lives in the jungle close to water under the roots of trees or in holes it has excavated. Its favourite food seems to be cockroaches, termites and various larvae, but it eats all kinds of insects and some vegetable matter, such as leaves and small berries. It has a peculiar offensive odour. When caught alive it is extremely savage and bites at anything within reach, snarling and growling.

Aji is one of the subsidiary omen animals, and is supposed to be a manifestation of Klieng, the war god and greatest hero of Iban legends. In the *S.D.D. aji* is also stated to be "a title of the Dayak fairy god Kling", and he is referred to as "The god Kling Aji who is brave". Ling Roth (I, p. 332) gives a tale from Brooke Low's notes in which Aji is the brother-in-law of Klieng and there is nothing to associate him with the moon rat. Klieng is a hero, not a god. Endless stories are told of this mythical being, most of them warlike and spectacular, and so representations of the shrew might be expected to confer bravery on the wearer of the garment, if it were not almost confined to *bidang*; perhaps the *aji* patterns refer in some way to the hero.

The well-known pugnacity of the animal is suggested in the fighting attitude of two shrews facing one another (pl. v, *g*), a favourite motive on shrew-patterned cloths.

Examples of characteristic shrew patterns are illustrated on pl. v, *a–e*; *f* is a shrew which occurs on a tiger cloth and is an example of the influence of one pattern upon another, as characteristic *remaung* paws are indicated in addition to shrew legs; the distinctive snout is clearly shown. Judging from the cloths the shrew appears to like the sweet-smelling *bangkit* fruit, for several designs show the *aji* on one (pl. vi, *a, d, e*). One shrew (pls. xxix; vi, *c*) has white spots, which may be rice grains, in its stomach and another (pls. xxx, A; vi, *b*) is actually depicted inside a *plangka*, "husking box", but there is a very different kind of *plangka*, see p. 78. There is no record of the shrew feeding on rice grains, and it seems very improbable that a jungle animal would enter the houses even if it could climb up the ladder.

Burong, *or bird, patterns*

The reason for the preponderance of bird patterns is evident, for mostly good omen birds are portrayed which will ensure success in whatever venture is being undertaken, although other birds are also represented. In the illustration on pls. VII, VIII, IX, no special types of birds can be distinguished, except pl. IX, *a*, which is a variety of swift or swallow and is always represented by a large wing, and *e*, which has distinctive tail feathers of the argus pheasant. Bird patterns are most often used in the narrow borders at the sides of the cloths and therefore have to fit into rather narrow parallel lines. Birds whose wings are covering their bodies are represented at pl. VII, *i, j, k,* and birds with "combs" at pl. VII, *l, m, n, o, p*; these seem to refer to the comb-like effect of the feathers on the wings rather than to a comb on a bird's head; *q* and *r* of pl. VII represent a bird with limbs outstretched.

Birds in action are figured on pl. VIII, where some are shown eating the sweet *bangkit* fruit, in *a* and *b* part of the fruit is seen with the bird almost hidden by it; others are depicted on a netting needle or spool of which a clear shape is seen at *e* and degenerate forms at *f* and *g*. Three birds are described as "rowing" or swimming, *h, i, j*. Those at *k* and *l*, which are dancing, are particularly interesting, as in one of the three ancient Dyak dances in which the chiefs leap up and down with extended arms in imitation of the flight of a soaring hawk. It will be noticed that these two figures are quite distinct from all the other bird designs.

Special types of birds are illustrated on pl. IX, but as their designations are obscure we are not able to discuss them; one (*h*) seems to be an omen for rain. We have a note that *burong belingkian* (pl. IX, *e*) is the argus pheasant, *Argusianus grayi*, which has two distinctively long tail feathers, but *ruai* is the common Iban name for the bird. The ocelli of the long wing feathers are perhaps represented on pl. XVII, *e*, and possibly on pl. XVII, *d*.

At the foot of plate IX are four young birds, *j–m*, and a fifth, *n*, has wings typical of swifts in other designs. A bird with long legs is shown in fig. 7 and in the bottom row of fig. 23, B.

The elaborate figures on pl. X are named after *Singalang Burong* himself, whose earthly form is *lang*, the kite, *Haliastur intermedius*, a sub-species of *H. indus*, the Brahminy kite of India. The striped feathers of the kite, *e, f*, are occasionally represented as independent designs and doubtless have the same significance as the whole bird. The obscure design labelled "*kengkang lang*", referred to on pp. 33, 35, 36, 37, 73, 84, 113, 118 and illustrated in fig. 18, *b* and in pl. XXVIII, B, is of peculiar interest.

Favourite designs, especially on *sirat*, are *mata puna*, "the eyes of the small green pigeon" ("*Treron*, all species except *T. capellei*", *S.D.D.*); perhaps it is represented for the purpose of protecting the crops from the pigeons (pl. xvii, *k, l, m*).

Crocodiles

Although the crocodile, *baya*, is frequently used as a decorative motive in war-boats and is carved on the posts of the long house, it seems only to appear on the textiles used as blankets.

The crocodile designs, as will be seen from those figured on pl. xi, are amongst the most life-like representations on the cloths. The blankets upon which they appear and other designs are used as wall decorations as well as for their more practical purpose. Crocodiles on *pua* are shown in Camb. Mus. photos. Indon. Born. 362, 387, 394.

"A special deity, Pulang Gana, presides over the rice-culture of the Ibans, but the crocodile also is intimately concerned with their rice-culture.... On going to a new district Ibans always make a life-size image of a crocodile in clay on the land chosen for the paddy-farm.... When the rites are duly performed this clay crocodile destroys all the pests which eat the rice.... Many Ibans claim the live crocodile as a relative and...will not eat the flesh of crocodiles nor kill them, save in revenge when a crocodile has taken one of their household. They say that the spirit of the crocodile sometimes becomes a man just like an Iban.... Another reason given for their fear of killing crocodiles is that Ribai, the river-god, sometimes becomes a crocodile", as may Klieng, who gives them heads in war and first advised the Iban to make friends with Pulang Gana (Hose and McDougall, 1901, pp. 198, 199; 1912, ii, pp. 88, 89). The belief that crocodiles are afraid to eat Iban is reported by the Rev. W. Chalmers as quoted by Ling Roth, i, pp. 348–350.

Lizards

Borneo abounds in lizards; Beccari mentions 49 species, one of which is the monitor lizard, *bayak, Varanus* sp., which reaches a yard in length; it is common and its flesh is highly esteemed. This is conventionally represented on pl. xii, *l*, but what is evidently the same lizard is realistically shown in shell-work on certain *kalambi*, pp. 51, 52. Large "lizards" adorn a *pua* (1905, 419) in the British Museum, which, if they are lizards, are probably monitors; and it is possible that the six reptiles on our cloth 35.931 are monitors and not crocodiles.

The much smaller green grass lizards which are represented from *a* to *e* as young ones, *anak lachau*, are depicted as full grown in *f*, *g*, *h*, but except at *h* the legs are not shown. This may possibly be due to the fact that the narrow borders in which they usually appear do not leave much room for them.

Examples of skink lizards, known as *engkarong*, are shown at *i* and *j* on pl. xii, and are interesting because they have distinct heads and tails. The stiff lizard or skink, *engkarong kejong*, figured at *k* occurs only once in the cloths.

Snakes

Snakes, as such, are not shown on our cloths, though several border stripes are said to represent banded snakes, pp. 29, 33, 55, 68, 73, 112. This seems to be more in the nature of a colour effect than an intention to delineate actual snakes. Two *pua* in the Sarawak Museum, nos. 244, 247 (Camb. Mus. photo. Indon. Born. nos. 357, 360) have six large snakes that extend along the whole length of each cloth.

Occasionally, as on a cloth, no. 407 in the British Museum, and on a *sirat* in the Sarawak Museum, no. 262 (Camb. Mus. photo. Indon. Born. no. 407), one finds a folded band termed *leku sawa*, "twining of the python or twisting like a python".

Perham says that the feeling of the Iban towards prominent members of the snake tribe is something more than reverential regard, much the same as is given to *antu*, but it is "a personal and not a tribal deity". The python, *sawa*, and the cobra, *tedong*, are the snakes generally selected by the *antu* for their habitation, but only individual ones.

Frogs

The frog designs naturally fall into two categories: (1) the true frog, *engkatak*, and (2) more or less mythical conceptions of it and those frog-like creatures known as *gajai*; we do not know why that shown in pl. xiii, *k* was labelled "*entilang gajai*".

(1) Of the first group one, a species of frog, known as *pamā*, is sometimes represented anthropomorphically, pl. xiii, *g*, but at *f* it is somewhat more like a frog.

Frogs are used for food and they are considered a great delicacy; quite life-like representations of them are not uncommon, such as the examples drawn on pl. XIII, *a*, *b*, *c*, *d*. The curious appendages on the fore-limbs of *d* cannot be accounted for.

(2) The other designs are of mythical creatures with more or less frog-like bodies and human heads, whose special significance is unknown to us. That on pl. XIII, *h* is labelled *engkaramba engkatak*. *Engkaramba gajai*, *i*, *gajai*, *j*, and *entilang gajai*, *k*, can scarcely be expected to look like frogs as they are mythical creatures. All these occur on *pua*.

Salampandai is a female spirit and the maker of men. Apparently she is never visible in her own person, but she is supposed to have a manifestation in a creature something like a frog, which is also called Salampandai. This creature is regarded with reverence and must not be killed. If it goes up into an Iban house, they offer it sacrifice and let it go again, but it is very seldom seen. The noise it makes is said to be the sound of the spirit's hammer, as she works at her anvil in the unseen regions hammering out children as they are born into the world. The creature is supposed to be somewhere near the house whenever a child is born; it approaches from behind if the infant is a girl and in front if a boy (see p. 115). The *S.D.D.* says: "*Selampandai*, a species of locust only heard at night. It is the manifestation on earth of Selampandai".

Kalambi gajai is a jacket with a frog pattern (*S.D.D.*) and it appears to us that this *gajai* may be a representation of Salampandai as a frog. If this be so its occurrence on a cloth worn by women would be very appropriate, but we do not know if this is a woman's *kalambi*.

INVERTEBRATES

Spiders

Many species of spiders exist in Borneo, and some are large and have a poisonous bite; it is probably as a protection from such harm that they are portrayed on the cloths.

Spiders, *emplawa*, usually are delineated correctly with eight legs, but exuberance in design and perhaps the speed at which they travel occasionally makes them appear as if they had more. They are sometimes represented with another animal inside them: (pl. XV, *a*), a lizard (pl. XV, *c*), a bird (pl. xv, *b*) and birds' heads (pl. xv, *d*). This is, of course, impossible, and may be due merely to the artist's urge to fill up a vacant space. Examples of young spiders are drawn on pl. xiv at *a* and *b* (these usually have but four legs), and of other spiders at *c*, *d* and *e* on the same plate.

Centipedes

This group of designs on pl. xvi, *a–f*, is very common on narrow border stripes of *bidang*, and its use is probably protective. The designs are very suggestive of the *embayar* itself, the so-called "hundred legs" making a definite appeal. In one cloth, 35.881, the centipede (pl. xvi, *d*) extends for half of the length of the cloth and finishes with a curly twist at each end. The ardent desire for bi-symmetry which the Iban designer possesses often results in the head and tail of a creature being represented as much alike, but in the centipede there is actually this similarity.

Scorpions, insects, etc.

There are other zoomorphs, some of which are not of very frequent occurrence in the cloths, such as those illustrated on pl. xvii. A scorpion, *kala*, is shown by *a*; and a scorpion's nippers, *spit kala*, by *b*. The *buyah*, a beetle or moth, is represented by *c*. *Pantak* is a wasp, the *S.D.D.* gives: "*Pantak*, a small dark-coloured wasp which inhabits holes in trees, or perhaps, more frequently holes in the banks of streams". *Pantak penandok* (pp. 74, 118; pl. xxvii, *d*) may be translated as the wound caused by the sting of a wasp, and *pantak penandok iku ruai* (p. 113; pl. xxvii, *e*) may be such a wound, or possibly the scarification preparatory to the cupping process (*nandok*), which may be likened to the ocelli on the feathers of the argus pheasant (p. 128); but *ruai* also means the verandah of a Dayak house. At one time we thought that the term on p. 113 might have reference to clay nests of solitary wasps sheltering under the verandah of a long house. Here we must leave it pending local information. A stylized wasp is shown in *f* on a flower pattern, *pantak lelambak*. A grub, *empetut*, *g*. Heads of locusts, *pala buntak*, *h*, *i*, are very commonly represented, perhaps for the purpose of protecting the crops. Crabs are eaten; young crabs, *anak ketam*, are shown in *n*, *o*, *p* with only four legs, and at *q*, the nippers, *spit*, of the freshwater crab, *grama*.

Leeches

All those who have travelled through the jungle in Borneo are unpleasantly acquainted with the land leeches, *lintah*, which stretch out from the foliage and fasten themselves not only on exposed portions of the body but find their way beneath the clothing; periodic examination of the whole person is sometimes necessary in order to remove these blood-suckers. It is rather surprising that these creatures are depicted, so far as we know, on but a few *bidang*. On pl. xvi, *j*, *k*, are seen leeches on a creeper and a flower. Leeches with interlocked mouths are called *betegam*, which means "to swallow all at once"; it is physically impossible for a leech to swallow anything except blood. Their coiled-up (*besimpan*) tails are shown at *l* and *m*; the former is from one of four *bidang* in the Sarawak Museum (nos. 213, 217, 219, 465; Camb. Mus. photos. Indon. Born. 324, 329, 330, 409).

We do not understand the significance of the hooks on the bodies of the leeches. It is tempting to assume that leeches are represented as charms to keep them away from the wearer of the *bidang*.

The *S.D.D.* gives "*Lintah*, the water leech", but the *lintah* on the cloths are certainly land leeches.

PHYLLOMORPHS

The *empili*, mast, drawn on pl. xviii, *a*, *b*, *c*, *d*, *e*, is a wild nut which is the favourite food of wild pigs; it, in conjunction with the arenga palm, *entibap* (pl. xxii, *a*, *b*, *c*, *d*), and ratan leaves is very frequently used as the decoration for the narrow patterned stripes at the sides of the cloths.

The arenga palm, *Arenga saccharifera*, has many uses: the juice from the inflorescence makes sugar and, when fermented, toddy or palm-wine; the black fibres around the trunk and the bases of the fronds make very strong and durable rope, preferred to ratan in house-building; the cotton-like down is used as tinder, *lulup*; and the trunks afford excellent sago.

There are many varieties of the climbing palm (*Calamus* sp.) known as *rotan* by the Skarang and Saribas Iban and as *wi* by other Iban: the thinner kinds are the more valuable. Baskets and mats are made of split ratan and pliable ratans are used as ropes. The thorny tendrils (*tangai*) and leaves of the ratan (*daun wi*) are very frequently represented in the narrow border patterns of *bidang* and occasionally in those of *pua* (pl. xxii, *j*, *k*, *l*, *m*, *n*).

Many other jungle plants and one species of ratan have very large thorns which make the clearing of the jungle very difficult; two crossed thorny stems of ratan, *unak wi bekait*, are illustrated on pl. xxii, *o*.

The *tangkong* "creeper" (? a climbing plant), which is a jungle plant with scented pendant flowers, provides many characteristic patterns. The designs *b, c* on pl. xix and all those on pl. xx are derived from this plant. The *randau* is some kind of creeper or climbing plant.

Illustrations of *bangkit* flowers are given in pls. xix, *a*; xxi, *e*; the fruit is always represented as lozenge-shaped (pls. vi, *a, d, e*; xviii, *i, j, k*) and is one of the most common motives on woven and embroidered cloths. The *S.D.D.* says, "*Bangkit*, a scented flower, scented leaves or fruit of certain jungle trees used as scent or ornaments to decorate the hair or body".

The fruit of the *beringen* tree is occasionally represented (pl. xviii, *l*) and much more often that of various species of mango (*Mangifera*): we illustrate *buah bunut*, "horse-mango" (pl. xxii, *r*) and *buah angkong* (pl. xxii, *q, s*). "*Angkong*, a tree bearing strong-scented diamond-shaped fruit (the horse manggo)", *S.D.D.*

A tree with its trunk and branches outlined by the light of fireflies dominates the surface of *pua* 35.922 (pl. xxi, *c*), and *pua* 35.928 is very similar. Species of large fireflies are common in Borneo, and when they settle in enormous numbers on a bush or tree it appears as if on fire; the white line round the designs suggests this remarkable phenomenon.

Very frequently repeated in all the kinds of cloths are the young shoots of the bamboo *pemuchok tubu*, which are used as a vegetable; we illustrate a few on pl. xviii, *f, g, h*.

The curled tops of the *rĕsam* fern, *gelong paku rĕsam*, are occasionally depicted in a realistic manner (pl. xviii, *m, n, o*). *Paku* is the general name for ferns, particularly for *Hollenium esculentum*, which is eaten as a vegetable. The *deman* is the fern *Gleichenia dichotoma*.

Other useful plants are represented on cloths, the most frequent being the *bingka lia*, "root of the ginger" (*lia* or *liah*), and gourds. Seeds, *leka*, are shown on pl. xix, *f* of the *labu*, "a white pumpkin, gourd, calabash (*Cucurbita lagenaria*)", *S.D.D.*, the dried fruit of which is used as a water vessel. The *serok genok* is shown on pl. xxii, *f*; the label says, "*genok*, a gourd with a long twisted stalk; the fruit is used by the Dayaks to rub their bodies in the place of soap". The *S.D.D.* says, "*Genok*, gourd, a white pumpkin (when dried these are used as water vessels)". *Bunga janggat*, flower of the *janggat*, "a white pumpkin, a fruit resembling a vegetable marrow", *S.D.D.*, is embroidered on jacket 35.904 and illustrated on pl. XXII, *g*.

Lelambak is a conventionalized flower very frequently plaited in mats and baskets; it is embroidered on jacket 35.918 (2) (pl. XXII, *i*).

It will be noticed that practically all of the plants represented are of value to the Iban in their daily life, though the thorny plants may form an exception.

OBJECTS IN DAILY USE

A small number of the designs, probably about 3 per cent., represent objects connected with the daily life of the Iban.

A plot of land, *ras*, and the balk or ridge of earth around a plot of land, *ladang*, are illustrated at *e* and *f* on pl. XXIII. A rocky ledge in swamp-land, *padong paya* or *paya bepadong*, *a*, *c*, and sown swamp-land, *tabor paya*, *b*, are shown on pl. XXV, and mentioned on pp. 91, 92, 95; we do not profess to understand the designs. Zigzag fences, *pempang lelingkok*, are sometimes shown (pl. XXIII, *g*).

Connected with houses are: the plank where the prop is tied, *papan penukoh*, and serrated notch in an upright post for a cross bar, *dabong betangkal* (pl. XXIV, *m*, *l*). Boards or planks and poles are represented on other cloths, and the notched steps of a pole-ladder, *tangkal tangga*, or *tebok tangga pantok*, on *bidang* 35.877 (27), 35.862 (21) respectively. The framework of an Iban cooking place, *entilang*, with its shelves and a bird on the middle shelf is depicted on pl. XXIII, *h*, two hearths, *entilang dapur*, *j*, *k*, and fire-tongs, *spit api behilak*, *i*. A tripod for cooking rice, *tanku asi*, is seen on pl. XXIV, *f*, and a "box" for paddy husking, *entilang pelangka*, at *i* and pl. XXX, A; see p. 78 for another kind of *plangka*. Hooks, *kait* (pl. XXIII, *o*, *p*, *q*), are frequent and also wedges, *pasak* (*r*, *s*, *t*, *u*).

Warlike pursuits are represented by the shield, *trabai bungkok* at *a*, the handle of a shield, *gelang trabai*, at *b*, and the sheath of a kris or dagger, *sarang kris*, at *d*. A canoe, *besampan*, with a suggestion of the stern platform, *dandan*, and oars, *dayong*, projecting from its sides is drawn at *c*, and a paddle, *ulu*, at *n*, and crutch-handles of paddles at *l*, *m*, all on pl. XXIII.

135

A hooked fish-trap, *sergang pala tangga beji*, is indicated on pl. xxiv, *k*, which seems to mean a bamboo fish-trap at the head of a staircase or ladder. We have no translation for *beji*. A description of the different nets, baskets and traps used for fishing is given by Ling Roth (i, pp. 454–464). Two barbed fish spears, *ruit gansai*, are shown on pl. xxii, *p*, and a barb, *ruit*, on pl. xxiv, *j*.

The pursuits of the women are represented by shaped pieces of wood upon which the spun thread is wound, *tayok gasing*, at *a*, *b*, pl. xxiv, and at *c* a more elaborate example which possibly includes the uprights of that part of the spinning wheel through which the driving thread passes to the spindle. A weaving spool, or "netting needle", *jengkuan*, is seen at *e*. The ridges on a mallet used for beating bark-cloth, *surik gran pemalu tekalong*, are indicated in or suggested by certain patterns on *bidang* 35.859 and on other cloths. Women's combs, *sugu*, are represented at *g* and *h* on pl. xxiv.

NATURAL PHENOMENA

Representations of natural phenomena occur very rarely in the cloths; all the examples, except the moon, are to be found on *bidang* 35.859, which has unusual patterns, and these include clouds, possibly cumulus, *miga dudok*, and cirrus, *rayok miga dudok*, literally, "the clouds in steps", figured at *i*, *j*, *k* on pl. xxv, with a bird in flight against the cumulus cloud at *j*. Clouds are shown on cloths nos. 416, 418 in the British Museum. The moon, *bulan* (pl. xxv, *h*), is an unsatisfactory design on one of the *pua*, upon which the chief motive is an ambiguous design which was termed in Sarawak "*simpang taribang*" or "*simang taraba*"; we have a note which we cannot trace describing it as "making obeisance to the moon" (pl. i, *j*). A rocky ledge upon which a tiger-cat is resting, *kaki padong remaung*, is shown at *e* on pl. xxv and occurs on the same cloth as the clouds. Tigers or tiger-cats are supposed to live in holes in the rocks and only the legs of the animal are seen in the design.

A very frequent design in borders of *bidang* and elsewhere is a zigzag which is constantly described as "crossing a river", *lelingkok semerai sungai*; it indicates the zigzag course frequently made by canoes when travelling along a river in order to avoid the stronger current (pl. xxv, *f*, *g*). "*Lelingkok*, crooked, zigzag", *S.D.D.*; it has been likened to the movement of a snake.

GENERAL CONSIDERATIONS

We now pass on to a brief consideration of the broader issues connected with the Iban cloths and begin with a quotation from Hose and McDougall (1, p. 244):

"We are inclined to suppose that the Ibans have copied many of their cloth-patterns from the Malays together with the crafts of dyeing and weaving. For their technique is similar to that of the Malays all over the peninsula, and the same is true of some of their designs. Only in this way, we think, can we account for their possession of these crafts, which are practised by but very few of the other inland peoples. The fact that plant derivatives predominate greatly over animals in their designs, whereas the reverse is true of almost all other tribes, bears out this supposition, for the Malays are forbidden by their religion to represent animal forms, and make use largely of plant forms."

We have quoted in full here and on p. 123 what has been written on the decorative art of the Iban (with the exception of tattooing) by Hose and McDougall in their authoritative book on Sarawak, but we venture to question some of their statements. It is true that the carvings and engravings of the male Iban show predominantly plant forms, and the textiles of the women depict predominantly animal forms. If the men were influenced by Muhammadan Malays, why were not the women? The Iban have not embraced Islam and there is no reason why their designs should be influenced by that religion, nor is there sufficient evidence that they have borrowed some of their designs from the Malays; what designs they have in common might as well be attributed to their supposed common ancestry. The vast majority of the decorative designs of the Iban are not only markedly different from those of other Bornean peoples but equally so from those of the Malay, and almost all are intimately connected with their environment, pursuits, or beliefs.

The technique of producing the pattern by tying up the warps before dyeing is used only in isolated cases in the Malay peninsula. Other resist methods are referred to later. The Iban loom is the simplest of the Indonesian looms and therefore is not likely to have been copied from the Malay type with its fixed frame, heddles, treadles and other refinements.

137

We have now to consider to what extent the Iban owed this part of their culture to other peoples, or if there is any evidence to show that the technical methods employed and the majority of the actual patterns have developed within the period of time in which they may be considered to have been a separate people.

A comparison has been made by L. E. Start between the cloths from Sarawak and the technical construction and patterns of the cloths of the Chinese, Hindu, Malay, or other inhabitants of the Indo-Chinese peninsula, as well as those of Java, Sumatra and the nearer island groups of Oceania.

The method of weaving is mostly carried out by the Iban in the simplest possible way on the most primitive type of Indonesian loom, the *tumpoh*, for although a few Iban use a simple Malay loom, the *tenjak*, they usually produce only coarse work upon it and that apparently in very small amount. We have no example of this in our collection, nor is there one in the large series in the British Museum, or in the collections in the Bankfield Museum, Halifax, or the Castle Museum, Norwich. The bulk of the Iban cloths and all the skilled weaving of the warp-dyed pattern cloths are done on the primitive *tumpoh*; this supports Ling Roth's argument that "if the Ibans had learnt [weaving] from the Malays I think we are more likely to have found among them an imperfect or degenerate form of loom, rather than a more primitive one than that used by the Malays" (1918, pp. 71, 72).

The patterned weaving in Europe and civilized Asia is based on employing coloured warp and weft threads, but this technique is lacking, or almost so, in Indonesia. There is one method of making designs on cloths in Great Britain and Europe in which the warp is printed before weaving and "shadow" patterns are produced. Cretonnes, linens, and silks may have "shadow" patterns.

In one technique in Indonesia the pattern is entirely developed before the actual weaving takes place and it is accomplished by tie-dyeing of the warp. This under skilful hands affords beautiful and elaborate patterns and it has a peculiar charm.

There are various terms for this tying technique in Indonesia. According to Loebèr (1903, p. 14) the Malay and Iban term *ikat* was first introduced into Europe by Prof. A. R. Hein (1890), who in 1901 turned it into a Dutch verb "ikatten". We suggest that the word "ikat" might be adopted in English for the finished product and "to ikat" for the technical process.

The method of producing patterns by tying-up the warps before dyeing is not in general use among the peoples of the Malay peninsula nor of those of southern China. The only account we have been able to find of the use of a similar technique is that by L. Wray (1902), who says that it is carried on to a limited extent by a few Malay women at Sitiawan in Perak. The fabrics are made of silk which comes from China in a raw state and is treated locally before dyeing.

The ikat method is nearly always used by the Iban and is carried by them to a degree of great excellence, but it is not confined to them in Indonesia.

Lamster (1929, p. 125) refers to the bold and effective ikat technique of the women of Sumba and Flores and to the delicately worked and beautifully tinted patterns of Roti, Savu, Timor, Alor and other islands. The art of ikat weaving is practised throughout nearly the whole of Indonesia. Two pieces of hempen cloth from Mindanao, Philippine Islands, in the Haddon collection in the Cambridge Museum also illustrate this technique.

The woof, and not the warp, is ikated on the silk fabrics of Palembang, south-east Sumatra, at Gresik in east Java, and in Bali. At Tenganan, a small mountain village in south Bali, and nowhere else in Indonesia, the warp and the woof are ikated, a very difficult technique that produces cloths, termed *kain gringsing*, of unequalled beauty; they are the most splendid and costly of Indonesian woven cotton fabrics. Their manufacture is associated with all kinds of precautionary regulations; it can be done only in secret and the girls or women must work naked. Formerly the cloth was dyed with the blood of a human victim: the blood of animals must not be used; now they employ the bark of the *kemiri* tree, *Aleurites triloba*, with shredded *Curcuma* (turmeric) stamped in water. On various important occasions a person (or a young couple) is engirdled with a *kain gringsing*, and one wrapped round a sick person ensures recovery. The designs are mainly plant motives. (Lamster, 1929, p. 126; Wirz, 1931.)

Loebèr points out that the material used for the tying is not unimportant. Winding cotton around cotton is ineffectual and the binding ribbon must be of some other material that takes the dye less readily than the cotton warp. The manner in which the warp is wrapped around is decisive for the character of the decoration. The simplest type is found on Flores, whence Prof. Max Weber in 1888 brought back bundles of yarn in various stages of "ikat". Each skein is tied round at regular intervals, and consequently uncoloured rings appear after the dyeing. That at any rate is what it looks like on the skein; when this is wound off the rings disappear and each thread is furnished with regular white dots. After the threads have been stretched on the frame of the loom they naturally come into a different order and an irregularly dotted background results—the parts that have been "reserved" from the dye have shifted their position.

The patterns in all these cases are different from those of the Iban and frequently the workmanship is less expert. Illustrations of patterns made by these techniques are given by the Dutch authors quoted and by others.

In some parts of Indonesia there is found another entirely different method of resist-dyeing, which is accomplished by applying wax to the fabric at those places where the dyeing is not desired. This highly developed *batik* technique, by which beautiful and elaborate patterns are made, is especially characteristic of Java. An analogous wax technique is used in southern China and by some Malays.

There are other methods of making patterned cloths in Indonesia, but these do not concern us here.

When Iban patterns are produced by other means than warp-tying, whether by floating shuttles, the use of more heddles or shed sticks, or by embroidery, the quality of the work is more variable and the patterns themselves differ from those characteristic of warp-tying. These technical methods may have been adopted by the Iban from other peoples, and their own patterns made by these techniques have suffered modification through these alien influences.

Among all the cloths in England examined by us, not more than 1 per cent. of the patterns are like those of the Malay peninsula or the surrounding islands. The designs on our Bornean cloths have been compared by L. E. Start with traditional Chinese and Hindu designs, with those of the hill tribes of southern China, the Shan, Kachin and Burmese printed and embroidered fabrics, as well as with the resist-dyed fabrics of Java and Sumatra. With the exception of the occasional tendency to make a fret-like completion to a design, which does not necessarily prove anything, there seems to be no outside influence in the style of the warp-dyed patterns of the Iban.

The motives chosen, with the exception of the crocodile, do not seem to be used by the other peoples mentioned. A strong argument against Malay influence is the predominance of animal forms, which are forbidden by Islam. The sources of the patterns themselves are all intimately connected with religious beliefs, daily life and environment of the Iban. The animals are those with which the island abounds, the plants drawn are in daily use and indigenous to Borneo, and the remaining subjects are connected with agriculture and other daily pursuits and domestic objects.

We would however refer to the ambiguous *gajah* motive (pp. 41–43), which certainly is not Bornean. It seems to us quite possible that it may be a dim relic of some higher culture that presumably had its origin in India, but we cannot pursue this conjecture further owing to lack of data. The correspondence between the spiritual personages of the Iban and those of Hinduism is discussed by the Venerable Archdeacon J. Perham (cf. Ling Roth, 1, pp. 181, 182).

It is a remarkable fact that the textile designs of the Iban women are quite distinct from the patterns carved by the Iban men on bamboo and wooden objects (see Haddon, 1905), and these are also very different from those carved by the Kayan, Kenyah, Murut and other peoples of Sarawak with whom the Iban come more or less into contact. These peoples do not practise the art of weaving to any extent and they do not make the patterns characteristic of the Iban women.

Taking all these points into consideration it seems reasonable to suggest that the traditional designs used by the Iban women in their textiles have been developed since the Iban became separated from other peoples, and thus the designs would be a native art peculiar to the Iban.

It has previously been stated (pp. 1, 2) that Dr Hose dates the migration to Borneo of the ancestors of the present Iban at less than three centuries ago. We wonder whether this highly developed technique could have reached such perfection within that period of time.

It is interesting to note that in some parts of New Guinea fibre skirts are tied in various places and dyed so as to produce horizontal stripes of a dark colour on the natural colour of the fibres. Loebèr (1903, footnote, p. 15) states that he saw, in Barmen in New Guinea, petticoats which had been dyed by this manner in three colours; probably one colour was the natural colour of the fibre. This method of resist-dyeing is probably an ancient one and doubtless will be found to have a wide distribution in scattered areas.

There are other methods of resist-dyeing in Melanesia in which the finished cloth is tied so as to resist the dye. Tie-dyeing of cloth is also practised in West Africa.

It does not appear unreasonable to regard the tie-dyeing of the warp of the cloth by the Iban as a development and refinement of the similar though crude technique now seen in certain fringe-like fibre skirts elsewhere. In the British Museum a fringe on a Konyak Naga *dao* (a knife-chopper) is of goats' hair with transverse bands of red dyed by this technique.

IBAN RELIGION AND ITS EXPRESSION IN DECORATIVE ART

A brief account of the personnel of Iban religion will help towards an understanding of some of the designs shown on the cloths. This is abstracted from Perham as quoted by Ling Roth (1, pp. 168–213).

The Iban believe in an indefinite number of spiritual beings termed *Petara*; these "gods" have their several functions. Some Iban say that there is only one *Petara*, but when confronted with the references to many gods in their incantations they explain this as merely implying a unity of origin, which does not amount in their minds to a conception of a First Great Cause. An *antu*, or spirit, causes sickness or wants to kill persons and so has to be scared away, but *Petara* is regarded as saving power, the preserver of men; in extreme cases *Petara* alone can help a man; if he dies it is *Petara* alone who has allowed the life to pass away.

The moon and stars are not invoked, but they have an "invisible belonging", a *Petara*, just as all parts of the earth have. It is probable that no inanimate objects themselves, not even the sun, are supposed to be divinities; "it is an underlying spirit in them which is adored, a hidden living influence in them which effects their operations" (Ling Roth, 1, p. 201).

Three beings with definite functions occupy a peculiar position in Iban belief. (1) *Salampandai*, a female spirit and the maker of men. (2) *Pulang*

Gana, the tutelary deity of the soil and the spirit presiding over the whole work of rice-farming. (3) *Singalang Burong*, whose name probably means the Bird Chief. The Iban trace their descent from him and from him they learned the system of omens, and through the flights or calls of the omen-birds, his sons-in-law, he still communicates with his descendants. "These birds", said he, "possess my mind and spirit and represent me in the lower world. When you hear them, remember it is we who speak for encourage-ment or for warning" (Ling Roth, I, p. 200). His earthly form is the kite, *Haliastur intermedius*, a sub-species of *H. indus*, the Brahminy kite, which is reverenced by Hindus as sacred to Vishnu. He may also be said to be the Iban god of war and the guardian spirit of brave men. Hose and McDougall (II, p. 86) state that the Iban say that *Singalang Burong* never leaves his house and that for this reason they do not take omens from the hawks when going on the warpath.

The observance of omens occupies a large share of the thoughts of the Iban, and the system as carried out by them is most elaborate. The birds "used" by them are: *Membuas* (a kingfisher, *Carcineutes melanops*), *papau* (a trogon, *Harpactes diardi*, or ? *Dendrocitta cinerascens*), *beragai* (a trogon, *Harpactes duvauceli*), *kutok* (*Lepocestes porphyromelas*), *katupong* (a wood-pecker, *Sasia abnormis*), *nendak* (a kind of thrush, *Cittocincla suavis*), *briak* (*Orthotomus cineraceus*, the tailor bird, or *O. ruficeps*), *bejampong* (a shrike, *Platylophus coronatus* or *Hydrocichla frontalis*), *Enkrasak* (the spider-hunter, *arachnothera*, three sp.). The system also embraces the *rusa* (the deer, *Cervus equinus*), *kijang* (barking deer, *Cervulus muntjak*), *plandok* (mouse-deer, *Tragulus*), and sometimes even *aji* (the moon rat), *tengiling* (scaly anteater, *Manis*), *sandah* (bat), the *sawa* (python) and *tedong* (cobra), *tuchok* (house lizard, *gecko*) ("a species of grasshopper", *S.D.D.*), and the following insects *rioh, rejah, burong malam* (a cricket, *Gryllacris nigrilabris*). All these may be omens in various ways and circumstances and therefore, in this connection, they are designated *burong* (birds), and to augur from any of them is *beburong*. But these other creatures are subordinate to the birds, from which alone augury is sought at the beginning of any important business. Augury is sometimes taken from other animals. In the *S.D.D.* (p. 16) it is stated that the eight relatives or followers of *Singalang Burong* are: *beragai, katupong, bejampong, membuas, kutok, nendak, papau, briak*. Called

143

"birds" but holding a lower place and not considered "sacred" (indeed they are often eaten) are the insects *rioh, rejah* (grasshopper) and *burong malam* (ground cricket); the snakes *tedong* (cobra), *sawa* (python); the animals *rusa, kijang, plandok, remaung, tengiling* (the Manis), *aji* (moon rat), *engkarong* (the skinks), and bat. Good accounts of the omen animals of Sarawak are given by Ling Roth from various sources (1896, I, pp. 191–197, 221 ff.), Haddon (1901, pp. 381 ff.), Hose and McDougall (1901, pp. 173 ff.; 1912, II, pp. 51–90), in all of which references are made to the Iban. The most authoritative account of the religion and the omen animals of the Iban is that given by the Ven. Archdeacon J. Perham (see Ling Roth).

The Iban has surrounded himself with thousands of *antu*, or spirits, which are supposed to fill earth and air, sea and sky; they are adversaries or helpers of men, and the difference between them and *Petara* is imperceptible. The good ones are nearly identified with *Petara*, of whom no evil is predicated; but the bad and angry spirits are far more numerous than the good ones. *Antu* may appear to men as animals, such as deer, python, crocodiles, etc. In order to communicate with the supernatural, an Iban may *nampok*, sleep on the tops of mountains with the hope of meeting with the good spirits of the unseen world, but this custom is now much less frequent.

Some Iban men, and they mainly or solely Ulu Ai Iban, have a *ngarong* or secret helper, usually the spirit of some ancestor or dead relative, who may or may not inform the individual Iban to whom he manifests himself in what form he will appear in the future. An Ulu Ai Iban of the Batang Lupar informed Dr Hose that every Iban who has no *ngarong* hopes to get some bird or beast as his helper at the *begawai*, the feast given to the *Petara*. As the *ngarong* is one of the very few topics in regard to which the Iban display any reluctance to speak freely (Hose and McDougall, II, pp. 90 ff. and *J.A.I.* XXXI, 1901, pp. 199 ff.), it is very improbable that the animal form of this mysterious secret, the *ngarong*, should be represented on a cloth. It seems probable that the *ngarong* is an institution related to the *nampok*. There may have been some connection between the gaining of a *ngarong* and *nampok*.

The *engkaramba* figures that ward off harm have been noted on p. 105.

Very many of the designs and patterns appear to have been adopted for some reason connected with Iban beliefs; the choice of the motive to some extent may correspond with the ultimate use to which the cloth will be put.

Pua, or blankets, which may be used on ceremonial occasions as well as for coverings, are frequently decorated with anthropomorphic and crocodile figures. We do not know whether there is any connection between the representations of crocodiles and the belief that spirits of the departed may choose crocodiles as abiding places.

The *kalambi*, or coats, particularly those worn by the men, are often ceremonial garments and are usually patterned chiefly with omen birds and animals, doubtless in order that their good influences may be experienced by the wearer. In such a highly specialised coat as 35.904 (pp. 37–46) the patterns suggest that it was worn by a man who conducted the most important of Iban feasts, and we suggest that it was the property of a *manang bali*.

The everyday garments, the *bidang* and the *sirat*, are decorated with less important motives.

Those on the *bidang* are more varied and interesting and consist chiefly of mammals, birds and other animals; there are also some plant motives, mostly the *bangkit* fruit and the *tangkong* creeper with its hanging blossoms. The crossed posts of houses and the wedge usually occur together, and there are examples of fire-places, a boat, and paddles. The arenga palm and mast ("acorn") patterns are frequently used in the borders and both are of importance in the daily life of the Iban, who make toddy and sugar from the juice of the flower and ropes from the black fibres of the trunk of the arenga. The pig is one of the animals always found in abundance near an Iban village, and the so-called "acorn" *empili* is really the nut-like fruit of a tree greatly liked by both tame and wild pigs, but "mast" is a better designation. The blossoms of the *bangkit*, and probably those of the *tangkong*, are sweet-smelling. The plants and flowers and the objects of material culture are all intimately connected with the needs of daily life, shelter, food and adornment.

Many of the designs or patterns on the *sirat*, or loin-cloths of the men, are mainly or solely confined to them, and doubtless have a special reference to the pursuits (such as the paddy fields), dangers or interests that more particularly affect men. Very common are parts of the creatures that injure crops, such as pigeons or other birds, and locusts. A curious design is that called "sleeping cats".

It is characteristic of the Iban, as well as of other peoples in Borneo, that the whole of their life is permeated with religious conceptions, and indeed no distinction can be drawn in their daily life between technical and religious operations: they are equally necessary.

In the background is the belief in *Petara* and in the associated lesser agencies, also known as *petara*, who appear to be in practice the executive staff of *Petara*.

It is futile to attempt any operation of importance without the assurance that *Petara* sanctions it, but this approval can only be ascertained by the messages that he conveys through omens. The most common of these messengers are omen birds, and anyone who has lived in Sarawak is fully aware of their importance.

The designs and patterns on the cloths clearly indicate this psychic attitude towards everyday life. They may be regarded in some cases as being protective, to ward off dangers of various kinds, in others as being a means to obtain blessings and good fortune. Thus they express a constant reliance upon supernormal power, and it is probably no exaggeration to say that these attractive people are literally clothed with prayers.

VOCABULARY OF IBAN WORDS USED IN CONNECTION WITH THE CLOTHS AND IN DESCRIBING THE PATTERNS

The English equivalents have been taken from the *Sea Dyak Dictionary*, from translations by Dr C. Hose on numerous labels and from information received in Sarawak. We have omitted those words for which we could not find a translation. We are painfully aware of the imperfections and inadequacy of this list of words, but it is the best we can offer to students from the material at our disposal.

A-a: an open slit

Adap: manner, way, from or on the side of, towards

Aji, aji bulan: white shrew, moon rat, a title for the god Kling (Malay *tikus bulan*, rat, moon), *Gymnura rafflesi* (pp. 72, 126, 127; pls. v, vi)

Akar: a creeper, anything that can be used for binding

Aki: grandfather

Aki Ungkok: Grandfather Ungkok, the man in the moon. He is also spoken of as "the ancient Ungkok, the brave leader" (pp. 64, 124)

Ambun: dew, fog, mist

Ampat: four

Anak: a child, young of animals and plants

Andi: rumour

Andin: ? fabulous, imaginary

Angkong: a species of *Mangifera* (mango); a tree bearing strong-scented, diamond-shaped fruit, the horse-mango (p. 134; pl. xxii)

Antu: ghost, demon, spirit (pp. 130, 142, 144)

Anyam: to weave, the plait (of baskets or mats); *anyam belebas*, woven stripes imitated by using a needle (p. 102)

Api: fire

Ara: stripes of different solid colours, to arrange different coloured stripes; to spread out

Ariniek: alternate markings

Asi: cooked rice; a victim, prey; fair, right, proper

Baju: a coat

Baku: a brass betel-box

Bala: a multitude, a war party

Balang: a bottle; unsuccessful; *leka balang*, an enemy's head

Bali, mali, bebali: to exchange, change colour, fade; an alteration

Baloi: a striped kind of bamboo

Balu: a widow, widower

Balut, bebalut: a band, small bundle; to wrap up, entangle

Bangkit: a scented flower, scented leaves or fruit of certain jungle trees used as scent or personal ornaments. Sometimes described as a creeping (? climbing) jungle plant (p. 134; pls. xviii, xix, xxi)

Bara: a tumour, a knot of wood

Batang: trunk or stem of tree, a tree, a stick, main branch of a river or road

Batebok: to make holes like a woodpecker

Batu: stone, rock

Baya, baia, jagu: crocodile (pp. 129, 145; pl. xi)

Bayak: the iguana, *S.D.D.* This is the monitor lizard, *Varanus* sp. (p. 129; pl. xii)

Be, bel, ber: the inseparable prefix which expresses a state or condition of being and thereby denotes the intransitive state of the verb

Bedayong, berdayong: to row with an oar, rowing

Bedong: a woman's girdle or waist band (p. 102)

Bejangkam: to squeeze (with thumb and finger), to nip

Bekait: to hook, hooked, ? crossed

Bekarong: to cover, conceal, enclose in a case

Bekatapu: wearing a war-cap

Bekaul, berkaul: twisted over one another, entangled, ? crossed

Bekengkang: to be striped

Bekikiang: crooked

Belambang: alternately, not regularly

Belingkian: the argus pheasant (p. 37)

Bendar: true, very

Bengkah: a division, class, lot, to put aside

Beparang: to cut (*parang*, sword, chopper)

Beprang: to make war, attack

Beradap: facing (*aji beradap*, shrews facing one another), to interview face-to-face. See adap (pl. v)

Beranak: to give birth to

Berasok: overlapping, to put on, fit together

Berayah: outstretched wings or hands; a ceremonial dance performed by chiefs leaping up with their arms extended in imitation of a soaring kite (p. 117)

Beringan: a collection of any articles tied together

Beringin: a fruit tree (p. 70)

Berkingking: a brass bangle

Berspit: grasp with claws

Besampan: a small native boat, a canoe (p. 135)

Besarang: to build a nest

Besarong: to encase, sheath

Besepit (bespit): to take between the fingers, or with a pair of tongs or pincers; provided with nippers or claws

Besi: iron

Besimpan: to pack up (coiled)

Besugu: with a comb

Besumpiang: to fill up, complete, finish off

Besurong: to push on

Betampong: a ceremony to cure sickness

Betangkal: to have a notch in a post for a cross-bar

Betangkin: to gird on a sword

Betayok: calling attention with the hand, to beckon ("to strike with the open hand", *S.D.D.*)

Betegam: to swallow all at once, to bolt food

Betong: a large bamboo used for carrying water

Betulak, betula: to push off, put aside, make a departure, to go in opposite directions

Betunga: face-to-face, opposite, interview

Betungku: to thresh paddy

Bidang: a petticoat (p. 52)

Bingka: a root

Bintang: a star

Biyak: see bayak

Brang: the upper arm

Brani: brave

Bras, brau: uncooked rice

Bruang: a bear, *Helarctos malayanus*

Buah: fruit

Buan: a small shrub whose fruit and flowers are the favourite food of the mouse-deer, *plandok* (p. 84)

Bubul: a collection, to add to, to fill up spaces; *bubul lapang*, a pattern so described as it fills up a space; *bubul jerit*, the pattern collected together to fill up the space; the pattern completed

Buchai: a fringe

Bujak: the monitor lizard, *Varanus* sp.; a spear

Bukang: a headless corpse

Bulan: the moon (pp. 122, 136, 142)

Buloh: a bamboo which grows very high; *buloh bala*, a yellow bamboo

Bulu: a feather, quill, hair

Bungai, bunga: a flower, the name of a snake

Bungkok: bent back, bent, hunchbacked

Buntak: a locust; *buntak balang*, a large yellow grasshopper

Bunut: the horse-mango, *Mangifera* sp.

Burak, borak: white

Buri: "cowry shells which are sewn as ornaments on jackets, petticoats, etc.", *S.D.D.* These are *Nassa*, not *Cypraea* shells (p. 49)

Burong: a bird (pp. 127–129; pls. VII, VIII, IX), an omen. For omen birds and animals see pp. 143, 144. *Burong belingkian*, the argus pheasant; *burong malam*, a night omen, a kind of cricket

Buyah: a beetle, a species of moth (p. 119)

Chayam: pig's whiskers?

Chelum, chilom: black

Dabong: serrated, notched, dog-toothed

Dadong: a shawl

Dandan: a platform at the stern of a war-boat

Dangdong: a shawl worn by a man in full dress (p. 103); "a Malay *sarong* or long skirt", *S.D.D.*

Dapur: a fire hearth, a cooking place

Daun: a leaf; *daun wi*, ratan leaves (p. 134, pl. XXII)

Dayong: an oar; shoulder blade, scapula

Deman: a species of fern, *Gleichenia dichotoma*
Di: at, on, in
Dilah, dila: the tongue
Dua: two
Dudok: in steps; to sit, settle, reside
Dulang: a wooden dish or trough

Embayar: a phosphorescent centipede (p. 132; pl. xvi)
Embun, ambun: dew
Empalai: a little garden, a small paddy farm
Empetut: a grub; alternate light and dark square markings as on the snake (*ular* or *urar*) called *empetut, Tropidonotus petersii*
Empili: a tree producing a species of wild nut, the favourite food of wild pigs. This is best translated by "mast", the fruit of various forest trees, especially as food for swine (pp. 62, 133, 145; figs. 28, 29; pl. xviii)
Empirjungau: a long-nosed fish
Emplawa: a spider (p. 131; pls. xiv, xv)
Engkaramba, engkramba: some kind of man or male personage; a representation of anything cut out of wood, used to prevent harm from coming to crops, etc. (pp. 40–44, 105, 106, 111–113, 124; pl. 1)
Engkarong: a species of skink lizard, *Lygosoma*, sp.; *engkarong kijong*, a stiff skink lizard
Engkatak: a frog (pp. 130, 131; pl. xiii)
Engkerbai: a shrub (pp. 11, 21)
Engklait: wild gambier, *Uncaria gambier*, a shrub which climbs by means of hooked spines; it is used medicinally and is extensively employed for tanning and dyeing. One of the most powerful of astringents
Engku, enk: my, mine
Engkudu: red; a plant of which the skin of the root produces a red dye
Entadu: a caterpillar
Entali: string
Entepa: outstretched wings or hands
Entibap: the palm, *Arenga saccharifera* (pp. 133, 145; pl. xxii)
Entilan: a boat shed
Entilang: a framework of an Iban cooking place (p. 65)

Gajah: an elephant (pp. 41–43, 141)
Gajai: a mythical creature, something like a frog (pp. 105, 106, 114, 115, 130, 131)

Gambar: a picture; *gambar mensia*, portraits of people
Gansai: a spear with one barb
Gari: a garment, clothes
Gasing, gasieng: a spinning-wheel, top, to spin (p. 7)
Gawai: a feast
Gelang: a handle (of a shield)
Gelegar: the flooring of a house
Gelong, giling: to roll up, to curl
Gelong paku resam: curled top of the *rěsam* fern (p. 134)
Genok: a gourd, white pumpkin (used as a water vessel); a gourd with a long twisted stalk, the fruit is used as soap (p. 134)
Gerunggong: a joint of the larger bones
Gigi: a step of a ladder; tooth
Grama: a fresh-water crab (p. 66)
Gran: to cut with a knife
Gran pemalu tekalong: grooves in the bark-cloth mallet
Grunong: small bells used as a fringe, "hawk-bells"

Home: a plant used instead of indigo (p. 20)

Igi: seed
Ikan: a fish
Ikat; ngikat, beikat or **bikat**: anything tied up; to tie, bind
Iko, iku: a tail
Imbai: horizontal, alongside, side by side, next to
Indang: soaring, to lift the arm; a sieve
Indu: a woman, female of any animal
Ipoh: a tree, *? Antiaris* sp., from which a white bark-cloth is made for *pua*; *A. toxicaria*, the sap of which is very poisonous (p. 4)

Jagu: the crocodile
Janga: an angle
Janggat: a white pumpkin, a fruit resembling a vegetable marrow
Jangkam, bejangkam: squeeze
Jangkit: a tree the bark of which gives a red dye *kara jangkit*, a tree, *Ficus* sp.
Jari: a hand
Jaul: twisted?
Jelu: wild, a wild animal
Jengam: to press with a forked stick
Jengkong: curved, to bend round, arch

149

Jengku: an artificial spur, curved, bent

Jengkuan: a netting needle; a weaving spool (pl. xxiv); a kingfisher

Jerit or jarit: the horizon

Jerit: many, in order, in series, a branch; *jerit betayu*, to beckon with the hand?

Jernang: a species of ratan, *Calamus*, employed in house-building; from the fruit is obtained the red "dragon's blood" which is used as a stain (p. 20)

Junggur: a snout, point of land

Kabu: the fringe of a *sirat*

Kain: cloth, clothes, woman's petticoat

Kait: a hook

Kaiu, ? kaiku: a kind of tree

Kaki: a leg, foot; foot of a hill or ladder

Kala: a scorpion (pp. 47, 132)

Kalambi: a jacket, coat (p. 22)

Kanggan: Chinese black calico

Kanji: rice gruel; sensuous

Kanulong: a long-nosed fish

Kapayang: a plant, *Pangium edule*

Karak, ? kara: scattered, spread or pour out

Karam: sunk, immersed

Karong: a coverlet, case, bag

Katapu: a cap, war-cap

Kebat, ngebat: tie, bind

Keberair: best

Kejong, kejoh: stiff

Kelabong: a scorpion

Kelalin: to interlace, tie, or fasten a wooden flooring with ratan; in-and-out plaiting like the *nibong* floor of a house

Kembong: swollen, full

Kendawang: a snake with a red head, red tip to its tail and body striped black, white, and red, *Cylindrophis rufus* (pp. 29, 36, 55, 112, 130), which is not poisonous; or doubtfully *Callophis flaviceps* (p. 68), this is a synonym for *Doliophis bivirgatus* which is poisonous

Kengkang: a stripe or knot

Kenyalang: the hornbill, *Buceros rhinoceros*

Kepong: cut off, amputate, surround, tailless

Kerchpaka: a kind of fruit

Ketam: a crab (pl. xvii)

Ketup, ketupang: bite

Klabumbu, kelamambang, klabembang: a butterfly

Klait: see engklait

Klapong, kelapong: the end or remnant of anything, a fringe; "*Tu klapong sirat iya*, this is the fringe of his waist-cloth", *S.D.D.*

Koali: a cotton-stretcher

Kris: a dagger

Kukut: a claw, talon, nail

Kumbu, pua kumbu: a coverlet or blanket

Kunding: nominally an omen bird, but really a cricket, *Gryllacris nigrilabris*, used as an omen (p. 143)

Kuning: yellow

Kunyit: turmeric, *Cucurma longa*, the plant from which the yellow dye is obtained; some species supply starch

Labang: white

Labong: a headkerchief, head-covering

Labu: the white pumpkin, gourd, *Cucurbita lagenaria*

Lachau, lachaur: a green grass lizard (p. 130; figs. 13, 30; pl. xii)

Ladang: a bulwark, bank of earth surrounding a paddy farm; (*beladang*, to separate, *S.D.D.*). A farm or a division of land. C.H. (p. 135)

Ladi, ladei: separate, ? a spot

Ladu: mud used as a black dye

Laki: a male of human beings or animals

Lalat: a fly

Lalau: a hand-rail; a bees' nest on a tree

Lalin: in-and-out (as of plaiting)

Lancham: pointed, cut to a point

Landak: a porcupine, *Hystrix*

Lang: a kite, the bodily form of *Singalang Burong*, the Bird king; *kengkang lang*, striped kite (p. 128; fig. 18b; pl. x)

Langgai: the extremity of anything, the longest tail feathers of a bird

Langgu: a pendant, young fruit; *langgu lungping*, earring

Langit: the heavens, sky

Langkiang: a kind of lizard with a long tail

Lantai, luntai: split bamboo or cane; the floor of a house

Lapang: spacious, roomy, an open space, an opening; *bubul lapang*, space-filling

Leka, lika: a seed, grain; give up, let go

Leka balang, leka nanga, leka mudan: an enemy's head

Leku: bend, curve

Lelambak: the flower pattern plaited in mats (pp. 31, 104, 135; pl. xxii)

Lelayang: a swallow, *Hirundo*; a swift, *Chaetura*; *lelayang bata, Collocalia fuciphaga* (fig. 13; pl. IX)

Lelingkok: curved, crooked, zigzag

Lemba: leaf of *Curculigo latifolia* used for tying warp threads preparatory to dyeing

Lemiding: a creeping fern, *Acrostichun scandens*; the tops are used as a vegetable by most tribes

Lensat: a fruit tree, *Lansium domesticum*

Lia, liah: ginger, *Zingiber officinale* (p. 134; pl. XIX)

Likau: a zigzag decoration, striped like a python or tiger

Lilit: gold embroidery, yellow, a binding

Lintah: a leech (p. 133; pl. XVI)

Long: a Kayan bark basket; a species of grasshopper

Luas: wide, spacious

Lunju: a spear with a narrow blade

Macham: sort, species, kind

Malam: night

Mampul: re-tying

Manah: good, beautiful

Manang: a medicine-man (or woman); *manang bali*, "a sham-female witch doctor", *S.D.D.*; a medicine-man who behaves as a woman (pp. 40–46, 145)

Manok: a domestic fowl

Mansau: ripe, red, cooked

Marau: a large cane, *Calamus* sp.

Marik, mariek: a bead, bead necklace

Mata: an eye, edge of a weapon; raw, unripe

Mayang, the blossom of palms

Mayau: a cat, a wild cat, *Felis bengalensis*; *mayau tindok*, sleeping cat (pl. XVII)

Melanjan: a wild species of *rambutan, Nephelium*

Melintang: crossways, across

Menaul: a hawk, kite

Mengkatak: a frog

Menyembang, Menimbang: *bulan menimbang*, name of a god in the heavens (p. 122)

Mensia: people, persons

Menyeti: the best kind of *pua*

Miga: clouds (p. 136)

Mudan, leka mudan: an enemy's head

Mulai: to twist back

Mulut: mouth, the lips

Munsang: a wild animal

Munti: a species of small bamboo the shoots of which are eaten

Nabu: rolled up in a ball

Nadai: no, not

Nakar, ngar: a special red dye

Nama: name, reputation

Nandok, betandok: to butt, to gore, to cup; cupping is done by gashing the flesh and sucking out the blood by means of a bamboo cylinder [or a horn?]

Nanga: the mouth of a river; *leka nanga*, an enemy's head

Nemaiar: a centipede (p. 104)

Ngelambai, lambai: to wave, beckon to, shout to

Ngelepan: a centipede (pl. XVI)

Ngikat: see ikat

Nibong: a thorny palm, *Oncosperma tigillaria*

Niga: the sky (white clouds in the heavens visible only on fine days or nights); *niga dudok*, clouds on the horizon on a fine day (*dudok*, sit)

Nya: that, those

Nyandih, penyandih: lean against

Nyang: sunset

Nyangking: ? by itself; *jerit nyangking*, a pattern by itself

Orang: a man, person, people

Padang: a cleared piece of land, field; renowned

Padi: rice in the husk

Padong: a bed place; rocky ledge across a river bed; shelf; *padong buah*, a fruit store

Pakan: the woof in weaving or plaiting, *S.D.D.*

Pakan belebas: a small striped pattern formed by grouping warp threads together with the weft or woof, so leaving spaces, as this is done with a needle it is termed needle-weaving (pp. 94, 96, 97, 102)

Paku: the general name for ferns, particularly *Hoplenium esculentum*

Pala: the head; *antu pala*, the smoke-dried head of an enemy

Pama: a species of frog; well, good

Pampul: to cover, cover the face with the hands

Pandin: a buckle

Panggal: a pillow, resting place

Panjai: long

Pantak: a small dark-coloured wasp (p. 132)

Pantak penandok: the wound caused by the sting of a wasp? or perhaps the clay nest of a wasp, or even scarifying the skin preparatory to the cupping process (pp. 74, 113, 118, 132)

Pantok, bepantok: the bite (of a snake, bird, etc.), peck (as a fowl); the shoot of a plant

Papan: a plank, board

Pasak: a wedge; a paddy-destroying insect

Pating, patieng: the stem of a flower, bunch of fruit with its stem, a twig

Patok: a beak or bill of a bird; tender shoot of a seed

Patong: the knee; *pala patong*, knee cap

Paya: swamp land, a wet-land paddy farm (p. 135; pl. xxv); *sirat paya* an especial kind of waist-cloth

Payong paya: cleared space in swamp land

Pe, pem, pen, peng: the inseparable prefixes used in the formation of derivative nouns

Pedalai: the bread-fruit tree, *Artocarpus incisa*, and also the jack-fruit tree, or *jaca* tree, *A. integrifolia*, from the wood of which a yellow dye is obtained (pp. 4, 19)

Pemadu, pemadam: the end of anything

Pemalu, permalu: a bark-cloth beater or mallet; *pemalu tekalong*, a mallet for beating the *tekalong* bark to make it into bark cloth

Pemigi: a cotton-gin

Pempang: a fence

Pemuchok: a shoot of a plant

Penan: a shelter, defence

Penandok: see nandok

Pendal: stuck fast

Pendawan, penawan: a fish-spear with a single barb

Penjuang: posts on either side of the staircase supporting railings, cross-pieces, wood or sticks in the shape of an **X**

Penukoh: possibly a flowering tree, but Hose says the meaning is uncertain; trestles

Penukok, punchok: a shoot

Penumboh: a growth, opening, foundation

Penuri, penori: thorns, spiky, hole made with the finger, pressed down

Penyadi: condition, existence

Penyandih: lean against

Petara: spiritual beings who have their several functions. Some Iban say there is only one *Petara* who has saving power (pp. 105, 115,

142, 144, 146). "A god, gods. It is probably a corruption of the Hindu *Avatara*", *S.D.D.*

Petik: spotted

Pinang: a palm, *Areca catechu*, "betel" nut

Pisang: the banana, *Musa sapientum*

Plangka, pelangka: the paddy foot-sieve through which by stamping paddy the grains fall through and the stalks and the ears remain. An oblong wooden frame about 6 ft. by 3 ft. enclosing ratan-work which is used for threshing paddy; a propitiatory offering on behalf of a sick person, the offering may be a common plate or a square wooden box without a cover standing upon four ornamental legs. When a person is taken ill the medicine-man, *manang*, sometimes recommends that the ceremony of *saut* be gone through, a *plangka* is then got ready for the *saut* ceremony (p. 78; pl. xxiv)

Plir: testes

Prut: a stomach, breast, intestines

Pua: a blanket, the old blankets of the Iban were made of bark-cloth; *pua tengkebang*, a blanket with a new pattern, the maker must not copy any other (p. 106)

Puchok, muchok; bepuchok: a point, top of anything; to attain the summit

Pun: a tree, stem, origin, basis, foundation, commencement

Puna: a green pigeon (*Treron*, all species except *T. capellei*) (p. 129)

Punggang, punggai: the end

Punggong: the waist

Pusat: the navel, centre

Raia: large; *burong raia*, a heron, *Ardea sumatrana*

Rambut: a fringe

Rambutan: a lofty fruit tree with hairy fruit, *Nephelium echinatum*

Randau: a creeping plant, a creeper of any kind, a parasite

Raras: a small stick or branch; likeness, picture; build

Ras: a farm, a cleared space

Ratan: a climbing plant, *Calamus* sp., the Skarang and Saribas Dayaks use the word *rotan*, but the other Dayaks call it *wi* (p. 133; fig. 13; pl. xxii)

Rawai: a Dayak woman's corset made of rings of ratan strung with brass rings

Rebong: a bamboo shoot; *muchok rebong*, cone-shaped
Rejang: to bore a hole, pierce or thrust upwards
Rekong: the neck
Remang: light fleecy clouds (not rain clouds)
Remaung: a tiger cat, *Felis nebulosa*; *remaung raras*, *F. marmorata*; *remaung bendar*, the true tiger (pp. 69, 71, 126; pl. IV)
Rĕsam: a species of fern, *Pteris arechnoiden*, which usually grows in secondary jungle where the primeval forest has been destroyed (p. 134; pl. XVIII)
Resam: to press down with the hand, make a hole with the hand or finger
Riang: a creeper the leaves of which are eaten
Rinik, renik: close to
Rotan: see ratan and sega
Ruai: the verandah or long reception room of a Dayak house; *burong ruai*, the argus pheasant
Ruat: stripped; pull out, overflow; numerous
Rumah: a house
Ruman: ears of grain after threshing, chaff
Rundai: hanging down, dangling (pl. xx)
Rusa: the deer *Cervus equinus* (p. 125; pl. III)
Ruyit, ruit: barb of fish spear

Sabaka: equal, alike
Sabong: fighting, butting, to match, to set cocks to fight
Salampandai, Slampandai: the maker of mankind (pp. 131, 142, 151)
Salapok: a skull-cap made of ratan or pandanus
Samak: a reddish brown dye obtained from the *samak* tree (p. 19)
Samoa: all, everyone
Sampan: a small native boat, a dugout canoe
Sampok: a white ant, termite
Sandong: a jungle tree with fruit
Sanggol, sanggul: a braid, roll, plait of hair, *S.D.D.*; a knot, a tendril
Sarang: a nest, dwelling-place
Saribu: a thousand legs, millepede
Sarong: a case, sheath
Satu: one, first, good
Saut: an answer, reply; a *manang* ceremony performed when a person is ill. The ceremony is fully described in *S.D.D.*
Sawa: a python, *Python reticulatus* (p. 130); paddy sown in a nursery plot and transplanted to the wet field

Sawang: an opening, hole, to enlarge a hole
Sayap: a wing
Sega: a species of ratan; there are two kinds of *sega*: *sega balau* (or *bulu*) and *sega enseluang* (*enseluai* or *ikan*), a smaller and more valuable kind of cane, *S.D.D.* See buloh, ratan and rotan
Selam: to dive, diving
Selampur: the whole, all; *serampor*, of one colour
Selempepat, sepepat, semperpat, slampepat: fireflies (pp. 117, 134; pl. XXI)
Semalau: a species of thrush, *Copsychus amaenus*
Sembrang, semberai, semerai: to go across water or a boundary
Semerai: to cross over
Sengayoh: a paddle
Senggang: a species of gigantic lily
Serepang, serpang: a fork, trident, split, slit
Sergang: a bamboo fish trap with a wide mouth, a bamboo receptacle for plates
Serok genok: a white pumpkin (used as soap by Dayaks)
Serpan, serpang: dark
Serundan: usually *kain serundan*, a petticoat with the central part plain and coloured borders (p. 85)
Siko: one person or animal
Siku: the elbow
Simbang: a corner; to sharpen a bamboo or piece of stick by cutting it on one side only into a point
Simbing, Simbieng: one-sided, crooked, aslant
Simpan: keep, put by, hide
Simpang: the branch of a path or a river, a junction
Simpong, besimpong, sesimpong: to cut in two; to cut off the top of anything
Singalang Burong: the Bird-king who once appeared in human form, but is manifest as a kite, *Haliastur intermedius*, a sub-species of *H. indus*, the Brahmin kite (pp. 33, 46, 128, 143, and *S.D.D.* p. 157)
Sirat: a waist or loin cloth, the *chawat* of the Malays (p. 91)
Sit: a cluster of *pinang* nuts
Skelat, sklat: red flannel
Skut: foundation
Slaku, selaku: a ratan used as a rope for climbing trees
Spiak: one side only, half

Spit, sepit: pincers, tongs, nippers, claws

Srepang: a spear with three points, a trident, a fork

Sugu, besugu: a comb (fig. 13; pl. xxiv)

Sulor nyang: break of day, the colours of the sky at dawn

Sungai, sungei: a river, stream, brook

Sungkit, sunkit: a bone needle used for embroidery; *kain sungkit*, an embroidered cloth (p. 88); *besungkit*, to prick, pierce, insert

Suri: a ripple on the water

Surik, suriek: stripes, striped

Surong: a temporary bridge or path made of poles; push on, push

Tabor: sprinkle, scatter, sow (seed)

Tali: string, rope

Tampok: a fruit stalk; ? a knot

Tampong: follow, join, splice, sew on, patch

Tanda: the stem of a palm blossom

Tanda: a sign, mark, figleaf ornament, ? decorated; *tanda sirat*, the embroidered end of a waist cloth

Tandok: horns, antlers, see **nandok**

Tangai: a thorny tendril?

Tangga, tanggai: the notched pole which serves as a ladder up to the floor of a house, a ladder

Tangga ubong: a tying frame (p. 9)

Tanggi: a sun-hat

Tangkai: a peduncle, fruit stalk, bunch of fruit; ear of paddy

Tangkal: a notch

Tangkin: a sword (scabbard and belt)

Tangkong: a jungle (? climbing) plant with scented pendant flowers (p. 133; pl. xx); the horny excrescence on the beak of the hornbill; ? a handle or knob (p. 134)

Tangku: the supports of a cooking-pot

Tanjong: *Mimusops elengi*, a tree with hard, heavy durable timber, the bark has astringent and tonic properties. A fragrant nectar can be distilled from the flowers. A cape, projection

Tanju: a platform

Tanka asi: a tripod for cooking rice

Tarum: indigo, *Indigofera tinctoria* (pp. 19, 20, 87)

Taya: cotton when growing; to clear away stumps

Tayok: to strike a person with the open hand, strike (of a flint and steel)

Tayok gasing: a hooked piece of wood for winding thread upon from the spinning wheel; the curves a top makes when spinning

Tebok: a hole, notch

Tekalong: a species of bread-fruit tree the bark of which is used for making *sirat*, *kalambi*, and *pua* (pp. 4, 69)

Teku, teko: curved; a kind of earring

Telu, telo: an egg (Malay, *telor*)

Tengang: a long and straight creeper, the bark makes durable cords; it is cultivated

Tenggak: a necklace

Tengiling, tengilang: the scaly anteater, *Manis javanicus*

Tenjak: a treadle loom with a rigid framework; the type used by the Malays

Tenyalang: hornbill, *Buceros rhinoceros*

Tetak, betetak: to cut; *setetak nadai tampong*, cut off with nothing to follow

Tiang: a post, pole, mast

Tiga: three

Tikai burit: a seat-mat

Tikal: fold up, tie, turn back

Tikup: to close, shut

Tindok: sleeping, asleep, to sleep

Tinggang: to fall upon, press

Tisik: scales of a fish or animal

Trabai, terabai: a shield

Trong: the egg-plant, *Solanum* sp.

Truju, trugu: push with violence

Tu: this, these

Tuboh: the body, people, a person

Tubu: edible bamboo shoot (pl. xviii)

Tugang: a decoration of various colours or coloured stripes

Tukal: a wooden frame about three feet long upon which cotton thread is strung ready for weaving (Malay, a skein)

Tulang: a bone

Tumpoh: the ordinary Iban loom (p. 11)

Tungku: the supports of a cooking-pot; *tungku asi*, tripod for cooking rice

Tunjing: a hoof

Tusu: the breast, udder, milk

Tutup: a lid, cover

Tutup long: the cover of a Kayan bark basket

Ubi: a yam, *Dioscorea*

Ubiara: the wild potato used as a dye

Ubong: cotton thread

Udah: finish, end

Udun: a species of fresh-water fish
Ujan: rain
Ujok: a feather or anything put in the headkerchief or hat as an ornament
Ujong: end, point
Ular, urar: a snake
Ulat: a grub, maggot, caterpillar
Ulu: a handle (of a sword, etc.); head waters of a stream, up river
Unak: a thorn

Ungki: edge of a pattern
Ungkoi: the red or black trimming to the collar of a jacket
Upeh: the spathe of palm blossoms
Upong: the spathe of palm blossoms, flower or fruit stalk
Urat: a root

Wi: the ratan, *Calamus* sp., see **ratan** and **sega**

BIBLIOGRAPHY

Beccari, O. *Wanderings in the great forests of Borneo.* London, 1904.

Brooke Low. *See* Catalogue.

Catalogue of the Brooke Low Collection in Borneo. Printed by D. J. J. Roderiguez at the Sarawak Gazette Office (? about 1890). 1890.

Catalogue to Lady Brooke's Collection. MS. in the British Museum, Department of Ethnology.

Chalmers, W. *Some account of the Land Dyaks of Upper Sarawak.* Singapore Mission Press, n.d.

Donop, L. S. von. *Diary of travelling through North Borneo.* London, 1882.

Driessen, Felix. "Tie and dye work manufactured at Semarang, Island Java." *Internat. Arch. für Ethnographie*, II, 1899, pp. 106–108, pl. VI.

Gomes, E. H. *Seventeen years among the Sea Dyaks of Borneo.* London, 1911.

Haddon, A. C. "The textile patterns of the Sea-Dayaks." *Journ. Anth. Inst.* xxx, 1900, Anth. Rev. and Misc. No. 73, p. 72.

—— *Head-hunters black, white, and brown*, p. 326. London, 1901.

—— "A sketch of the ethnography of Sarawak." *Arch. per l'Antr. e l'Etnol.* xxxi, 1901.

—— "Studies in Bornean decorative art: 1. Patterns derived from the roots of the fig-tree." *Man*, 1905, No. 39.

—— "The physical characters of the races and peoples of Borneo." Appendix to Hose and McDougall, 1912, II, pp. 311–341, with 10 tables of measurements.

—— *The races of man.* Cambridge, 1929.

Haddon, E. B. "The dog-motive in Bornean art." *Journ. Anth. Inst.* xxxv, 1905, pp. 113–125.

Hein, A. R. *Die bildenden Künste bei den Dayaks auf Borneo.* Wien, 1890.

—— *Catalogus der tentoonstelling van Indische kunstnijverheid*, Juli, 1901.

Horsburgh, A. *Sketches in Borneo.* London, 1858.

Hose, Charles. *A descriptive account of the mammals of Borneo.* Diss (Norfolk), 1893. Out of print.

—— *Natural Man, a record from Borneo.* London, 1926.

Hose, C. and Shelford, R. "Materials for a study of tatu in Borneo." *Journ. Anth. Inst.* xxxvi, 1906, pp. 60–91.

Hose, C. and McDougall, W. "The relations between men and animals in Sarawak." *Journ. Anth. Inst.* xxxi, 1901, pp. 173–213.

—— —— *The pagan tribes of Borneo.* 2 vols. London, 1912.

Howell, W. "The Sea-Dayak method of making thread from their home-grown cotton." *The Sarawak Mus. Journ.* I, No. 2, 1912, pp. 61–64.

Howell, W. and Bailey, D. J. S. *A Sea Dyak Dictionary.* American Mission Press, Singapore, 1900–1902.

—— —— *An English–Sea Dyak Vocabulary.* S.P.G. Printing Office, Kuching. Sarawak, 1909.

Huebner, Julius. *Bleaching and dyeing of vegetable fibrous materials.* London, 1912.

Lamster, J. C. *The East Indies.* Droste's Cocoa and Chocolate Manufactory Ltd., Haarlem, Holland, 1929.

Leggatt, F. W. Notes supplied by Mr Leggatt with his collections, now in the Ling Roth Collection in the Bankfield Museum, Halifax.

Loebèr Jr., J. A. "Het 'Ikatten' in Nederlandsch-Indië." *Onze kunst,* Amsterdam, 1902, pp. 17–33 (privately printed).

—— "Het Weven in Nederlandsch-Indië." *Bulletin van het Koloniaal Museum te Haarlem,* No. 29. Amsterdam, 1903.

Meyer, A. B. and Richter, O. "Webgerät aus dem Ostindischen Archipele mit besonderer Rücksicht auf Gorontalo in Nord Celebes." *Abhandl. und Berichte des K. Zool. und Anth. Ethnogr. Mus. zu Dresden,* x, No. 6, 1902–3, pp. 19–67, 1903.

Mijer, Pieter. *Batiks and how to make them.* London, 1919.

Nieuwenhuis, A. W. *Quer durch Borneo.* 2 vols. Leiden, 1904.

—— "Figuurknoopen (ikat)-verven en -weven in Oost-Indië." *Nederlandsch Indië oud en nieuw,* I, 1916. Amsterdam.

Nouhuys, J. W. van. "De oorsprong van de toempal-kapala der Javaansche bakiksaroeng." *Nederlandsch-Indië, oud en nieuw,* XIV, The Hague, 1929, pp. 195–208.

Perham, J. Various papers, *Journal of the Straits Branch of the Royal Asiatic Society,* Nos. 2, 6, 8, 10, 14, 16, 19 (1878–1887). "Petara, or Sea Dyak Gods", 8, 1882, pp. 133–152; "Sea Dyak Religion", 10, 1883, pp. 213–243; 14, 1885, pp. 287–304; "Manangism in Borneo", 19, 1887, pp. 87–103.

Perkin, A. G. and Everest, A. E. *The natural organic colouring matters.* London, 1918.

Roth, H. Ling. "The natives of Borneo", edited from the papers of the late Brooke Low, Esq. *Journ. Anth. Inst.* xxi, 1892, pp. 110–137; xxii, 1893, pp. 22–64.

—— *The natives of Sarawak and British North Borneo.* 2 vols. London, 1896.

—— "Indonesian looms." *Journ. Roy. Anth. Inst.* XLVII, 1917, pp. 323–366. Reprinted in *Studies in primitive looms,* Bankfield Museum Notes, 2nd series, 1918, No. 10, pp. 65–108. Obtainable at the Museum or from F. King and Sons, Halifax.

S.D.D. *A Sea Dyak Dictionary,* see Howell and Bailey.

St John, Sir Spencer. *Life in the forests of the Far East.* 2 vols. London, 1862.

Skeat, W. W. "Notes on the ethnography of the Malay Peninsula" (spinning and weaving on the east coast; tie-dyeing of warp-threads; (p. 179), pl. M showing the various kinds of apparatus employed). *Man,* 1901, No. 142.

Start, Laura, E. "Coptic cloths." Bankfield Museum Notes, 2nd series, No. 4, 1914. F. King and Sons, Halifax.

—— "Burmese textiles from the Shan and Kachin Districts." Bankfield Museum Notes, 2nd series, No. 7, 1917. F. King and Sons, Halifax.

Wirz, P. "Die magischen Gewebe von Bali und Lombok." *Jahrbuch des Bernischen Historischen Museums,* Bern, XI. Jahr, 1931.

Wray, L. "Notes on the dyeing and weaving as practised at Sitiawan in Perak." *Journ. Anth. Inst.* XXXII, 1902, pp. 153–155, pl. XI.

PLATES
I–XXXV

Plate I

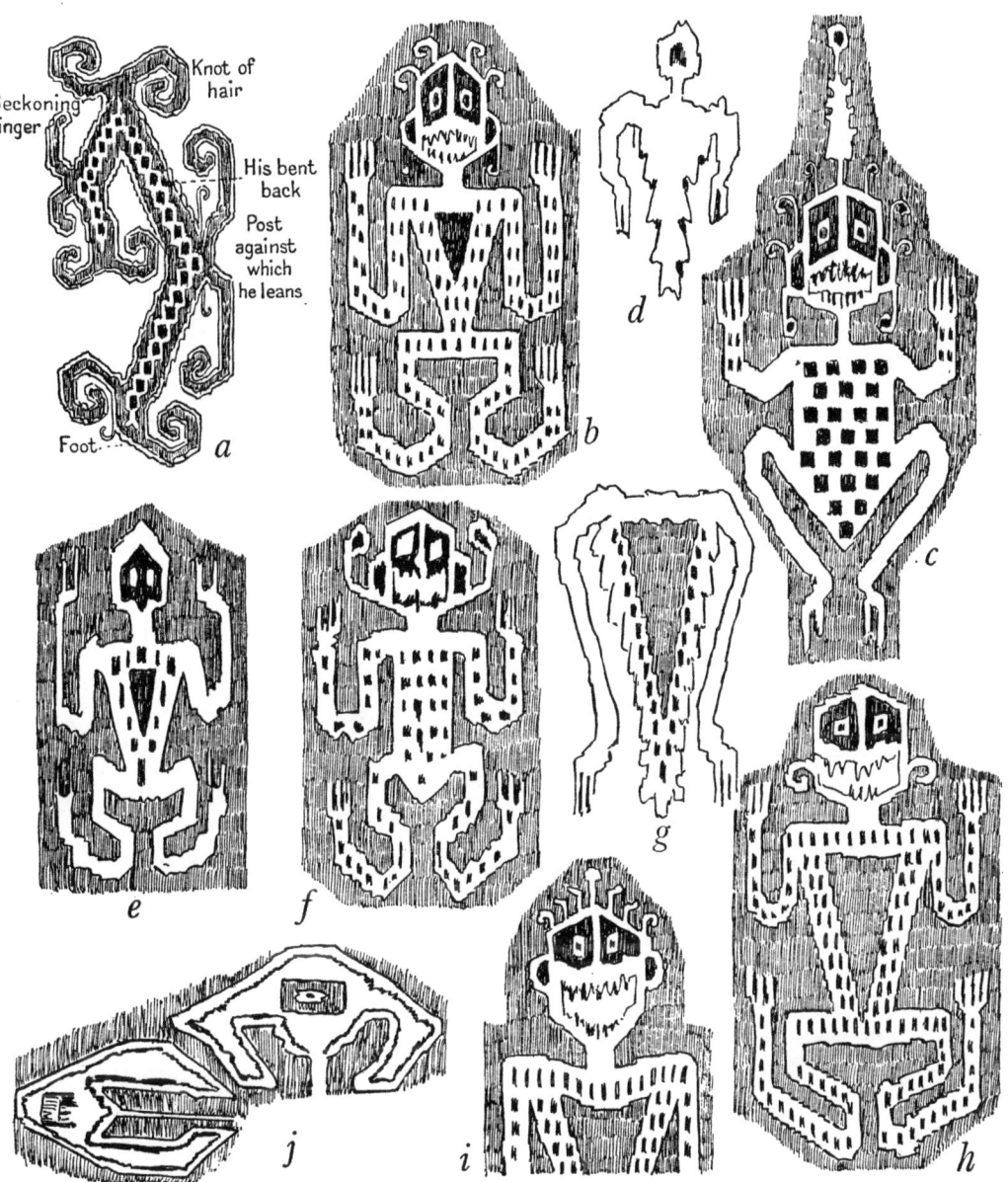

Knot of hair

Beckoning finger

His bent back

Post against which he leans

Foot

ANTHROPOMORPHS

a, Aki Ungkok: "Grandfather Ungkok, who lives in the moon". 35.854 (13).

b, f, h, Engkaramba. b, 35.923 (9); *f,* 35.924 (36, 38); *h,* 35.926 (2).

c, Engkaramba. 35.923 (17); perhaps an *engkaramba engkatak,* frog figure.

d, g, Bukang engkaramba: headless *engkaramba. d,* 35.924 (14, 15); *g,* 35.924 (46).

e, Anak engkaramba: young *engkaramba.* 35.924 (22, 23).

i, Engkaramba besugu: "a female figure with a comb in the hair". 35.926 (7).

j, Bulan menyembang. 35.921 (7).

[Many of the drawings on pls. i–xxv were made from the opposite side of the cloth than that to which the labels are attached, so in these cases the design appears reversed when looking at the labelled side.

The numbers in brackets indicate the numbered patterns on the cloths. A complete list of the numbered and named patterns is entered in a book in the Museum. A star after a number in brackets denotes that the identification was made by us. The translations in quotes are taken from labels.]

Plate II

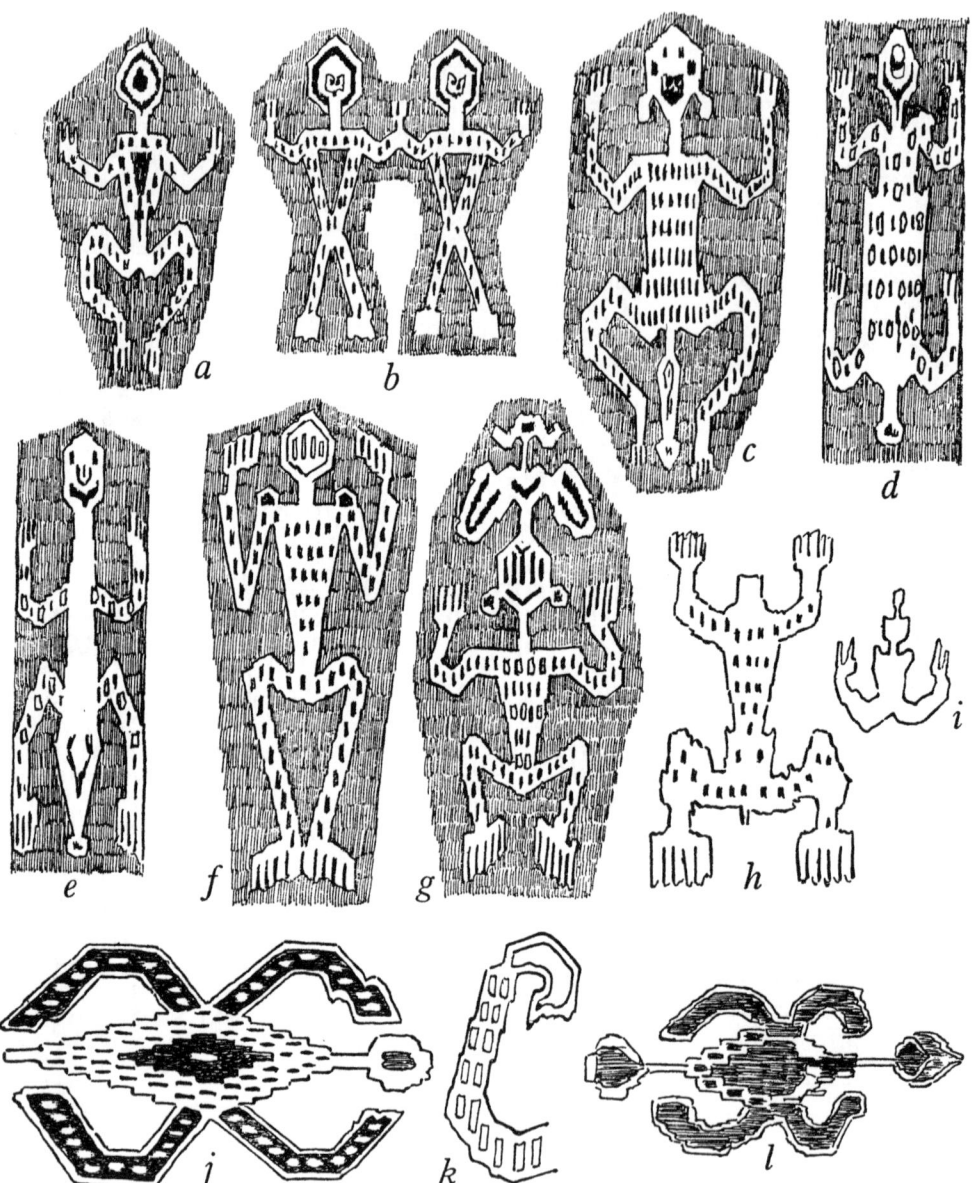

ANTHROPOMORPHS

a–g, Human figures (*? engkaramba*). *a,* 35.931 (1*); *b,* 35.931 (2*); *c,* 35.930 (1*); *d,* 35.930 (2*); *e,* 35.930 (3*); *f.* 35.929 (1*); *g,* 35.929 (5*).

h, Bukang: a headless corpse. 35.929 (3*).

i, Gari enk (engku): my clothes. 35.924 (7).

j, l, Selam: "diving pattern". *j,* 35.882 (1*); *l,* Sarawak Museum, *pua,* No. 251 (Camb. Museum photo. Indo. Born. 365).

k, Betayok: "calling attention with the hand, to beckon" ("to strike with the open hand", *S.D.D.*). 35.859 (8).

Plate III

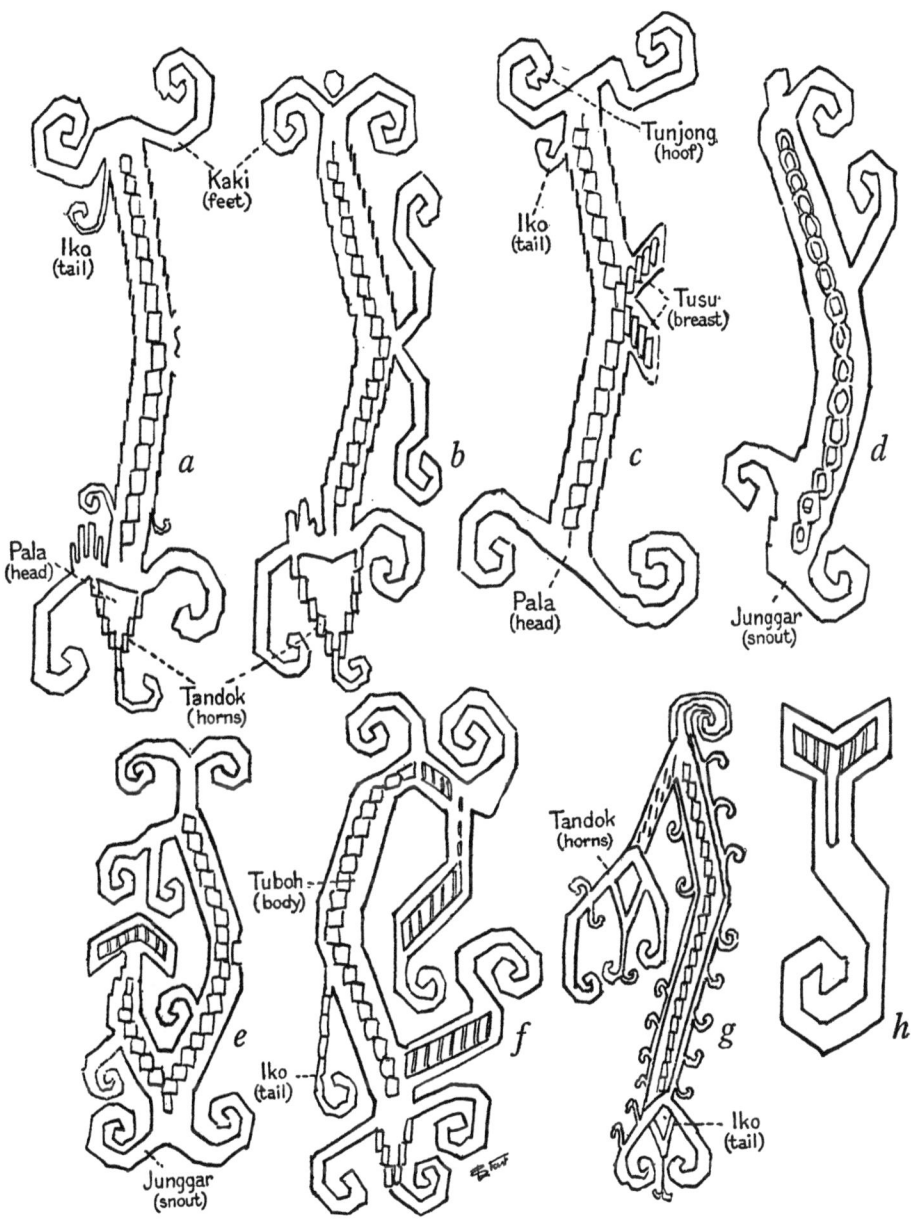

DEER

a, b, *Rusa*: "deer". a, 35.854 (44); b, 35.854 (45, 51).

c, d, *Rusa indu*: hind. c, 35.878 (11, 13); d, 35.870 (15).

e–g, Deer curled up. e, 35.870 (25, 29); f, 35.878 (17, 27, 29); g, 35.863 (31, 34, 38, 42).

h, *Anak rusa*: young deer. 35.878 (2, ?9).

d and e, *junggar* (snout) should be *junggur*.

Plate IV

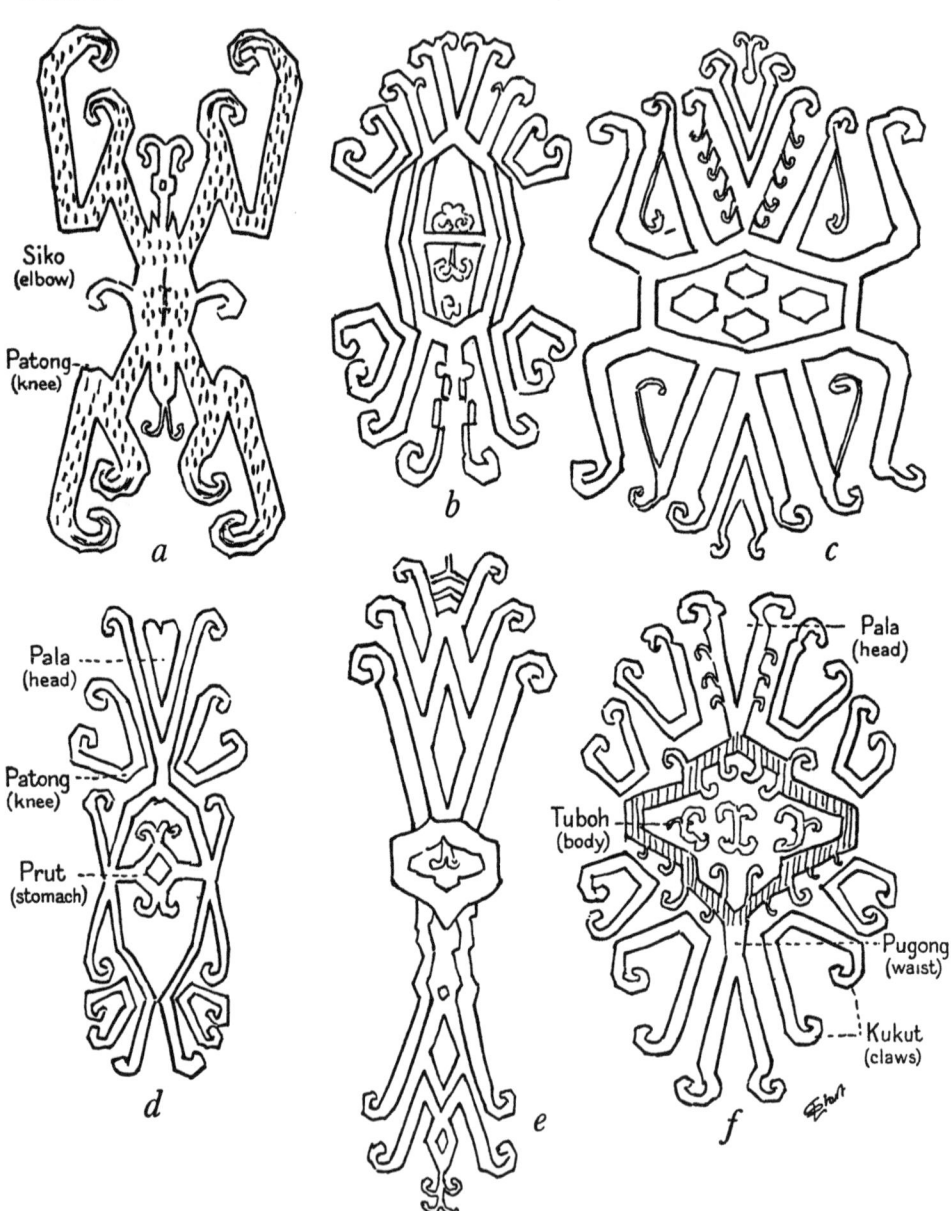

Siko
(elbow)

Patong
(knee)

a

b

c

Pala
(head)

Patong
(knee)

Prut
(stomach)

d

e

Pala
(head)

Tuboh
(body)

Pugong
(waist)

Kukut
(claws)

f

TIGER-CATS

a, Remaung: "tiger". 35.862 (3, 6).

b–f, Remaung: "tiger-cat" (*Felis nebulosa*). *b,* 35.868 (12, 16, 21); *c,* 35.866 (45, 46, 48, 53); *d,* 35.868 (2, 5); *e,* 35.859 (11, 13, 14, 17, 20, 22); the head is towards the foot of the page; *f,* 35.873 (4, 7, 13); *pugong* (waist) should be *punggong*.

Plate V

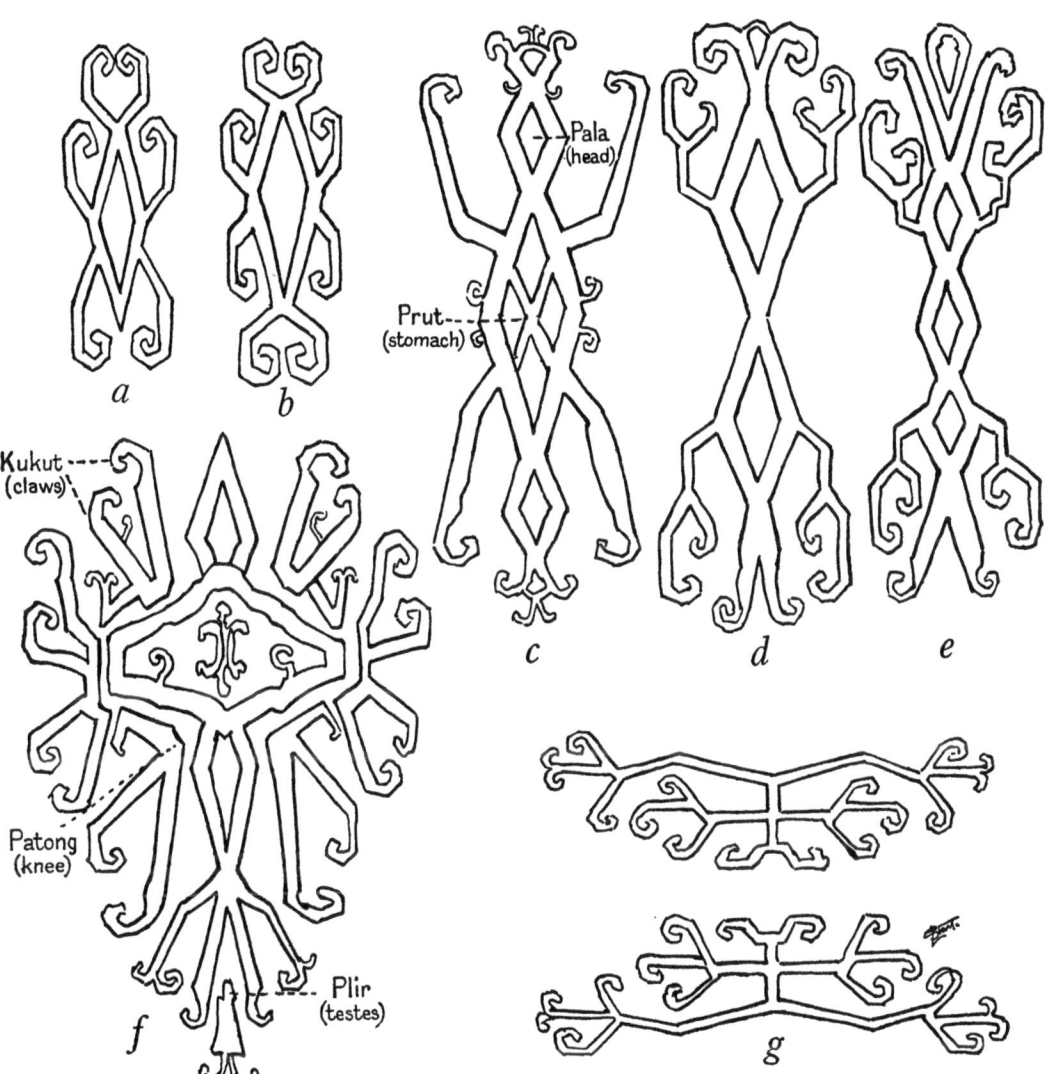

Pala
(head)

Prut
(stomach)

Kukut
(claws)

Patong
(knee)

Plir
(testes)

a

b

c

d

e

f

g

SHREWS

a, Anak aji: young shrew. 35.877 (19).

b–f, Aji: "shrew". *b*, 35.865 (18); *c*, 35.866 (27, 32, 38); *d*, 35.895 (1*); *e*, 35.894 (1*); *f*, 35.862 (25, 28, 38); this is labelled "*aji bulan*".

g, Aji beradap: "shrews face to face". 35.865 (17).

Plate VI

SHREWS

a, d e, Aji bulan buah bangkit: white shrew on a *bangkit* fruit. *a*, 35.862 (22); *d*, 35.855 (39); *e*, 35.865 (2, 4) see pl. xxix. The lozenge outside the *aji* is the fruit, *buah*, of the *bangkit*, the stepped outline is labelled "*tebok tangga pantok*, pole-ladder with notched steps, *pantok* means to peck as a fowl", the scrolls outside are *jerit nyangking*, "a pattern of itself".

b, Aji pelangka: shrew in a "husking box (*plangka*)". 35.872 (17) and pl. xxx, A.

c, Shrew with white spots (rice grains?) in its stomach. 35.865 (6, 7, 8, 11, 14), see pl. xxix.

Plate VII

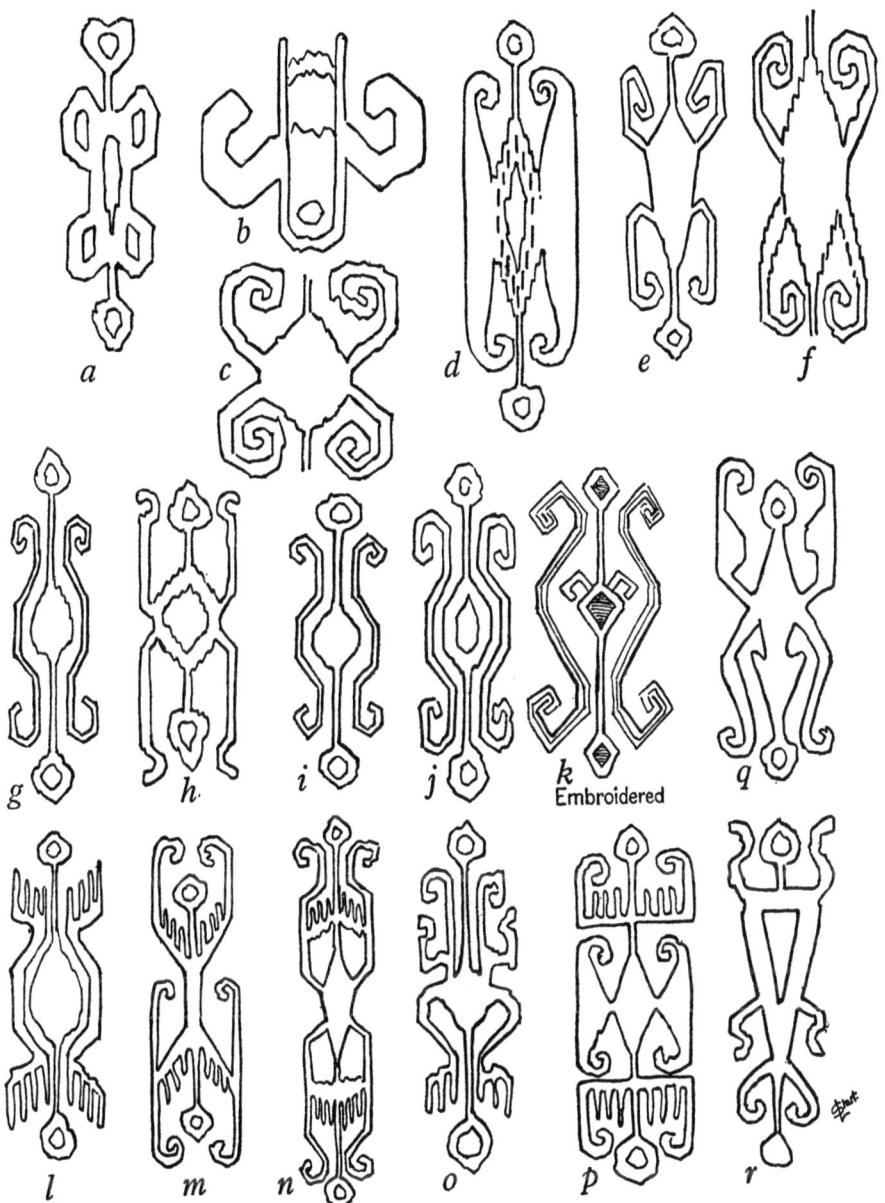

BIRDS

a–d, Burong: "bird". *a*, 35.854 (35); *b*, 35.870 (19); *c*, 35.928 (46); *d*, 35.862 (20).

e, Burong burak prut: "bird with white breast". 35.860 (31).

f, Burong burak: a white bird. 35.924 (3).

g, h, Burong sawang prut: "bird with opening in breast". *g*, 35.907 (7); *h*, 35.860 (26).

i–k, Burong bekarong: covered or concealed bird. *i*, 35.904 (31); *j*, 35.905 (5); *k*, 35.906 (13).

l–p, Burong besugu: "bird with comb". *l*, 35.926 (4); *m*, 35.856 (17); *n*, 35.860 (27); *o*, 35.872 (5); *p*, 35.908 (54).

q, r, Burong entepa: bird with outstretched wings. *q*, 35.908 (47); *r*, 35.908 (43, 44).

Plate VIII

BIRDS IN ACTION

a–d, Burong buah bangkit: "bird with the *bangkit* fruit". *a*, 35.903 (18); *b*, 35.855 (2); *c*, 35.908 (45); *d*, 35.856 (13).

e–g, Burong jengkuam: bird and the netting needle or spool. *e*, 35.858 (8); *f*, 35.856 (16); *g*, 35.923 (14).

h–j, Burong bedayong: "bird rowing". *h*, 35.860 (22); *i*, 35.926 (1); *j*, 35.856 (15).

k, l, Burong berayah: "bird with wings extended". *k*, 35.922 (30); *l*, 35.859 (1, 4).

m, n, Gajai burong: gajai-bird. *m*, 35.920 (27); *n*, 35.920 (5–8).

o, entilang gajai. 35.920 (16, 17, 19).

Plate IX

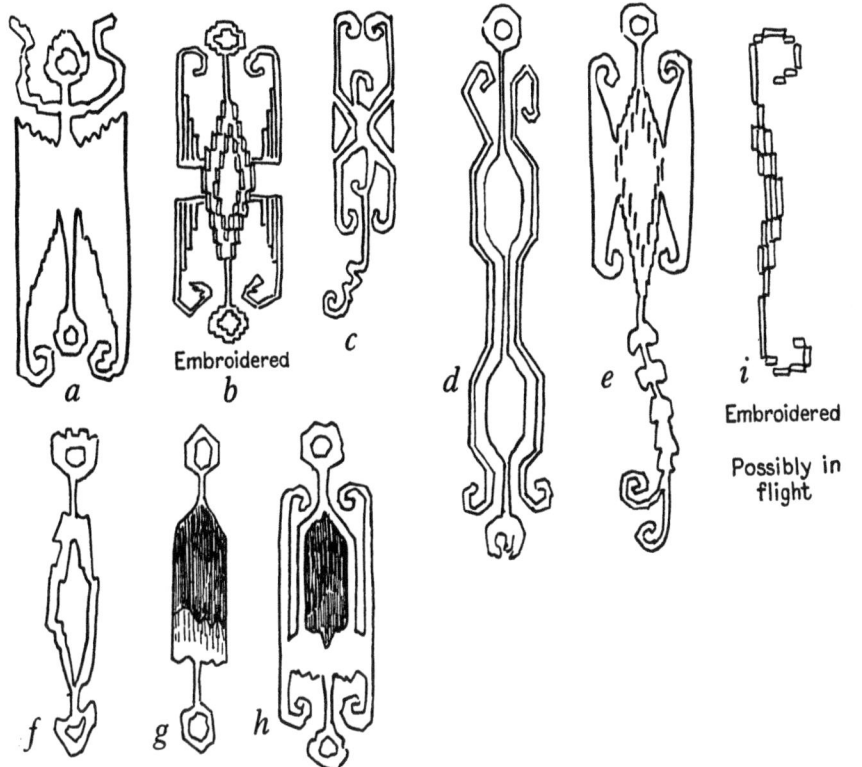

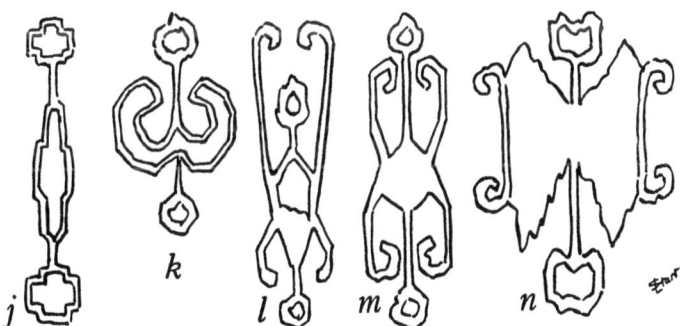

SPECIAL BIRDS AND YOUNG BIRDS

a–c, Burong lelayang: "swallow". *a*, 35.928 (49); *b*, 35.904 (30); *c*, 35.872 (26).

d, Burong betampang: a ceremonial bird. 35.907 (3).

e, Burong belingkian: argus pheasant? 35.908 (39, 40).

f, Burong andin: a fabulous bird? 35.923 (16).

g, Perhaps a variant of the next one on the same cloth.

h, Burong enchoyok (tinggang ujan). We cannot find a translation for *enchyok*; the following words are "falling rain". 35.905 (11).

i, Burong jagi. 35.904 (40).

j–m, Anak burong: "young bird". *j*, 35.904 (43); *k*, 35.881 (7); *l*, 35.856 (11); *m*, 35.873 (3).

n, Anak burong: "young bird" (the large wings indicate a swallow). 35.870 (7).

Plate X

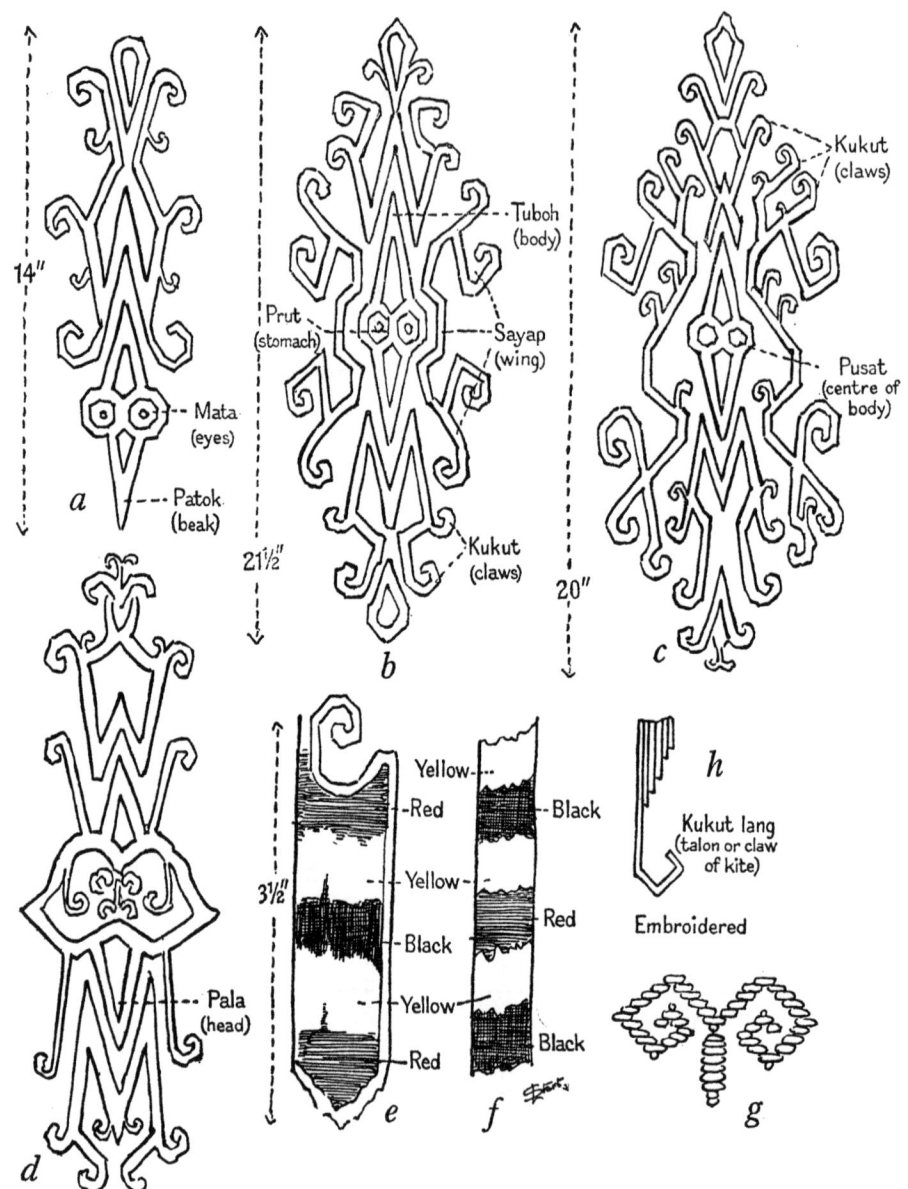

KITES

a–d, Lang: "hawk", the kite. a, 35.881 (15, 17, 19, 20); b, 35.881 (22, 26, 28, 30, 33, 34);
  c, 35.877 (2, 4, 5, 7, 10, 11); d, 35.857 (7, 9, 11).

e, f, Kengkang bulu lang: striped feather of kite (Singalang Burong). e, 35.924 (17); f, 35.922
  (22, 23).

g, Kukut burong: "bird's claw". 35.915 (5).

h, Kukut lang: talon of kite. 35.904 (33).

a, b, c have their heads towards the foot of the page. The eyes and beak of a are so labelled, but
in c this lozenge-shaped device is the centre of the kite's body, and in the cloth there is, as in c, a
continuation of the pattern which is not drawn.

Plate XI

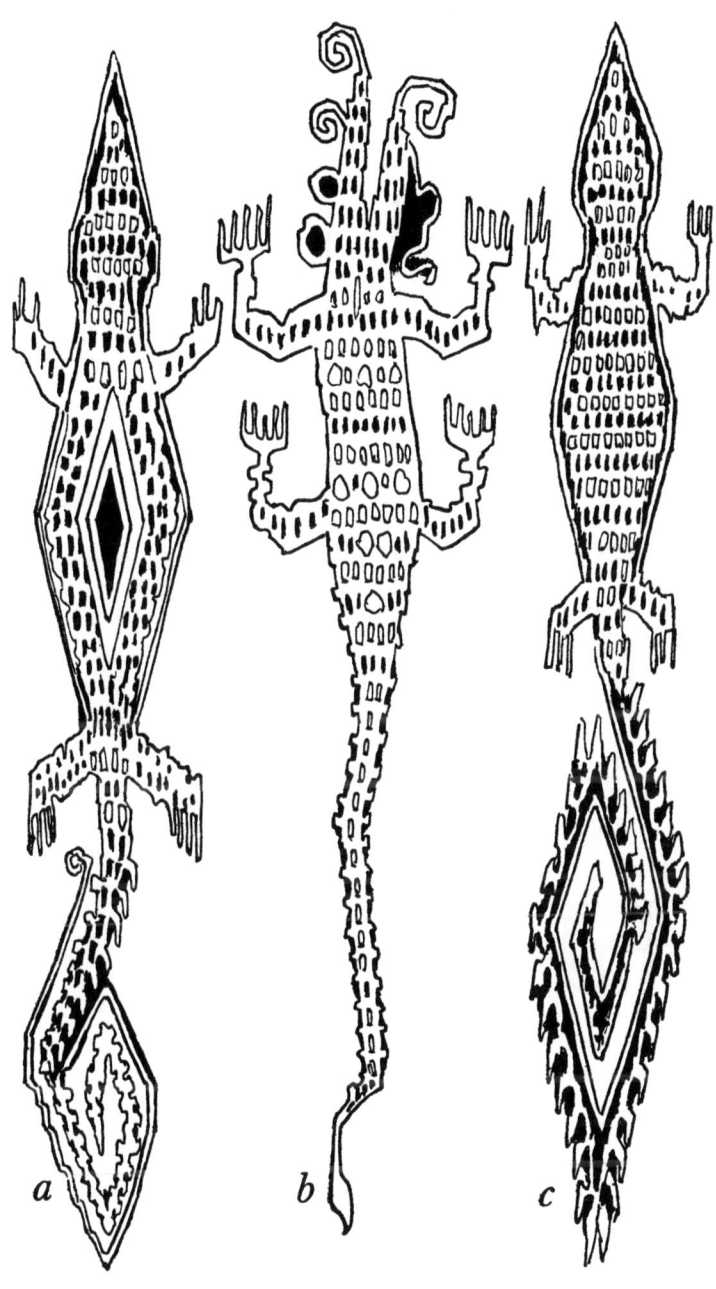

CROCODILES

a–c, Baya or *baia*: "crocodile". *a,* 35.931 (3*); *b,* 35.929 (4); *c,* 35.931 (4*).

Plate XII

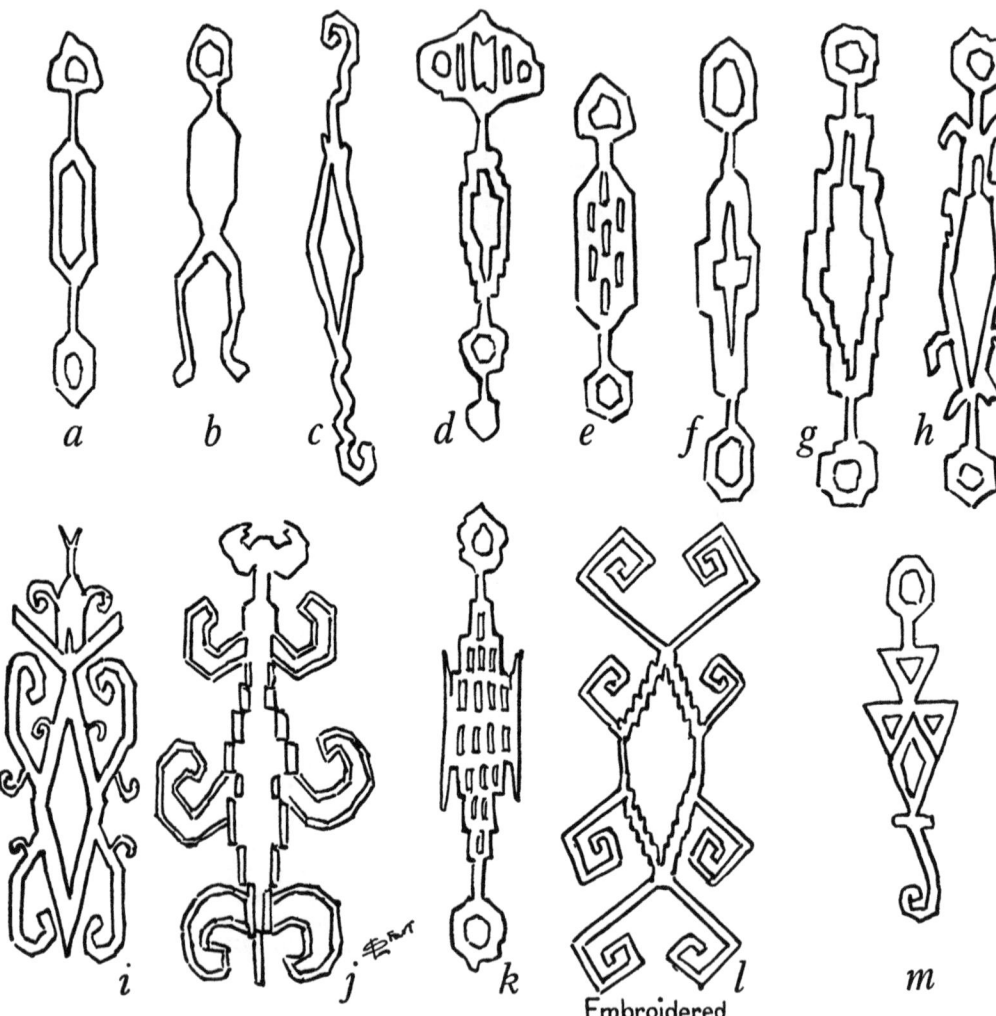

a b c d e f g h

i j k l m

Embroidered

LIZARDS

b–e, Anak lachau: young grass lizard. *b*, 35.858 (6); *c*, 35.923 (12); *d*, 35.922 (45); *e*, 35.908 (12, 13, 14).

a, f–h, Lachau: "green grass lizard". *a*, 35.906 (10); *f*, 35.903 (3), fig. 13 *g*; *g*, 35.922 (27); *h*, 35.924 (12).

i, j, Engkarong: lizard (skink). *i*, 35.880 (4, 5, 8, 9); *j*, 35.861 (6, 7, 8).

k, Engkarong kejong: a stiff skink lizard. 35.871 (1, 8).

l, Biyak: monitor lizard (*Varanus* sp.). 35.918 (1).

m, Engkarong tisik: lizard with scales. On a *bidang* drawn by Haddon at Baram.

Plate XIII

FROGS

a–e, Engkatak: "frog". *a*, 35.923 (4), labelled *anak engkatak*; *b*, 35.924 (42); *c*, 35.924 (23),
   labelled *anak engkaramba*; *d*, 35.908 (16); *e*, 35.906 (8).

f, Pama: a species of frog. 35.868 (13).

g, Although this is labelled *pama*, we think this is an *engkaramba engkatak*. 35.929 (2).

h, Engkaramba engkatak: frog figure. 35.926 (9).

i, Engkaramba gajai: *gajai* figure. 35.926 (13).

j, Gajai. 35.920 (16); these figures are spotted.

k, Entilang gajai. 35.920 (4).

l, Telu gajai: egg of *gajai*, it looks like frog spawn. 35.920 (18).

Plate XIV

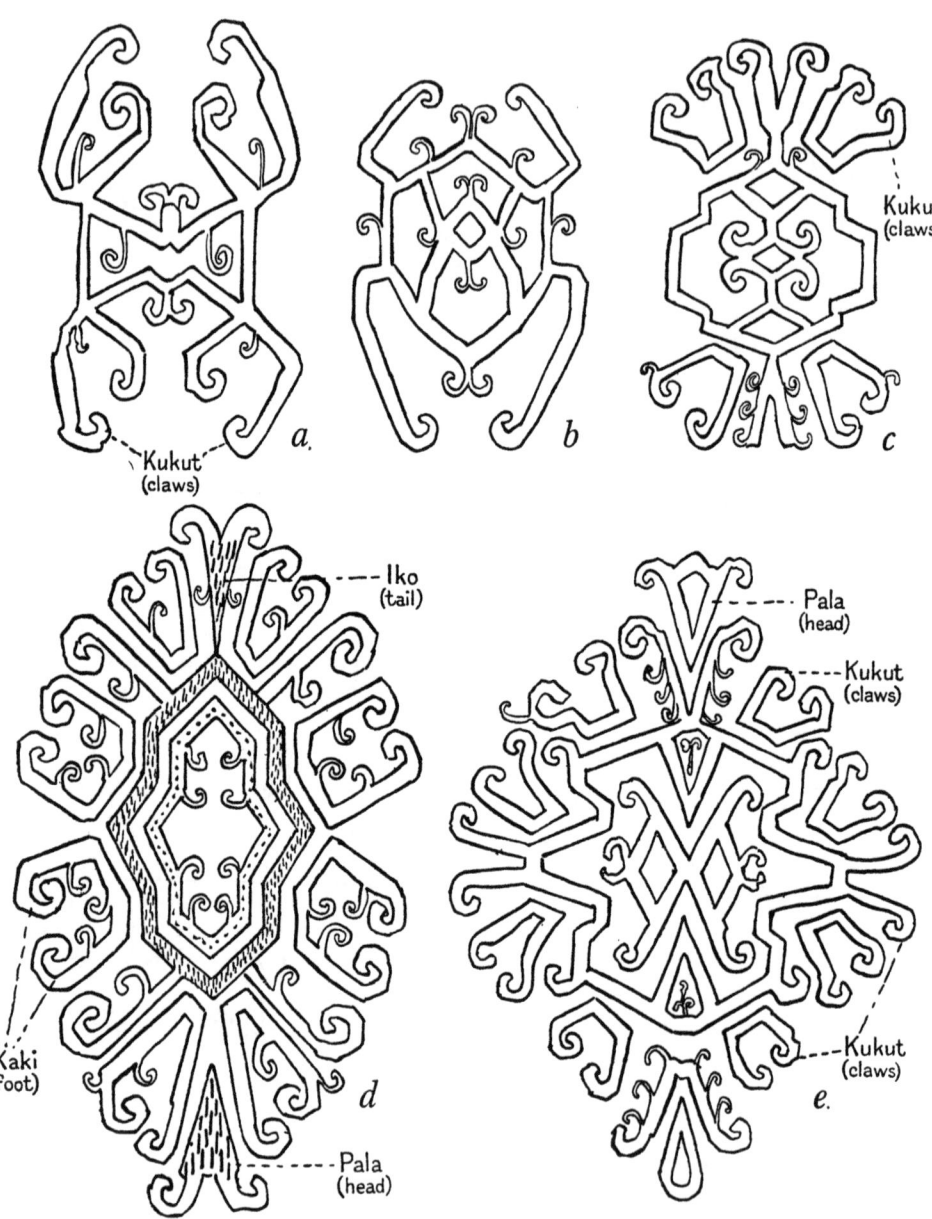

SPIDERS

a, *b*, *Anak emplawa*: "young spider". *a*, 35.862 (43); *b*, 35.857 (19*).
c, *d*, *e*, *Emplawa*: "spider". *c*, 35.862 (42); *d*, 35.857 (14); *e*, 35.866 (13, 15, 24).

Plate XV

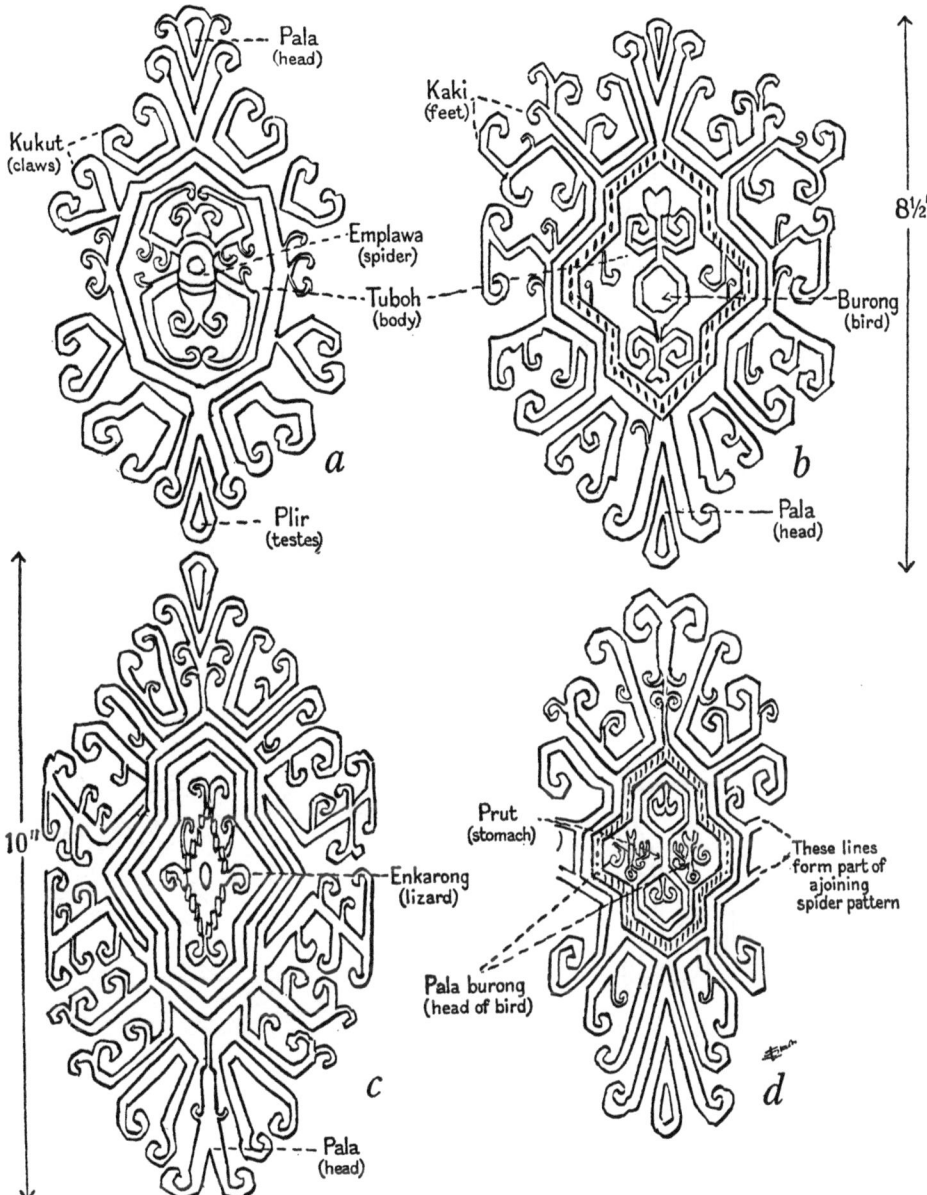

Pala
(head)

Kukut
(claws)

Kaki
(feet)

Emplawa
(spider)

Tuboh
(body)

Burong
(bird)

8½"

a

b

Plir
(testes)

Pala
(head)

10"

Enkarong
(lizard)

Prut
(stomach)

These lines
form part of
a joining
spider pattern

Pala burong
(head of bird)

c

d

Pala
(head)

SPIDERS

a, Spider with another spider on it. 35.866 (21, 25, 31).

b, *d*, *Burong di tengak tuboh emplawa*: "a bird in the body of a spider". *b*, 35.857 (4); *d*, 35.879 (14, 16, 17, 18, 20, 21); the marks in the outline of the stomach, *prut*, are labelled "*tebok igi bras*, rice grains".

c, *Engkarong empakap di tuboh emplawa*: "the grass lizard on the body of the spider". 35.857 (29). *c*, *enkarong* (lizard) should be *engkarong*.

Plate XVI

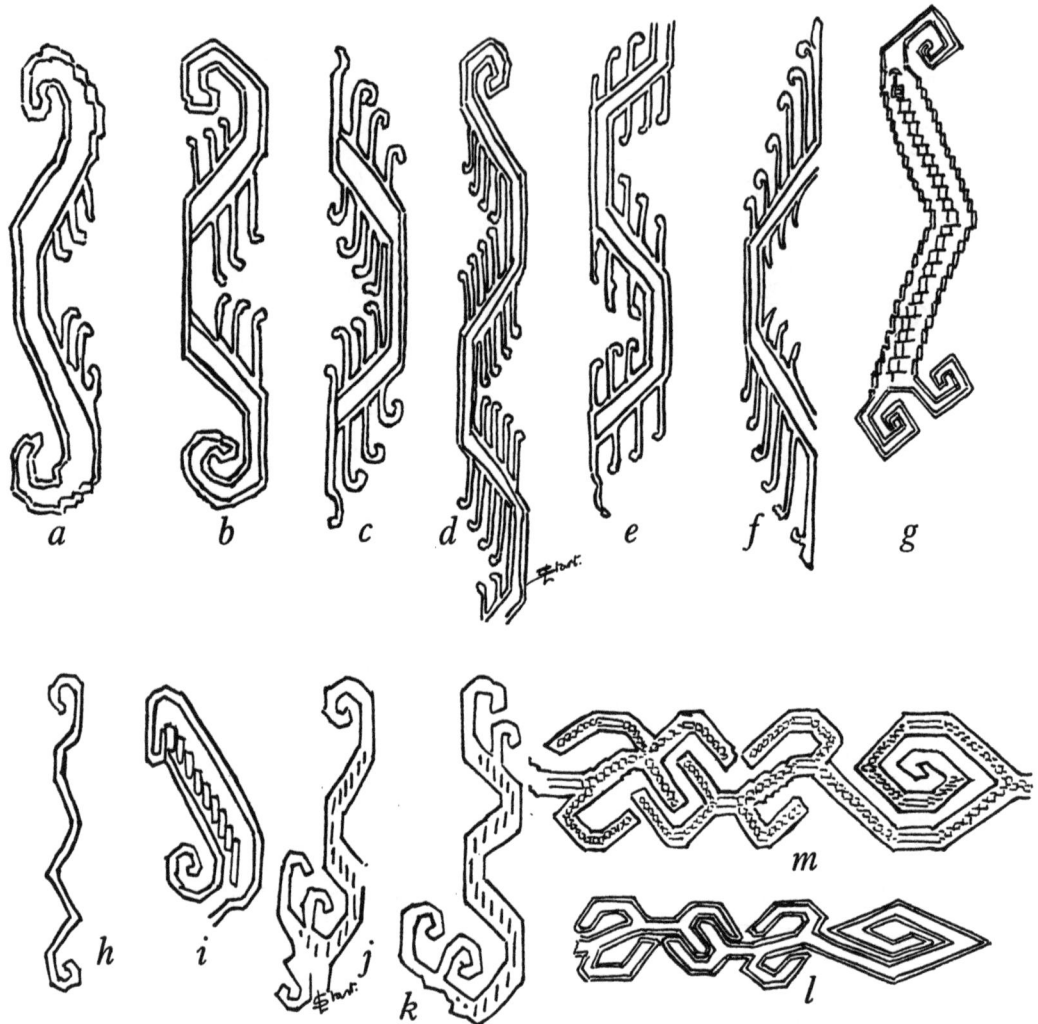

CENTIPEDES AND LEECHES

a, Anak embayar: young centipede. 35.856 (2).

b–d, Embayar: "centipede". *b*, 35.868 (3); *c*, 35.872 (12); *d*, 35.881 (6, *ngelepan* 10).

e, Embayar semerai sungai: "centipede crossing a river". 35.857 (31).

f, Kaki embayar: feet of centipede. 35.856 (7).

g, Nemaiar: "centipede" (from embroidered cloth). 35.918 (6).

h, i, Lintah: "leech". *h*, 35.906 (14); *i*, 35.860 (14).

j, Randau lintah: leech on a creeping plant. 35.877 (23, 24, 26).

k, Bungai lintah: "flower of the leech". 35.881 (8, 14).

l, m, Lintah betegam: "leeches swallowing" (one another). *l*, Sarawak Museum. Saribas *bidang* No. 219; Camb. Mus. photo. Indo. Born. 330 A; *m*, 35.886 (Pl. xxxi, B).

Plate XVII

SCORPIONS, INSECTS, ETC.

a, Kala: "scorpion". 35.906 (12).

b, Spit kala: scorpion's nippers. 35.872 (21).

c, Buyah: "beetle" ("*buyah*, a species of moth", *S.D.D.*). 35.928 (11, 12, 14).

d, Pantak penandok: the wound caused by the sting of a wasp? It might even represent the clay
    nest of a wasp (see p. 132). 35.865 (4).

e, Pantak penandok iku ruai: *iku*, tail; *ruai*, argus pheasant, or the verandah of an Iban house
    (see p. 132). 35.924 (4).

f, Pantak lelambak: wasp and flower pattern. 35.903 (16); cf. fig. 14.

g, Empetut: "grub". 35.881 (9, 11).

h–j, Pala buntak: "head of a grasshopper". *h*, 35.855 (10, 14); *i*, 35.913 (4); *j*, drawn by
    Haddon from a *sirat* at Marudi.

k, l, m, Mata puna: eye of green pigeon. *k*, 35.912 (10, 12, 15); *l*, a *pua* border pattern, Kuching,
    Camb. Mus. photo. Indo. Born. 415; *m*, from the badge of a Saribas Iban *kalambi* at
    Limbang, Camb. Mus. photo. Indo. Born. 403, a similar pattern covers *bidang* 35.883.

n–p, Anak ketam: "young crab". *n*, 35.928 (25); *o*, 35.928 (39); *p*, 35.922 (15, 16).

q, Spit grama: "crab's nippers". 35.855 (30).

r–u, Mayau tindok: "sleeping cat". *r*, 35.927 (17); *s*, 35.927 (13); *t*, 35.927 (15); *u*, 35.913 (5).

Plate XVIII

Upong

MAST, BAMBOO SHOOTS, FRUITS, AND FERNS

a–e, Empili: mast ("acorns"). *a*, 35.854 (32); *b*, 35.868 (9); *c*, 35.867 (7); *d*, 35.860 (6, 8); *e*, 35.856 (9).

f–h, Pemuchok tubu: "bamboo shoots". *f*, 35.921 (2); *g*, 35.905 (6); *h*, 35.928 (51).

i, Burong buah bangkit: bird and *bangkit* fruit. 35.928 (47).

j, Buah bangkit: fruit of the *bangkit*. 35.855 (5).

k, Buah bangkit bebunga: fruit and flower of the *bangkit*, hanging from *upong bunga*, flower stalk. 35.928 (19).

l, Upong buah beringin: "bunch of *beringin* fruit". 35.860 (2, 3, 4).

m–o, Gelong paku resam: "curled tops of the *resam* fern". *m*, 35.854 (5); *n*, 35.854 (74); *o*, 35.860 (5).

p, Daun resam: "leaf of the *resam*". 35.927 (5).

Plate XIX

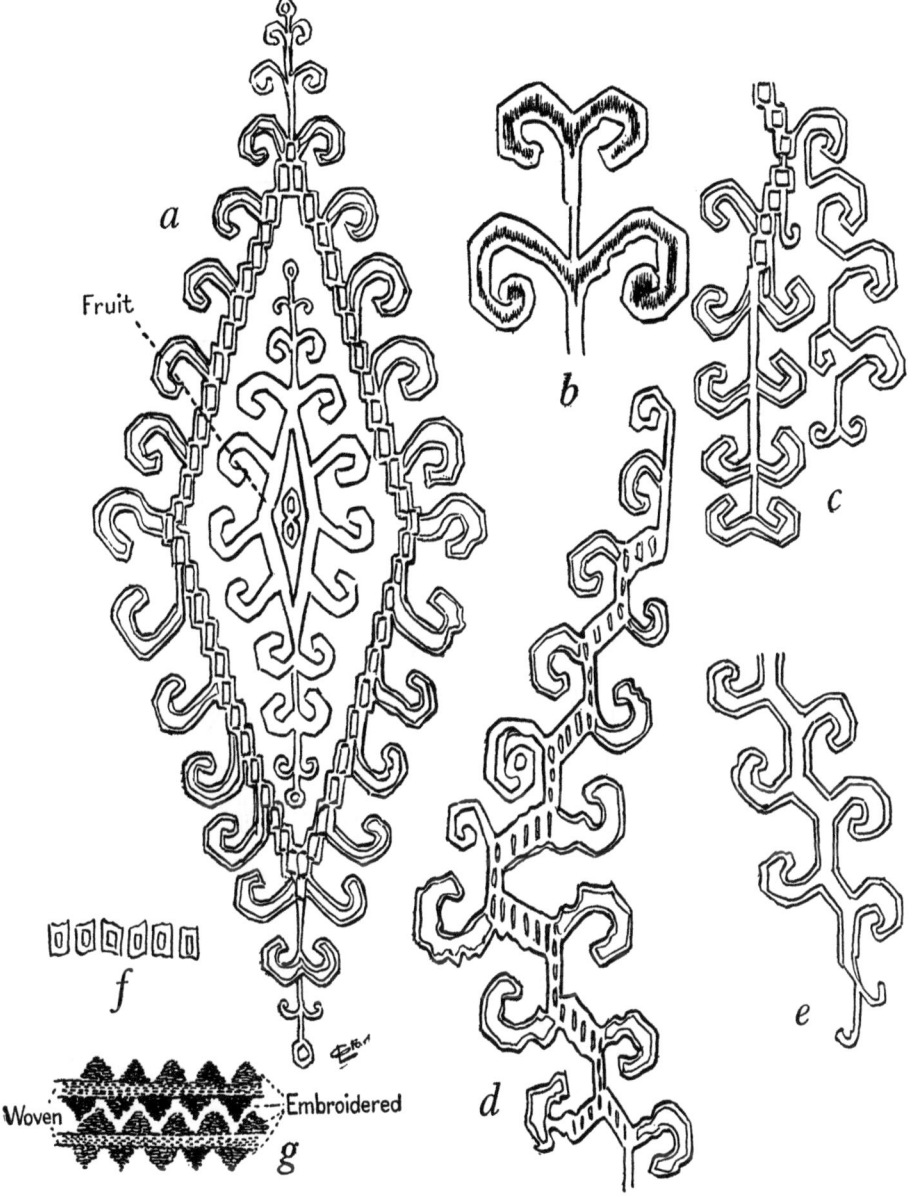

BLOSSOMS, GINGER ROOT, AND GOURD SEEDS

a, Jerit tangkai bunga: "blossoms [of the *bangkit*] completely covering the bunch" (*jerit*, "many, in series"; *tangkai*, "stalk"); the fruit, *buah bangkit*, is in the centre. 35.855 (3, 5).

b, Sanggul sesimpong: "tendrils of a creeper which has been cut in two". 35.928 (2).

c, Rundai bunga tangkong: "dangling flower of a creeper". 35.855 (21).

d, e, Bingka lia: "ginger root". *d*, 35.863 (19); *e*, 35.869 (4) (labelled "*bingka liah bubul lapang*", ginger root to fill up a space).

f, Tebok leka labu: gourd seeds with holes. 35.875 (14).

g, Dabong mayang: serrated *mayang*, blossom of a palm. 35.913 (17, 18).

Plate XX

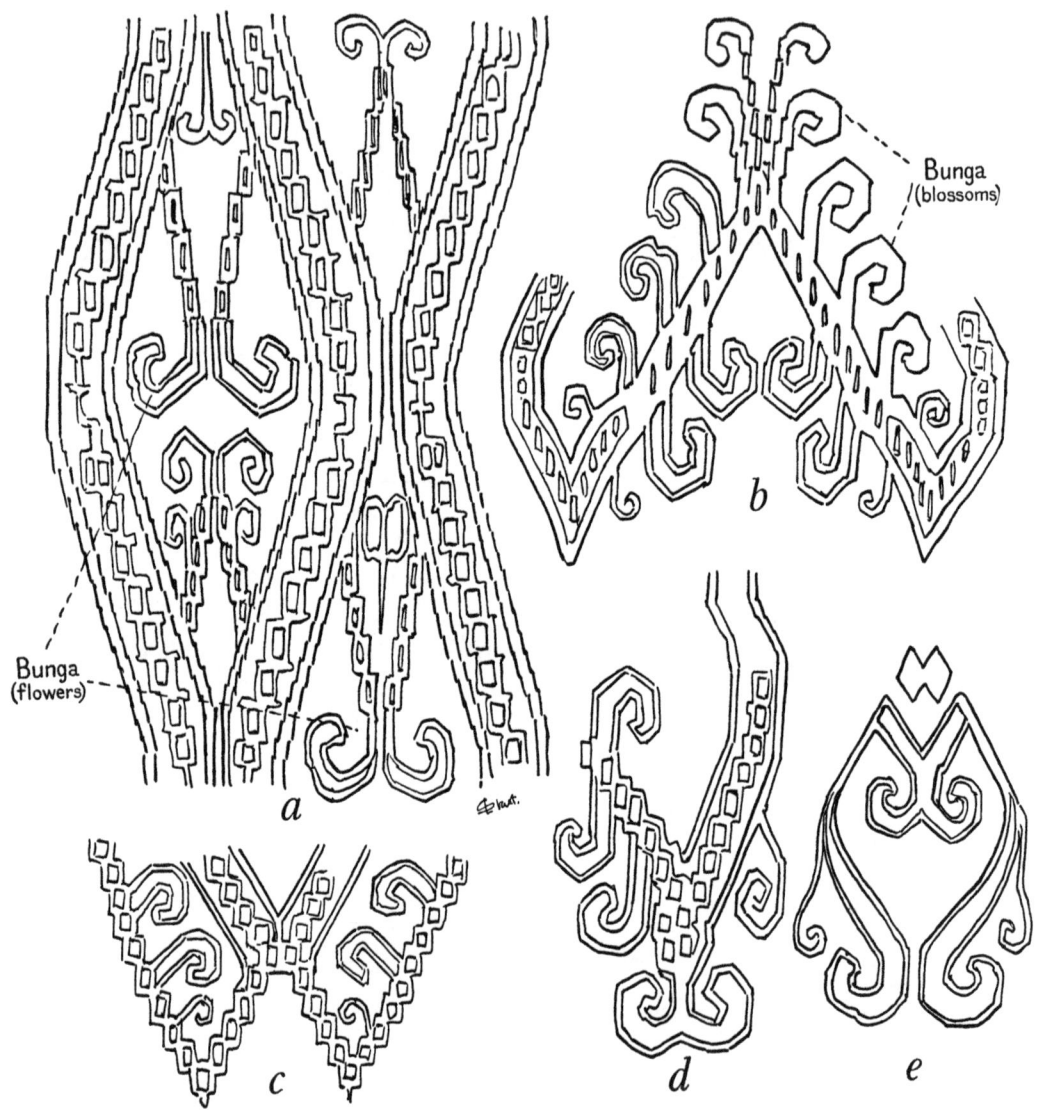

Bunga
/(blossoms)

Bunga
(flowers)

a

b

c

d

e

THE *TANGKONG*

Randau tangkong, "a creeping (climbing) jungle plant with scented pendant flowers".

a, Randau tangkong bi penyuang: "the lattice-work pattern of the *tangkong* creeper". 35.871 (6).

b, Bunga tangkong: "flowers of the *tangkong*". 35.863 (7).

c, Tangkong mulai: "a creeper which bends back from where it started". 35.855 (18).

d, Daun tangkong mulai: "leaf of the *tangkong* twisted back". 35.863 (24, 27).

e, Upong bunga tangkong: the spathe of the spadix (cluster of flowers) of the *tangkong*. 35.863 (26).

Plate XXI

BRANCHES, FIREFLIES ON A TREE, AND FRUIT

a, Pating betulak: "branches pushing one another back". 35.863 (6).

b, Pating: "branches". 35.870 (6).

c, Batang sepepat [selempepat] tebok igi bras: tree with branches outlined by the light of fireflies, and holes with rice grains. 35.922 (14); *tangai sepepat*: "branch with fireflies" (12).

d, Sanggul simpong: at the top of the drawing are the tendrils, *sanggul*, of a creeper; at the bottom, "the creeper cut off", *simpong*; the marks on the creeper are called *igi bras*, "rice grains". 35.927 (2).

e, Flower and fruit of a *bangkit* tree. 35.928 (19, 20).

f, Buah anyam: woven or plaited fruit. 35.916 (3).

g, Tangkong bara: "knob of wood". 35.881 (18).

Plate XXII

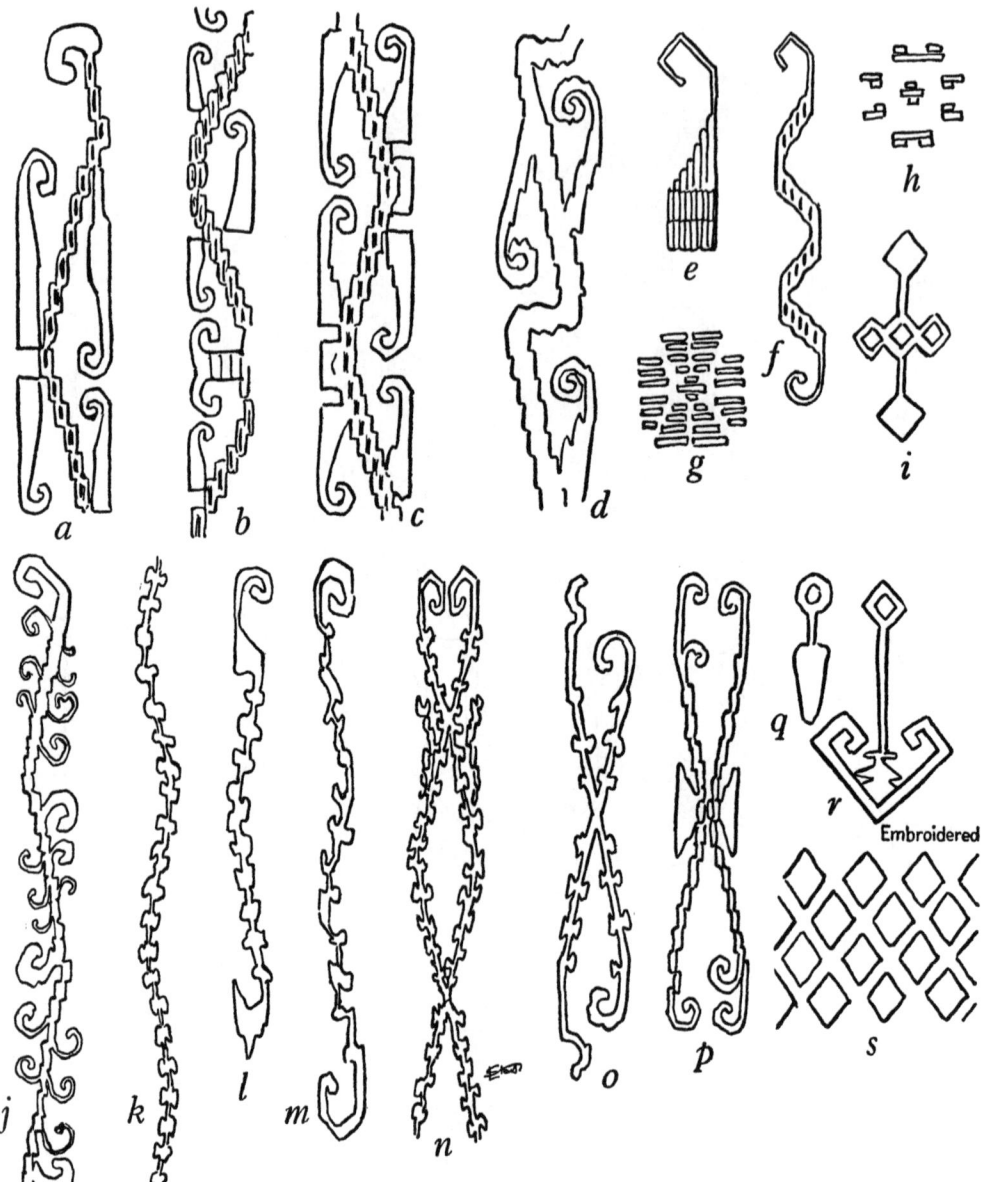

ARENGA PALM, PUMPKIN, RATAN, THORNS, AND MANGO FRUIT

a–d, Entibap: "arenga palm". *a*, 35.862 (15); *b*, 35.860 (13); *c*, 35.856 (19); *d*, 35.868 (7).

e, Daun entibap: "leaf of the arenga palm". 35.904 (5).

f, Serok genok: "a gourd". 35.860 (20).

g, Bunga janggat: flower of a white pumpkin. 35.904 (11).

h, i, Lelambak: a flower design plaited on mats. *h*, 35.906 (17); *i*, 35.918 (2).

j–n, Daun wi: "ratan leaves". *i*, 35.926 (6); *k*, 35.863 (12, 13); *l* (*unak wi*), 35.920 (22); *m*, 35.903 (7), see fig. 13 *d*; *n*, 35.921 (5).

o, Unak wi bekait: crossed thorny ratan. *o*, 35.856 (3).

p, Ruit gansai: barbed fish spear. 35.887 (1).

q, s, Buah angkong: fruit of a species of *Mangifera* (mango). *q*, 35.921 (6); *s*, 35.918 (4).

r, Buah bunut: "fruit of the horse mango (*Mangifera* sp.)". 35.918 (5).

Plate XXIII

Platform at stern (Dandan)

Oar (Dayong)

Rice grains

Bird

OBJECTS IN DAILY USE

a, Trabai bungkok: shield. 35.870 (10).
b, Gelong trabai: "handle of shield". 35.871 (2, 3).
c, Besampan: canoe. 35.875 (9, 13).
d, Sarong kris: "kris sheath". 35.927 (7).
e, f, Ladang: "a farm, a division of land". *e*, 35.931 (5); *f*, 35.927 (6).
g, Pempang lelingkok: zigzag fence. 35.854 (4, 75).
h, Entilang: "framework of an Iban cooking-place". 35.855 (23–26).
i, Spit api behilak: fire-tongs. 35.922 (17–19).
j, Entilang dapur: "fire-hearth". 35.928 (24).
k, Baku entilang: "fire-hearth without the earth for firing on". 35.928 (9, 10).
l–n, Ulu sengayoh: "(crutch) handle of a paddle". *l*, 35.923 (6); *m*, 35.855 (31, 32, 42);
    n, "a complete paddle with extra scrolls", 35.855 (37).
o, p, Kait: hooks. *o, Gelong bekait*, "a hooked scroll or curve", 35.854 (16); *p, kait betulak*,
    "a hook pushing another back", 35.863 (3).
q, Jengku ruyit: a curved barb. 35.880 (35).
r, s, Pasak serpang: "the wedge of the fork". *r*, 35.861 (31); *s*, 35.867 (8).
t, Serpang bekait: "hooked wedge" [*serpang*, a trident, fork]. 35.872 (3).
u, Pasak: "wedge". 35.865 (39).

Plate XXIV

OBJECTS IN DAILY USE

a, b, Tayok gasing: a hooked piece of wood on which thread is wound from spinning wheel. *a*, 35.865 (40); *b*, 35.869 (39).

c, Part of spinning wheel with spindle. 35.918 (3); it is labelled "taio [? *taya,* cotton] *gasieng,* thread driving the spinning wheel".

d, Tukal jengkuan: "frame for winding cotton", "a wooden frame about 3 ft. long upon which cotton thread is strung ready for weaving", *S.D.D.* 35.878 (1, 3, 4).

e, Serpang jengkuan: "the slit in the weaving needle"; a netting needle with forked ends or a spool with slit ends. 35.861 (22, 27).

f, Tunku asi: "tripod for cooking rice". 35.870 (13, 14).

g, h, Sugu: "comb". *g*, 35.903 (10); *h*, 35.854 (30, 40).

i, Entilang plangka: "box for padi husking". 35.872 (14, 15, 16, 18, 20). No. 15 is labelled "*pelangka (manang besaut)*" which indicates a box without a lid; a *plangka* of this kind is used by a *manang*, medicine man, at the *saut* ceremony, which is performed when a person is ill (see p. 78).

j, Ruyit: barb of a fish spear. 35.924 (41).

k, Serang pala tangga beji: bamboo fish trap, head, pole-ladder, —? 35.924 (43, 44).

l, Dabong betangkal: a serrated notch in an upright post for a cross-bar. 35.903 (14).

m, Papan penukoh: "the plank where the prop is tied". 35.855 (34).

Plate XXV

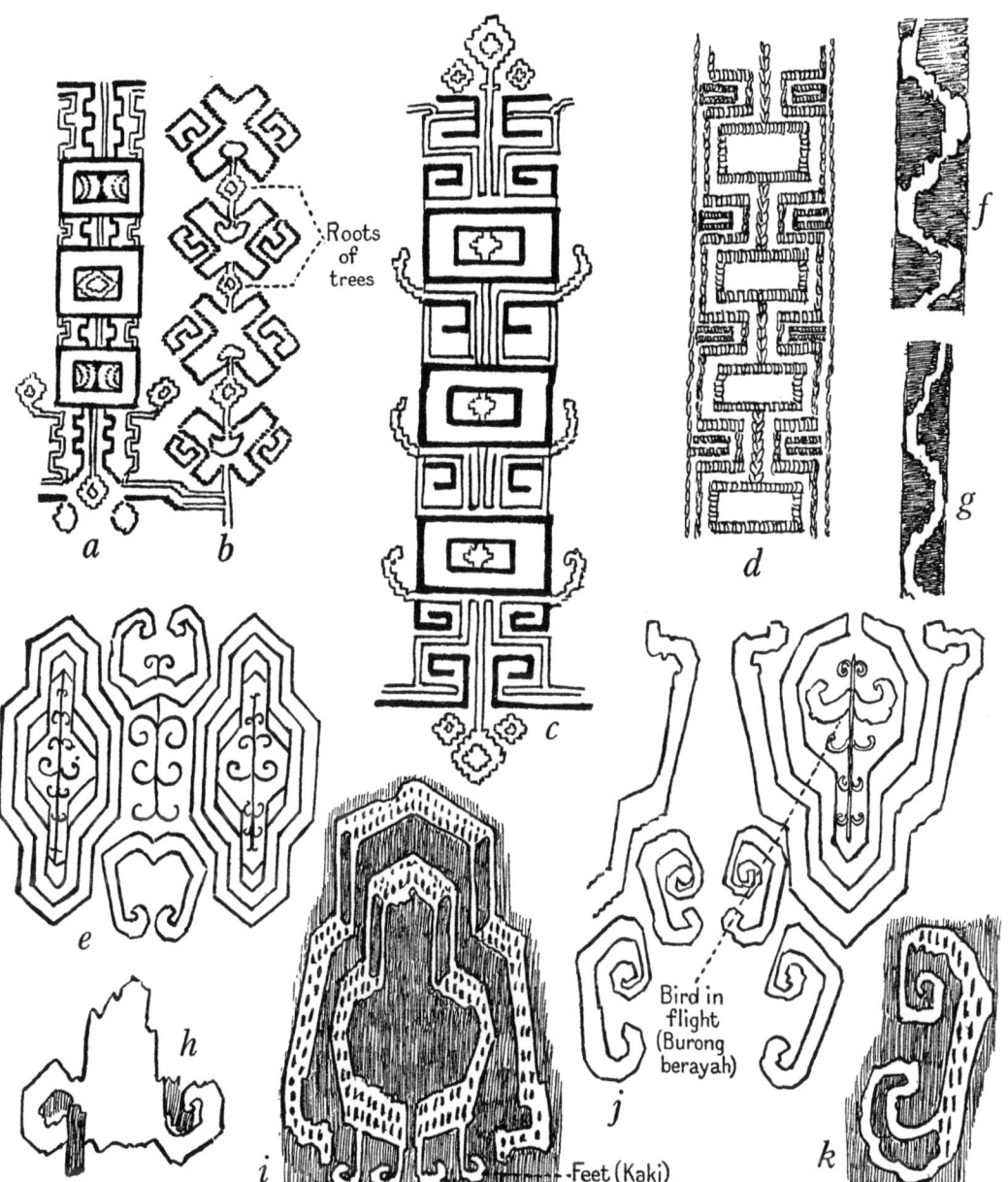

NATURAL PHENOMENA

a, c, Padong paya: a rocky ledge in swamp land. *a*, 35.913 (10, 12); *c*, 35.917 (8, 10).

b, Tabor paya: sown swamp land. 35.913 (11).

d, Bengka senggang. 35.915 (12).

e, Kaki padong remaung: foot, rocky ledge, tiger. 35.859 (27, 28, 33, 34).

f, g, Lelingkok semerai sungai: "crossing backwards and forwards across a river". *f*, 35.871 (10); *g*, 35.857 (13).

h, Bulan: the moon. 35.921 (16).

i, Kaki miga dudok: "foot of the clouds in steps". 35.859 (2).

j, Burong berayah: bird with extended wings on *miga dudok*, between this and the next clouds in steps are four *rayok miga dudok*. 35.859 (4, 9).

k, Rayok miga dudok: "clouds in steps". 35.859 (12); one only is drawn which varies from those in *j*.

Plate XXVI

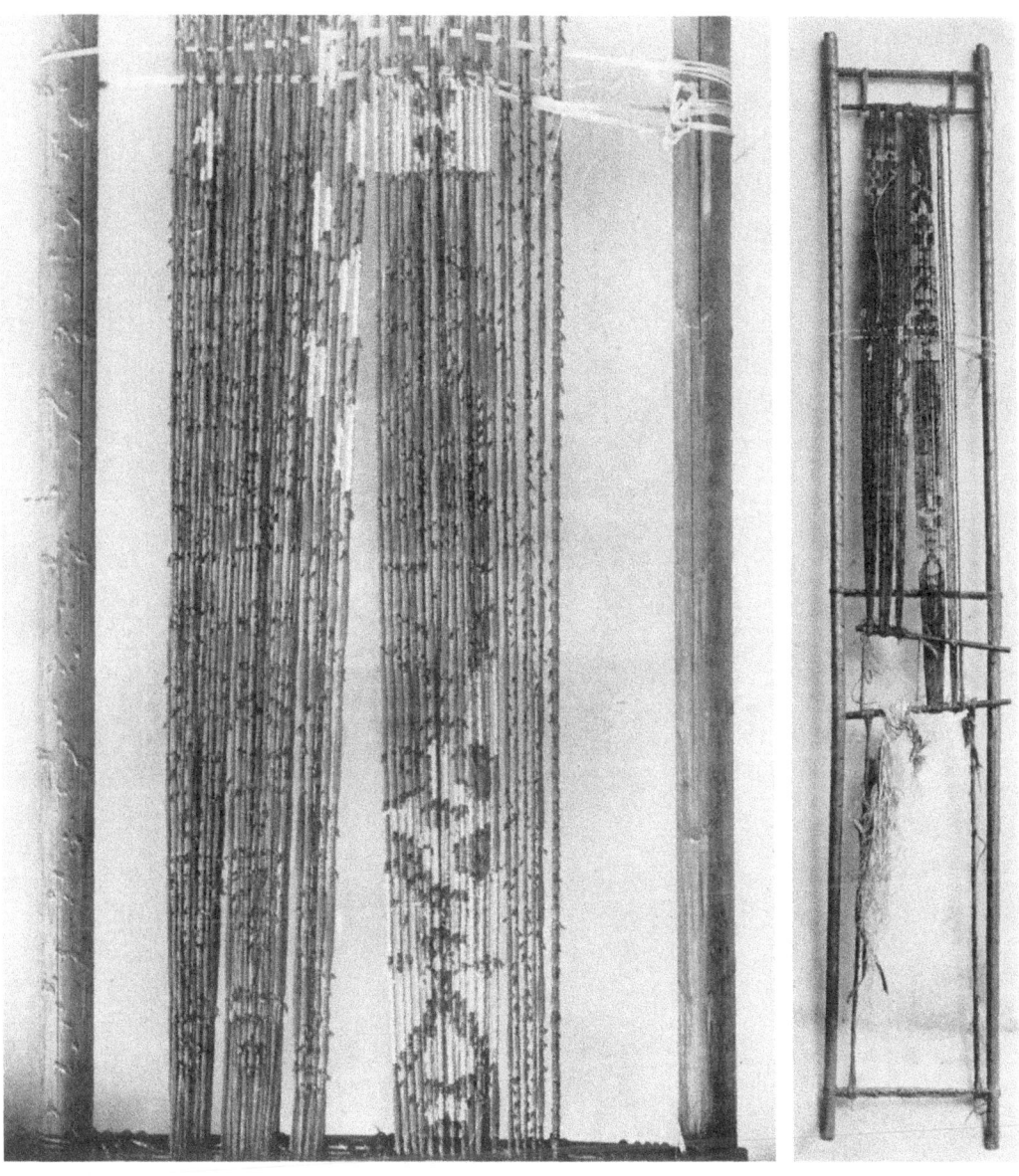

B   A

A. *Tangga ubong*, tying frame. Museum of Ethnology, Cambridge. B. Detail of a portion of the tied and partly dyed warp threads of A, p. 9.

Plate XXVII

Cloth for a *kalambi* as taken from the loom, 35.919, pp. 35, 36.

Plate XXVIII

A. *Bidang* 35.859, pp. 68, 69.

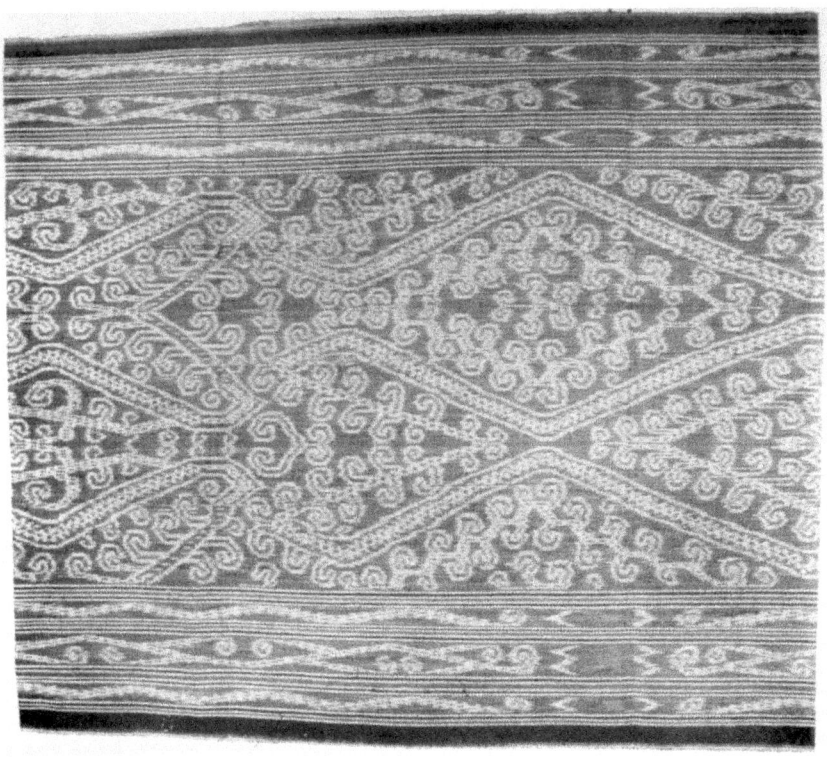

B. *Bidang* 35.863, pp. 72, 73.

Plate XXIX

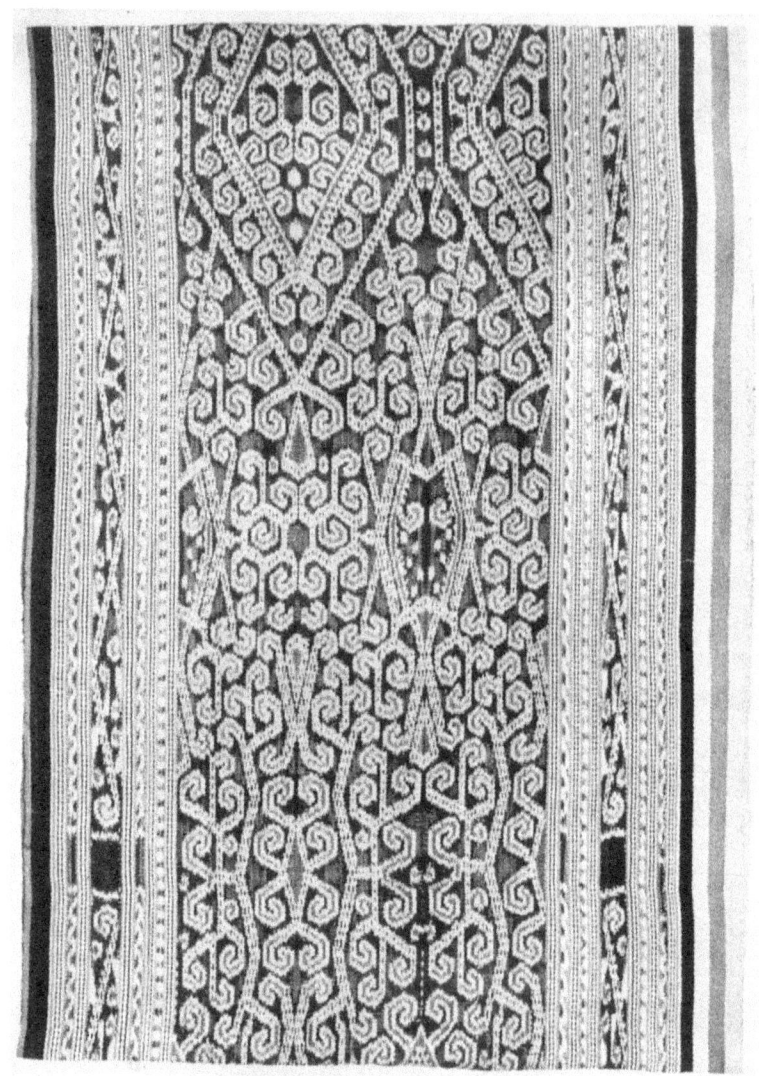

Bidang 35.865, pp. 73, 74.

Plate XXX

A. *Bidang* 35.872, pp. 78, 79.

B. *Bidang* 35.878, pp. 81, 82

Plate XXXI

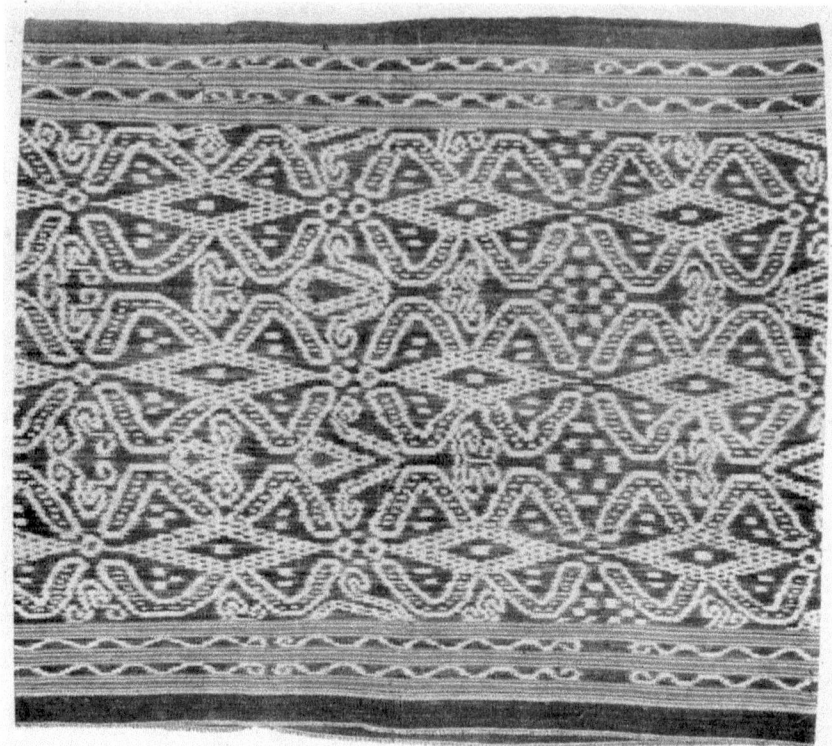

A. *Bidang* 35.882, pp: 83, 84.

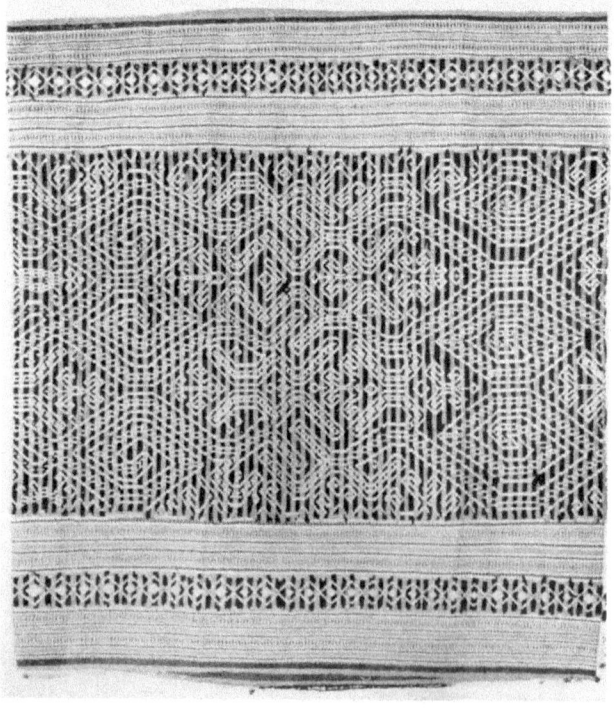

B. *Bidang* 35.886, pp. 89, 90.

Plate XXXII

B. *Klapong sirat*, type 2, Z. 2345, pp. 100, 101.

A. *Klapong sirat*, type 1, 35.913, pp. 94, 95.

Plate XXXIII

Pua 35.929, pp. 107, 108.

Plate XXXIV

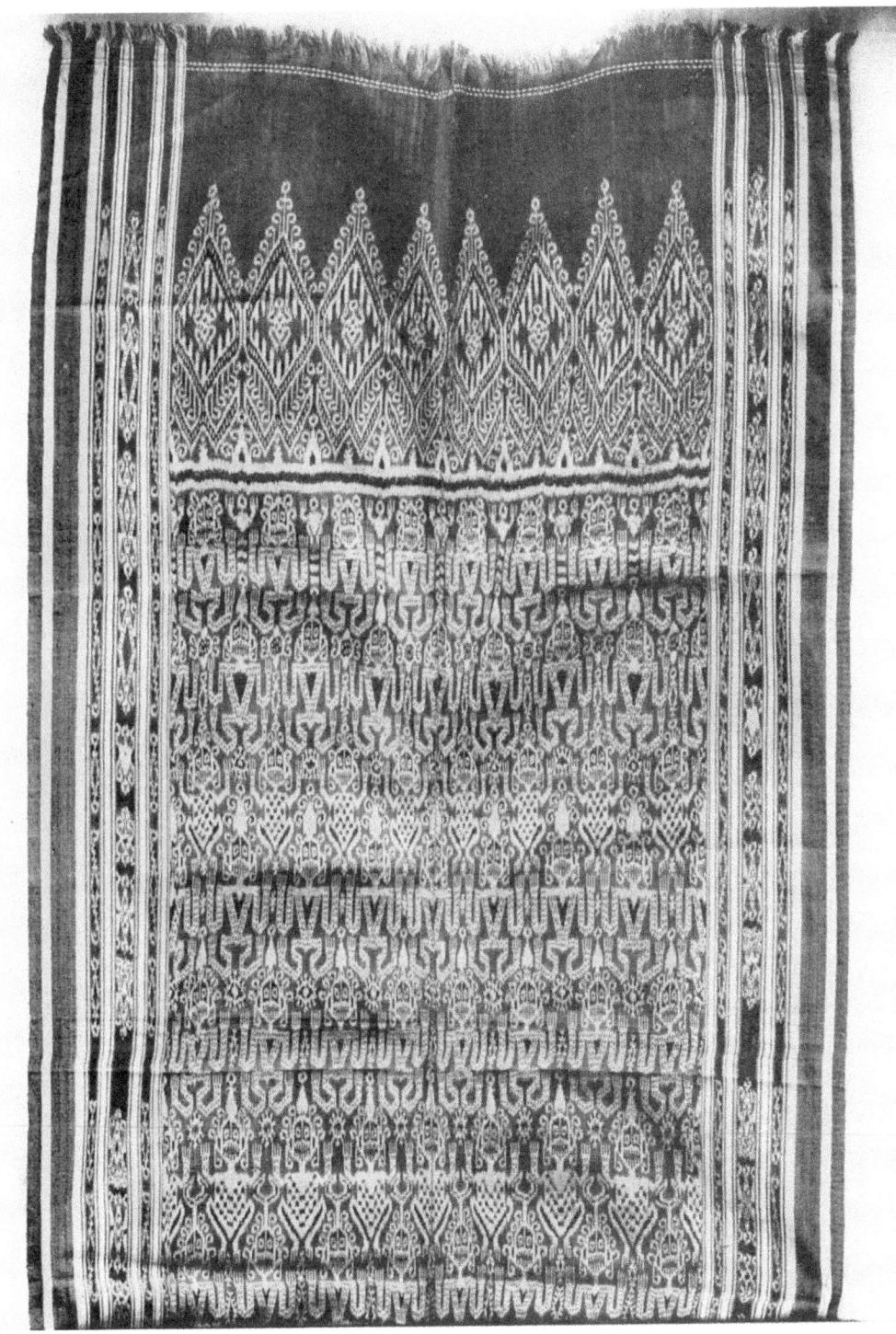

Pua 35.923, pp. 111, 112.

Plate XXXV

Pua 35.922, pp. 116–118.

For EU product safety concerns, contact us at Calle de José Abascal, 56–1°,
28003 Madrid, Spain or eugpsr@cambridge.org.

www.ingramcontent.com/pod-product-compliance
Ingram Content Group UK Ltd.
Pitfield, Milton Keynes, MK11 3LW, UK
UKHW051009240426
470322UK00018B/575